Transforming Higher Education
in Asia and Africa

SUNY series in Global Issues in Higher Education
———————
Kevin Kinser, Jason E. Lane, and Ş. İlgü Özler, editors

Transforming Higher Education in Asia and Africa
Strategic Planning and Policy

FRED M. HAYWARD

Cover map from iStockphoto.

Published by State University of New York Press, Albany

© 2020 State University of New York

All rights reserved

No part of this book may be used or reproduced in any manner whatsoever without written permission. No part of this book may be stored in a retrieval system or transmitted in any form or by any means including electronic, electrostatic, magnetic tape, mechanical, photocopying, recording, or otherwise without the prior permission in writing of the publisher.

For information, contact State University of New York Press, Albany, NY
www.sunypress.edu

Library of Congress Cataloging-in-Publication Data

Names: Hayward, Fred M., author.
Title: Transforming higher education in Asia and Africa : strategic planning and policy / Fred M. Hayward.
Description: Albany : State University of New York Press, 2020. | Series: SUNY series in global issues in higher education | Includes bibliographical references and index.
Identifiers: LCCN 2019028101 | ISBN 9781438478456 (hardcover : alk. paper) | ISBN 9781438478463 (pbk. : alk. paper) | ISBN 9781438478470 (ebook)
Subjects: LCSH: Education, Higher—Planning—Asia—Case studies. | Education, Higher—Planning—Africa—Case studies. | Universities and colleges—Asia—Administration—Case studies. | Universities and colleges—Africa—Administration—Case studies. | Educational change—Asia—Case studies. | Educational change—Africa—Case studies.
Classification: LCC LA1058 .H38 2020 | DDC 378.1724—dc23
LC record available at https://lccn.loc.gov/2019028101

10 9 8 7 6 5 4 3 2 1

Contents

List of Illustrations	vii
Preface	ix
Introduction	1
Chapter 1 The Critical Role of High-Quality Higher Education for National Development	13
Chapter 2 Prelude to Planning in Higher Education	29
Chapter 3 Leading Change in Pakistani Higher Education	33
Chapter 4 Afghan Higher Education: Change in a War Environment	53
Chapter 5 Bringing National Higher Education Transformation to South Africa	77
Chapter 6 Three Cases of Institutional Transformation in South Africa	93
Chapter 7 Challenges for Higher Education Change in Sierra Leone	123

Chapter 8
Fostering Higher Education Change in Uganda ... 137

Chapter 9
Madagascar: Higher Education Change Efforts Thwarted ... 151

Chapter 10
Ghana: Building Transformational Change at the University for Development Studies ... 161

Chapter 11
The University of Malawi: Coalition and Team Building for Effective Change ... 169

Chapter 12
Strategic Planning Challenges at Kabul Polytechnic University ... 181

Chapter 13
Implications for Leadership and Leading Transformational Change in Developing Countries ... 189

Chapter 14
The Nature of Change and Transformation in Higher Education in Developing Countries ... 213

Conclusion
What Does This Study Suggest for Higher Education in Underdeveloped and Developing Countries in the Future? ... 229

Notes ... 245

Works Cited ... 257

Index ... 269

Illustrations

Tables

4.1	Increase in Female Students at Public Higher Education Institutions: 2001–2016	60
4.2	Ordinary and Development Budgets for Higher Education: 2010–2016	64
5.1	Funding Formula 'Cost of Failure' for Peninsula Technikon, M. L. Sultan Technikon, and the University of Natal in 2008 and 2009	87
10.1	UDS Strategic Plan: Inputs from Stakeholders and Constituents	163

Figures

1.1	Strategic Planning Model	25
3.1	Projections of Costs Related to Increased Access and Enhanced Quality	39
4.1	Growth of Public and Private Higher Education in Afghanistan: 2001–2016	55
5.1	South African Higher Enrollment by Race	88

5.2 Participation Rate in Higher Education in South Africa: 1986–2005   91

13.1 Leadership in Strategic Planning   209

Preface

This study grows out of my interest in institutional development going back to my early efforts on political party formation, study of national integration, quality assurance, accreditation, and strategic planning. It builds on work I did at the American Council on Education (ACE),[1] with colleagues on higher education policy and internationalization, and in Africa and Asia on strategic planning and change. We were remarkably successful in our efforts with South African higher education to help foster change, and a case that seemed unique at the time made me aware of the many lessons it had for others. It also emphasized, as did the case of strategic planning in Pakistan, the central role of funding—one I thought was self-evident but didn't see as such a defining factor in success or failure. Thus, I began to gather data about each of these cases two decades ago, looking closely at leadership, breadth of participation, obstacles, and successes. It also required me to think more clearly about the term *transformation*, building on work I was involved in at ACE. I began to look at the higher education policy changes that were critical to strategic plans, interview leaders and others involved in these processes in each of the countries where I worked on strategic planning. I began to look again at some of my earlier experiences, go back and interview people involved, and gather data about what had happened with their strategic plan over time—in one case after more than eight years.

My involvement in each of these cases began with a request to assist the higher education system or institution with strategic planning and related policy issues, including establishment of quality assurance, accreditation, upgrading curriculum, and gender issues. The first of these was in Sierra Leone, where I had done PhD research in the 1960s, had a teaching Fulbright in 1980–81, and began work on strategic planning in 1987 when MUCIA (the Midwest Universities Consortium for International Activities) was requested by President Joseph Momoh of Sierra Leone to help prepare a strategic plan for the University of Sierra Leone (then including both Fourah Bay College [FBC] and Njala University College [NUC]). The advisor to the president, Dr. A. K. Turay, was a major driver behind this effort—someone I had gotten to know when teaching and doing research at FBC earlier. He had been to the United States on a State Department tour and was familiar with MUCIA.

The work in South Africa, which began in 1993, was originally funded by a grant from the Ford Foundation to the American Council on Education with a request that ACE work with the heads of five historically black universities and technikons on strategic planning. USAID later joined that effort and the number of institutions was expanded to twelve historically black institutions in South Africa plus the University of Namibia. I worked closely with all the vice chancellors, rectors, and senior staff, plus the Ministry of Education in South Africa, especially under the leadership of Minister Sibusiso Bengu, whom I had also worked with when he was vice chancellor of the University of Fort Hare. ACE also cooperated and worked closely with the Center for Higher Education Transformation (CHET).

My work in Afghanistan, Pakistan, and Madagascar was initiated by the World Bank when they asked me to assist the higher education systems in each of these countries in setting up a strategic planning effort and policies. Part of that work included quality assurance, upgrading the curriculum, and related issues respectively in 2003, 2005–06, and 2006–07. I returned to Afghanistan with USAID support through the University of Massachusetts, Amherst, to work on strategic planning and accreditation from 2007–2016. In all three of these cases, I worked closely with senior officials in the ministries (Higher Education Commission [HEC] in Pakistan), ministers, as well as senior administrators and academics. In Pakistan, I was part of the World Bank team working with the strategic planning committee at the HEC. In Afghanistan, I worked especially closely with Deputy Minister M. O. Babury, was listed as an advisor to the ministry, and have published several articles with him (Babury and Hayward, 2017, 2015, and 2013; Hayward and Babury, 2015 and 2014). Some of my later work in Madagascar was funded by the Government of Madagascar. I worked especially closely in Madagascar with the minister of education, Haja Nirina Razafinjatovo, and was listed as an advisor to the minister.

Preface

Work on strategic planning in Uganda took place during 2004 and was the result of an invitation from the National Council for Higher Education (NCHE) through its director A. B. K. Kasozi at the recommendation of the World Bank, which the NCHE funded. I was asked to review their draft strategic plan and comment on it at a week-long workshop with chancellors and higher education officials in Uganda plus give presentations on various aspects of strategic planning. My work there was limited to participants in the conference and leaders of the National Council. My work on strategic planning in Ghana at the University for Development Studies (UDS) during 2002–03 was initiated and funded by the Carnegie Corporation. I worked closely with the UDS strategic planning committee, Vice Chancellor Kaburise and Pro-Vice Chancellor Dittoh.

This work over the years has benefited from the generous assistance and encouragement of a large number of people, some of whom are mentioned in the text. I want to particularly mention and thank Prof. Teboho Moja of New York University, my long-time colleague, co-author, and friend, for reading the whole manuscript, for many comments along the way, and for invaluable suggestions. Also, very important is Dr. Daniel Ncayiyana another long-time colleague and co-author who participated with me in several of the projects detailed here, read a draft of this document, and as always contributed valuable ideas and suggestions. Dr. Madeleine Green is another important influence on this work, my former boss at ACE, someone who has read almost everything I have written in the last decades, and is a powerful critic and inspiration. I want to thank Prof. Jimmy Kandeh, of the University of Richmond, for his suggestions and updates on Sierra Leone. Finally, I owe a great deal to the comments and support of Prof. Joseph Berger of the University of Massachusetts, Boston (formerly of the University of Massachusetts, Amherst). I am also indebted to three former colleagues, now graduate students at U. Mass. Amherst for help with data gathering and tables: Mujtaba Hedayet, Razia Karim, and Hassan Aslami. I am deeply indebted to three anonymous readers who provided excellent comments and suggestions after their careful reading of the draft manuscript. I especially would like to thank SUNY editors and staff Rebecca Colesworthy, Diane Ganeles, and Kate Seburyamo for their excellent suggestions and the care they took in preparing this manuscript. None of these people are responsible for any of the errors here—they are my own—but they all bear a great deal of credit for any successes.

Finally, I owe a deep debt that I can never repay to my wife Linda Hunter, who has encouraged and inspired me throughout this process and who carefully read the whole manuscript several times, corrected errors, and gave me excellent advice and support along the way. It could not have been done without her.

Introduction

This is a story about hope, about a belief in a better future, about people who sought major change in higher education in eight underdeveloped countries. In this study, I explore efforts to improve lives by building high-quality higher education in more than a dozen cases that faced a variety of difficult challenges: war, underdevelopment, economic crises, corruption, mismanagement, racism, repression, external interference, gender discrimination, selfishness and greed, or a combination of the above. It is a story of dedicated, committed, and often fearless leaders who initiated strategic planning efforts and higher education policy for change and those who worked with them to make it happen. Most of these change efforts were successful, though not always. And there were several major failures—efforts that were unsuccessful through mistakes of their own or because of events over which participants had no control, including war, coups d'état, international economic crises, disease, and other calamities.

These strategic planning efforts take place in a variety of different places in Africa and Asia ranging from the struggle to reorganize, upgrade, and transform higher education in Afghanistan in the midst of a war, to the successful fight against apartheid in South African higher education with its amazingly open and participatory process both at the national and institutional levels. They include ongoing efforts to improve higher education in Malawi in a situation of weak government interest in higher education, political turmoil, drought, and internal crises. Each case represents a major strategic planning effort to improve and upgrade higher education by a group of educators, academics, politicians, students, faculty members, and citizens with a wide range of goals—efforts that are complex, fraught with challenges, and with varying results. At the same time, the reader will not find a model strategic plan as a result of this study. I and others have found, as Tony Strike et al. (2018: 37) emphasize, "[T]here was no normative or 'right' way . . . to deliver strategy and planning, and that many variations existed on how SP was devised and delivered." Even in the most successful cases we will see variations in the process—something that is important for practitioners to understand.

Each of these examples describes a major human effort to improve conditions for the citizens of each of these countries, to enhance the life chances for young people by providing quality higher education for them, to help national development by building strong knowledge centers in higher education institutions that can respond to local needs, foster creativity, innovation, and development and build open and free societies in which knowledge and discovery will operate in a free and hospitable environment. Some of the people discussed in these pages have put their lives on the line in the process of these change efforts. Many of these leaders have made the kinds of commitments that have given hope to young people for the future, laid the groundwork for growth, and been models for countless others who will follow them. Others have focused on narrow, specific problems and worked to resolve them. In some cases, their efforts have largely failed. Yet even those struggles have brought hope for a better life and memories of triumphs in that direction—if only for a moment—that cannot be erased. Some of these sacrifices will resonate at some point in the future and serve as a basis for real, sustainable change. Several of the cases examined here suggest reasons for failure which have broad applicability. Others provide examples of the hard work and commitment often required to bring about change and transformation. A few have been incompetent and/or corrupt with lasting damage—though there have not been many like that.

This study is written for those interested in higher education change and the policies that fostered it, whether as participants in the process, students, or as observers. My primary audience is a general one of people concerned about higher education in underdeveloped and developing countries, but the cases explored here will be relevant to anyone involved in or interested in higher education in any part of the world, including students who far too often have little knowledge of foreign countries. The cases examined focus on challenges, failures, and successes in strategic planning for change in higher education similar to those in any part of the world, since they explore themes, policies, and strategies that have general applications. Each in its own way, of course, is unique. Yet, all of them have lessons for anyone interested in bringing about change. This is especially the case for those doing so using strategic planning as the vehicle for change since these cases demonstrate its importance to success. Some of the cases examined here confront problems of an enormity few people will face, yet they too are suggestive. Those successes under especially difficult circumstances explored here should give courage to anyone who has to meet challenges in higher education and may, for some, suggest strategies that might not have occurred in other settings. Four of these cases represent striking examples of higher education system transformation. All of them deal with problems that have relevance to higher education in general.

In this study of higher education change, I examine twelve cases of strategic planning, the policies that drove them, both national and institutional, in eight different countries in Africa and Asia where I have worked over the last thirty years. Indeed, except for South Africa, little has been written on strategic planning and policy change in the developing and underdeveloped world.

As we think about the leadership of strategic planning, it is worth going back to the Prologue of James MacGregor Burns's 1978 classic *Leadership* where he writes

> that leadership is nothing if not linked to collective purpose; that the effectiveness of leaders must be judged not by their press clippings but by actual social change measured by intent and by the satisfaction of human needs and expectations; that political leadership depends on a long chain of biological and social processes, of interaction with structures of political opportunity and closures, of interplay between the calls of moral principles and the recognized necessities of power; that in placing these concepts of political leadership centrally into a theory of historical causation, we will reaffirm the possibilities of human volition and of common standards of justice in the conduct of people's affairs. (Burns, 1979: 3–4)

This description of leadership sets a high standard, but indeed that is what is being called for in the demands for change in most of the cases we have examined here—a range of fundamental changes in higher education to be led by people expected to have extraordinary capabilities and characteristics, or where the demands are not quite so great, where the reality of success requires some of these characteristics. We will assess a number of higher education leaders and the strategic planning processes and policies in the pages which follow. Some of the leaders were remarkable in their ability to mobilize people to foster change and transformation. We will see others who fail, sometimes because of limitations of their own, sometimes because of problems with followers or other leaders, sometimes because of events over which they have no control. Nonetheless, Burns provides an excellent introduction to the strategic planning processes we are examining with a clear description of ideal expectations, which are still valid after all these years.

As I revisited the literature on leadership I was struck by the fact that most of it focuses on what could be done to build strong leadership—books such as Jim Kouzes and James Posner's *An Administrator's Guide to Exemplary Leadership* (2008), which identified what the authors saw as five keys to successful leadership. At the same time, some of the literature was downplaying the role of leadership, as does Barbara Kellerman in *The End of Leadership* (2012), who concludes that: "[L]eadership is in danger of being obsolete—but leadership as being more consequential than followership, leadership as learning we should pay to acquire, leadership as anything better than business as usual, leadership as a solution to whatever our problems, and leadership as an agreement of which merit is a component" (Kellerman, 2012: 200). Linda Hill and Kent Lineback (2011) see three critical characteristics of successful leaders, which include managing your team, managing yourself, and managing your network. Added to that are a host of other "how to" books such as Yukl (2014).

Most of the work on leadership and change focuses on the United States, and I thought it important to explore the process in the underdeveloped world. I began to look at the processes of change and higher education policymaking from that perspective and to relate it to the strategic planning work I had participated in working in the United States and elsewhere. There are many similarities in the underdeveloped world, but also areas, such as security, which are not as serious an issue in most of North America or in Europe.

One of the criticisms of work on higher education leadership is the failure to look at leaders over a long period of time (Lumby, 2013:18). Several studies have tried to overcome that problem by returning to their case studies after a period of time.[1] I have had the luxury of being able to do that both in terms of the time I was able to observe the process of change in each of these countries and my ability to go back to reexamine the conditions of the process at a later date. In the cases of South Africa, Afghanistan, Madagascar, Malawi, Sierra Leone, and Pakistan, I was able to conduct additional interviews and reexamine earlier conclusions about what transpired in the face of more recent information.

In the course of this study of higher education strategic planning, I examine what seem to me to be key characteristics of successful higher education leaders in the underdeveloped countries examined. For example, Lumby asks, What role does vision play (Lumby, 2013: 2)? How do we show that? I try to answer that and related questions. What about organizational skill? Integrity? How do these attributes work in practice? What other characteristics of leaders seem to be important? At the same time, I am aware of the caution emphasized by Birnbaum to avoid "[t]his tendency to attribute influence to leaders, even when it may not be objectively warranted, [which] distorts the way we think about leadership, and obscures the actual relationship between leaders and outcomes" (Birnbaum, 1992: 7). Similarly, I find useful James MacGregor Burns's definition of leadership as "leaders inducing followers to act for certain goals that represent the values and the motivations—the wants and needs, the aspirations and expectations—of both leaders and followers." He goes on to say that "the genius of leadership lies in the manner in which leaders see and act on their own and their followers' values and motivations" (Burns, 1978: 19). In higher education it is the link between goals of leaders and followers that is much more important than concerns about power or control.

Especially important as well is "strategic thinking," the ability to consider and evaluate a variety of possible actions to deal with challenges—to think strategically about the challenges to the institution or the system (Pritchard, 2018: 52). Pritchard emphasizes the importance of "enabling strategic thinking and the other active engagement of stakeholders" (Pritchard, 2018: 49). As we will see, that is an important part of success in many of the cases we examine here. We will return to strategic thinking later in this study.

I also look at the role played by context and the conditions of the individual education systems. What different challenges have planners faced? How successful were their efforts to bring about change? What do those successes teach us about the strategic planning process? Are there critical parts of that process that affect success? Are there particular types of leaders who seem to be more successful than others at achieving change? We will return to these questions in what follows.

Several of these leaders had to contend with especially difficult crises. That is a particularly powerful test of their leadership abilities and the strategies they employed. As we will see, their responses to these challenges are often creative, sometimes exceptional, and frequently suggestive of mechanisms some of the rest of us might find helpful.

These cases demonstrate why strategic planning is so important to successful higher education change and transformation, how it focuses attention on critical needs, helps foster strategies and policies that work and abandonment of those that do not, can mobilize support, and often provides the basis for the change and transformation that is critical to quality improvement, national development, political stability, and the development of democratic values. In several cases, the process was in many respects more important than the actual changes in that it created agreement on conditions for cooperation at the institution or in the system for years to come (for example, between students and administration, or between faculty members and staff). Several of the less successful cases suggest weaknesses in the planning process, critical areas that were neglected, the cost of the inability to foster agreement about basic goals or strategies, lack of support from critical actors, financial shortfalls, or the failure to develop a viable plan.

I define educational change as *the alteration of major policies and values that guide higher education.* These range from minor changes in one program to major shifts in policy and values, such as new requirements for students to demonstrate facility in a foreign language or math, changes in recruitment and promotion policies, such as a move from appointment and promotion based on who you knew to one based on merit. M. O. Babury and I (2014: 2) discussed transformation and change as noted below:

> A few words about change and transformation might be useful here. There are many types of change as we are all aware. I find it useful to think about change along a continuum from minor modifications of the system at one end to total transformation at the other. By transformation, we mean that *the system is fundamentally altered in its structure and in some of its major values.*[2]

I find some of the discussions about transformation by other writers particularly useful. Eckel describes transformation as change that is pervasive and deep (Eckel, 1999: 16). Somewhere along the low end of the continuum are isolated changes[3] (one unit, one department) that may be extensive but do not affect the rest of the university or system. Farther along, moving to the high end of the continuum are various degrees of more extensive changes. Finally, at the high end of the continuum is transformational change—*change that is pervasive and deep in a way that fundamentally alter its structure and some of its major values.*

Others define transformation somewhat differently. The Center for Higher Education Transformation, in its study of transformation, identifies four main "pillars of transformation" as being equity, democracy, efficiency, and responsiveness (CHET, 2002). Burton Clark identifies the five common elements of successful institutional transformation as: (1) a strengthened steering core; (2) an expanded developmental periphery; (3) a diversified funding base; (4) a stimulated academic heartland; and (5) an integrated entrepreneurial culture (Clark, 1998: 3–8).

In assessing transformation, following this definition, I suggest that in a transformed higher education system or institution:

- There is a move from a traditional hierarchical system to one that is primarily merit-based and relatively flat.
- The system enshrines equity including gender equity.
- It is knowledge-based.
- The system is responsive and efficient.
- It has an active stimulated academic heartland (following Burton Clark, 1998).
- It is open to the world of ideas and enshrines academic freedom.
- It operates in a supportive environment.
- It is sustainable.

I will use these characteristics to examine higher education change and transformation in the pages that follow.

One of the dangers of studies that focus on leadership is a tendency to overglorify the role of the leader(s) in any successes,[4] attribute powers to the leader that did not exist, or give leaders credit for things they have not done or successes that were a result of the work of many people. Indeed, separating the impact of leaders on change from other factors that may be responsible for it is difficult. I have tried to avoid that problem, to be cautious in attributing cause and effect, to be self-conscious about both my close connections with some of these leaders, my involvement in some of these cases, the tendency to assert causality where there is none, and the too easy tendency to overlook weaknesses and failures especially when memories may be blurred by time. What are most important for this study are the processes used in successful strategic planning that lead to major change efforts and the changes that occurred rather than attempts to demonstrate causality. Furthermore, in every case of success, the successes were collective efforts involving many people, over a significant period of time.

And, of course, context and timing also have a lot to do with success. Some of the successes chronicled here were significantly aided by the timely availability of funding, or the fact of limited opposition. In several instances, excellent plans were undone by sudden events that the leaders had no control over, such as the coup in Madagascar, the crisis of an invasion, the Ebola epidemic in Sierra Leone, international economic downturns, and other unforeseeable disasters. These were not the fault of higher education leaders. Some leaders were able to work through or around disasters, as we will see. Those cases make especially interesting reading. Indeed, sometimes it seems that "the context is everything." While that is not the case in any of these examples, it is a critical variable in several cases and plays a significant role in many of these examples in very different ways, as we shall see.

What is especially striking about most of these cases is the level of success even in the most difficult of environments—amidst civil strife, war, economic crises, hunger, disease, and poverty. Many of these examples take place in fragile states[5]—Afghanistan, Sierra Leone, Madagascar, among others. Some take place in environments highly stratified by both race and economics—as was the case for South Africa. All but two of these examples took place in an environment tainted by war, civil strife, or military intervention.

It is also important to recognize that none of these examples happened in a vacuum. While some of these countries were more isolated than others, Afghanistan in particular during more than thirty years of war, all are influenced by the events in higher education going on around them, both in the academic sense of the findings in various fields of importance to them, but also in the higher education community and the world. It is not just the effects of the communications revolution of the twentieth century, the growth of network societies,[6] the development of knowledge societies (World Bank, 2002), but the effect of the constant interaction of academics, administrators, and students—many of whom have studied abroad, are involved in joint programs with foreign scholars, have worked in other countries, read the *Chronicle*, the *Times Higher Education Supplement*, or *University World News*, or are linked to others in education by the powers of the Internet. The power and influence of the networking constantly going on in higher education internationally should not be underestimated. The search for quality improvement, in some cases defined as "world-class standards," has been aided by the Internet, which allows faculty members to look at and draw from the syllabi and reading material of the best courses in the world. And as the Arab Spring demonstrated more than ten years ago, the impact of networking about ongoing events in societies and in higher education around the world can be enormous.

The choice of the cases examined here is purposive—chosen because I have worked in all of them. I have worked with higher education in fifteen countries, taught at the university level in Ghana and Sierra Leone, as well as the United States, and have worked with universities and ministries of higher education (or their equivalent) on strategic planning in Afghanistan, Algeria, Cameroun, Ethiopia, Gambia, Ghana, Kenya, South Africa, Madagascar, Malawi, Mauritius, the Netherlands, Bangladesh, Pakistan, and Uganda, among others. That has allowed me to experience strategic planning in a variety of higher education systems over a period of time (in some cases several years), see the plans being developed and observe conflicts about goals and how they were resolved, witness a large number of challenges to higher education in many different environments, look at a wide range of leadership styles in higher education, and follow plans for higher education change in all of them—often under very difficult circumstances. This has given me a major window into the work of planning, regular discussions of the process, and the ongoing work of a system or institution, over several months and in several cases a number of years. I have been careful not to divulge confidential events or policies (of which there were few) and have shared my findings with many of the people involved in follow-up discussions or visits. Collectively, these cases have served as excellent learning environments for a study of higher education planning in underdeveloped and developing countries.

In chapter 1, I briefly describe the focus of the study as strategic planning for higher education change and transformation in twelve cases in eight different countries in Africa and Asia in which I have worked. We will see the critical role of careful strategic and budget planning in the most successful change efforts in these underdeveloped and developing countries, as well as the importance of strong multi-level leadership, broad consensus on goals, and an open and democratic environment. My aim overall is to illustrate how careful strategic and budget planning can bring about major changes in higher education with each of these cases providing quite different examples of strategic planning for, and experience with, higher education change as well as to illustrate several failures. I look at the decisive role of high-quality higher education in fostering economic growth and social development in underdeveloped and developing countries. No nation has achieved significant economic development without a high-quality higher education system. I focus on the potential role of strategic planning in fostering higher education change and transformation. In chapter 2, I discuss some of the problems of slow and fluctuating growth and economic change in Africa and in much of the developing world in the 1960s and 1970s, focusing particularly on an overall assessment of the problems and their implications for higher education. The Asian economic situation began to improve significantly by the year 2000, while growth in Africa, after brief improvements in 2012–14, began to stall in 2015 but is now growing (Jerven, 2015: 124).

Chapter 3 begins an examination of specific cases of higher education change focusing on the case of Pakistan, a major strategic planning success in the transformation of higher education after years of decline and inaction. It is a model of careful strategic planning, budget development with risk assessment that proved its worth during a later slump in the economy. In chapter 4, I examine the higher education change process in Afghanistan—a particularly interesting and successful case taking place in the midst of war. It suggests a great deal about the leadership of strategic planning under difficult conditions—providing examples that have broad implications. In chapter 5, I look at the strategic planning process in South Africa—the difficult effort to end apartheid and produce a higher education system that is open, nondiscriminatory, and of high quality. It provides some of the most remarkable examples of national and institutional strategic planning success I have studied and suggests a great deal about the importance of process as well as goals. In chapter 6, I look at three interesting institutional cases in South Africa, the University of the North, University of Fort Hare, and Peninsula Technicon. Each of them in very different ways suggests the importance of process to successful planning.

Chapter 7 is focused on efforts to bring about higher education development and change in Sierra Leone, home of Fourah Bay College, the oldest university in Sub-Saharan Africa, and the devastating challenges encountered following a series of coups and other disasters including the Ebola epidemic. Chapter 8 is focused on strategic planning for change in Uganda, facilitated by the National Council for Higher Education, in a context fraught with dissension and a government with little interest in higher education. It has important lessons for financial planning, risk assessment, and consensus. In chapter 9, I examine the promising higher education strategic planning change efforts in Madagascar, the long struggle to gain broad support, early successes and then their derailment by a military coup d'état, and the aftermath of those events.

In chapter 10, we move to an unusual institutional level of strategic planning at the University for Development Studies (UDS) in Ghana. This example of higher education transformation serves as a model for student-centered development. UDS developed a unique third term program where teams of students worked on rural development projects during their whole undergraduate career in cooperation with local communities.

In chapter 11, in contrast, we look at the very difficult higher education strategic planning process at the University of Malawi and its aftermath—a process that was successful in developing an excellent strategic plan, one that illustrates the importance of team building and consensus on goals but also the critical need for strong government support. That case also illustrates how external consultants can sometimes help resolve conflicts that have created impasses locally. That is followed in chapter 12 by an examination of an institutional strategic planning endeavor in Afghanistan at Kabul Polytechnic University—demonstrating what can be achieved institutionally even in a war environment in which strategic planning is new and experience lacking generally and showing the importance of paying attention to writing quality in a strategic plan.

In chapter 13 I look at the leadership of change, the characteristics of leaders, the skills that seem to have been especially useful, and strategies used by various leaders. In chapter 14 we look at what we have learned about successful change and transformation in higher education in underdeveloped and developing countries focusing on several major themes. Chapter 15 presents the conclusions of this study and what it suggests for strategic planning in higher education in underdeveloped and developing areas for the future.

Chapter 1

The Critical Role of High-Quality Higher Education for National Development

As we look at the state of higher education in underdeveloped and developing countries today we see a starkly varied picture with some countries having made phenomenal progress over the last few decades and others slipping farther behind the rest of the world in quality, creativity, and effectiveness (see Sierra Leone and Madagascar below). What has become even clearer than when it was first highlighted in 2002 (World Bank, 2002) is the fact that national economic and social progress is increasingly dependent on having a high-quality higher education system. As emphasized in the World Bank's *Higher Education in Developing Countries: Peril and the Promise* (2000: 17) and further discussed and elaborated in UNESCO's 2006 study *Toward Knowledge Societies*, "Institutions of higher education are destined to play a fundamental role in knowledge societies, based on radical changes in the traditional patterns of knowledge production, diffusion and application" (UNESCO, 2006: ch.2). The authors go on to emphasize that "[w]hile there is no single organizational model, it is important to ensure emerging systems of higher education achieve a high enough level in terms of quality, relevance and international cooperation if they are to play their full role as key components in building knowledge societies."

In some countries, as Carnoy and other (2013: 2) emphasize for the BRICS,[1] it is the state and the political system that are the main drivers of the effort for quality improvement and the key to change and transformation in higher education. They note that

> [t]heir governments must negotiate complex political demands at home, including ensuring domestic economic growth, social mobility and political participation. Because more and better higher education is perceived by the public to be positively associated with all the elements of a developed society, BRIC governments' focus on their university systems has become an important part of their domestic economic and social policy. (Carnoy et al. 2013: 2)

In most of the countries examined here, public demands have not reached that state, though in several countries, including South Africa, they are moving in that direction. Nonetheless, the role of the state and public policy in the effort to raise quality in higher education has been critical in a number of the cases we will examine including Pakistan, South Africa, and Afghanistan. As Altbach notes, "All Universities cannot become world class in the sense of competing for top positions in the global ranking and league tables. But they can be world class in serving in the best way possible their particular mission, region, or country" (Altbach, 2011: 2).

Unlike the BRICS, as we will see, far too many governments and their leaders in underdeveloped and developing countries fail to understand the critical importance of high-quality higher education to national development and economic growth and thus do not understand the consequences of the serious underfunding of higher education and the failure to promote plans for quality improvement. This holds true of some donor organizations, NGOs, businesses, the general public, and even some educators as well—a failure to realize the long-term consequences of funding shortfall for higher education, which are having an additive negative effect on national development in far too many underdeveloped areas as we will see.

The demand for higher education has grown tremendously in the underdeveloped and developing world in the last several decades. That is a consequence of population growth, the expansion of primary education encouraged by the Education for All program,[2] the recognition that university graduates' salaries are substantially higher than those of high school graduates, and the understanding of some leaders that university education is essential for economic growth (Carnoy, 2013: 5). Part of the solution to the demand in too many places has been to increase access with little regard to quality or the relevance of the academic programs and little funding to accommodate the additional students.

Altbach has suggested that "all universities can be world class if they are provided with wise leadership and the resources to their mission" (Altbach, 2011: 2). That is probably too optimistic but both excellent leadership and ample resources are essential. As we will see, many of the leaders discussed here demonstrate what Northouse describes in his assessment of the skills approach to leadership as having the "knowledge and abilities [that] are needed for effective leadership" (Northouse, 2016: 366–371). In addition, success requires an effective leadership team. To paraphrase Northouse, an effective team needs to have a unifying goal, be results driven, have a unified commitment to goals, members who identify with the goals, and a collaborative climate. On the other hand, the problem of a lack of such leaders and teams was demonstrated starkly in Afghanistan at the outset of the strategic planning period in 2009 where Minister Dadfar's and Deputy Minister Babury's effort suffered from a shortage of competent leaders in the ministry and in the institutions. The loss of half the faculty and staff over the years of war and because of political rivalries had decimated leadership at every level. We will see this problem in several other cases, including Uganda and Sierra Leone.

These conditions produced a large number of poorly educated graduates hurting the chances of student employment and leading to broad unemployment. A large number of students have substandard degrees and do not meet employers' requirements. This problem is widespread internationally. For example, in India it is estimated that of the 450,000 engineers graduated every year only 25 percent have the skills to be employed (Aring, 2012: 6). The percent of firms identifying labor skill level as a major problem is 50 percent in Egypt (Aring, 2012: 6). These problems result in part from the rapid expansions of higher education without concern for its quality or relevance to employment. As the skills gap grows so does unemployment and the conditions for instability and violence. Added to that is the growing number of young people who are not getting a higher education at all. In South Asia, it was estimated that 31.1 percent of the population between fifteen and twenty-seven years old is unemployed or not in education (Economist Intelligence Unit, 2014: 4). That compounds the problem of potential anger and unrest as these high school graduates are unable to find employment.

The failure to focus on improving the quality of higher education puts these countries farther and farther behind the developed nations of the world year after year. As this gap grows, catching up becomes increasingly difficult, unrest grows among the uneducated, young people begin to leave, and even well-educated graduates look abroad to environments that offer greater opportunities for their future success, employment, and growth.

Among the goals of almost all leaders were major changes in, or transformation of, the system as Babury and I have noted elsewhere and I spelled out in the "Introduction" (Babury and Hayward, 2014). One powerful route to transformation is through careful strategic planning to ensure that change is tied to providing high-quality programs that are relevant to employment or foster entrepreneurship by graduates. Establishing high-quality higher education requires adequate funding, as Altbach has noted and as we will see. That remains a challenge even in those systems that are paying attention to the quality and relevance of higher education programs.

Most of the cases we will examine demonstrate significant successes in improving higher education quality through careful strategic planning and investment—encouraging universities to focus on meeting international expectations of high quality, produce employable graduates, contribute nationally and locally, and undertake research into some of the nation's critical problems. Among them are Pakistan from 2002–08 and beyond, South Africa, especially from 2001 to 2012, and Afghanistan from 2009 to 2016. However, as Daniel Ncayiyana and I noted in an article on graduate education in Sub-Saharan Africa in 2014 (Hayward and Ncayiyana, 2014), African higher education on the whole has been slow to make much progress, with a few exceptions, among them South Africa and Ghana. For many African countries there have been periods of growth followed by stagnation, as Jerven had emphasized. Nonetheless, he correctly emphasizes that the decline and stagnation many writers emphasize is a misreading of the data (Jerven, 2015: ch. 1), as noted earlier. The response in Asia has also been mixed, with early successes in India and later ones in Pakistan, Afghanistan, and elsewhere with the current situation looking very promising.

As we will see, a number of countries have worked to improve higher education and to begin to meet international standards with a wide range of both narrowly focused plans and, for some, comprehensive multiyear efforts to make significant advances in the quality and effectiveness of the system of higher education generally. They have been assisted by a number of donors in recent years, including the World Bank, Carnegie Corporation, Ford Foundation, USAID, several donor countries, and other donors. This has led to a major planning effort in these countries over the last twenty years with a number of significant successes, as we will see. The challenge has been especially difficult in fragile states.

Change in Higher Education in Underdeveloped and Developing Areas

The literature on change in higher education in underdeveloped and developing countries is extensive and illustrates the challenges faced by higher education systems and institutions in bringing about even the most basic changes given the political, economic, and social problems confronting many countries. Daniel Ncayiyana and I have chronicled the challenges in building and improving graduate education in Africa in our 2014 piece "Challenges of Graduate Education in Sub-Saharan Africa," where we note the difficulties and limited success of the efforts to build high-quality graduate education in that part of the world. There is also the World Bank's *Revitalizing Universities in Africa: Strategy and Guidelines* (1997), *Fixing Failed States: A Framework for Rebuilding a Fractured World*, by Ashraf Ghani and Clare Lockhart (2008), *The Bottom Billion: Why the poorest Countries Are Failing and What Can Be Done about It*, by Paul Collier (2007), UNESCO's *Toward Knowledge Societies* (2006) and *Constructing Knowledge Societies: New Challenges for Tertiary Education* (2002), among others. More recently a critique especially of Collier by Morten Jerven (*Africa: Why Economists Get It Wrong*) suggests that the comments about African economic stagnation and decline are wrong (Jerven, 2015: 2–3). This view has attracted strong support since then including by this author, with Jerven's criticism being borne out by a number of examples of recent growth in countries including Ghana, Ethiopia, and Senegal.[3]

All this work points to the challenges of development and change in higher education. We will see in the pages that follow that significant higher education change is possible, as examples of success in Pakistan, South Africa, Ghana, Afghanistan, and several other countries demonstrate. I will explore what leads to success in those cases and try to identify what distinguishes these efforts from those that have failed.

Challenges for Higher Education in Developing and Underdeveloped Countries

As we explore those questions it is useful to detail some of the major challenges that are being faced by higher education in developing and underdeveloped countries, based on my work in more than a dozen of them over the last twenty years and work on change that Madeleine Green and I did in 1997 (Green and Hayward, 1997: 3–26), which I have drawn on here. While many of the challenges are similar to those of higher education anywhere, their degree of importance in the daily operation of higher education is often especially critical because they can create an environment that is unpredictable and presents major obstacles to progress, reflecting the fragility of many of these states. Let's look at some of these challenges.

Effective Governance

Many of the countries we will be looking at in the examples below suffer from the instability of their governments. That may be a function of war (as in Afghanistan), fluid political crises (as in Sierra Leone), or a general weakness and ineffectiveness of the political system (as in Malawi). This instability makes it hard for higher education institutions to plan, to obtain support when needed, and to be assured of the long-term support required to effectively operate over time. We will see its consequences in several of the cases to be examined.

Financial Support

All of the cases examined here are of public higher education institutions, dependent on government for most of their financial support. Most are in countries with serious financial shortfalls. Many of them do not know what their allocations are likely to be from year to year, and when they do receive funding its amount can vary widely from year to year. Again, that makes long-term planning difficult, especially decisions with long-term impacts such as size of the student body, hiring of faculty members, construction of infrastructure, and expansion of programs. We will see that in far too many of these cases, higher education is starved for funds. One of the problems in general is that higher education worldwide has not done a very good job of making the case for adequate funding for higher education. Higher education leaders have generally made the case that higher education is important to the success of students—and their parents know that—but they have not done a very good job in helping both the public and politicians understand that high-quality higher education has real costs, which far too often governments are unwilling to meet.

Recruitment and Retention of Top Faculty Members

When we talk about the leadership of higher education and strategic planning, it is easy to forget that it is the quality of the faculty members that defines the quality of higher education in the long run. Faculty quality depends on their training, their ability to keep up in their field(s), their teaching load and other expectations of them, teaching and research support, and their salaries. The latter is too often ignored as not critical to high-quality higher education in developing economies. However, all too often salaries are so low that faculty members are forced to have outside jobs to survive, as in several of the cases examined here. That takes away from the time these faculty members can devote to teaching, research, participating in governance, service, and advising students. In the long run, it also often leads to the flight of the best faculty members, as we will see in Sierra Leone and several other cases.

While faculty members are sometimes paid at a higher rate than civil servants, the fact is that in most of the world the market for the best faculty members is at least regional if not international. Faculty members are generally more mobile than most other employees. Measures must be taken to ensure that good faculty members are retained if a system is to thrive.

Developing good teachers and researchers takes time. Too few higher education organizations in developing economies have any rewards systems, financial or otherwise, for their outstanding faculty members. That is a mistake. Higher education, like other employers, must value and guard its well trained and most effective employees. Only a few systems examined here have effective mechanisms to reward and retain high-quality faculty members.[4] While I am not arguing for extraordinary salaries for faculty members, they must have remuneration high enough for them to live reasonably comfortably with their families without taking second and third jobs to survive. These are issues that leaders and administrators must consider when thinking about building a high-quality higher education system.

Academic Freedom

The freedom of faculty members to teach, discuss, and carry out research without interference is key to their productivity and effectiveness. One of the hallmarks of success in several of these cases is that positive changes were facilitated by a free and open academic environment that allowed people to explore a wide range of possibilities as they sought to transform their systems. This was particularly striking in South Africa after years of oppression under apartheid, but was also very important to the transformation that took place in Afghanistan, even in a war environment. Those changes were possible because higher education operated in a remarkably free environment in spite of some limits on press and other freedoms in other parts of the system, as we will see in the discussion below.

Autonomy

The struggle between higher education and government for control over decisions and policymaking is a frequent challenge. We will see that especially in the cases of Pakistan, Uganda, and Malawi at various times during the planning and implementation processes. It is clear that in the most successful of the cases examined, high levels of autonomy facilitated the change agenda and its implementation. Autonomy is also important to quality improvement, which has to be free from outside interference of the sort that threatened quality in Afghanistan, especially regarding private higher education. On the other hand, we will see that some sort of overarching authority is important to the success of the system as a whole, putting limits on how many institutions offer PhDs, master's, and other degrees, controlling student to faculty ratios, and providing a rationale for new programs to prevent needless duplication. That became an issue in both Afghanistan and Pakistan during the strategic planning process, with institutions in both cases demanding more autonomy, and in the latter case, pushed by provincial demands to have greater control of higher education institutions in their areas.

Access

In all of the cases examined here the issue of access was a major one. In the case of South Africa, it was key given the skewed access under apartheid, which discriminated against students of color and women. Access was also an important issue in almost all the other cases. Increasingly, people have begun to recognize that access to higher education in most countries is badly skewed by income—even when it is free or highly subsidized. That poses problems of fairness, with most governments heavily subsidizing the middle and upper classes, which can afford to make significantly greater contributions to the education of their children.

In some countries, the problems of access were related to pressure to increase the number of students faster than they could be absorbed by higher education without lowering quality. In other cases, the problems were related to political pressure to admit favored individuals or groups, thus depriving students whose merit would have otherwise qualified them for university admission. In some cases, the access issue related to a desire to open the universities to everyone without thinking about the cost or the effects on quality. There were issues of access for disadvantaged groups in several cases—those with disabilities, those in war-torn areas, and those discriminated against on the basis of gender or some other factor. Every system faced some access issues, but the issue of gender was especially difficult in a number of cases. This was especially the situation in Afghanistan as we will see. In other cases, the issue was admission by race, which became a major driver in the struggle against apartheid in South Africa. All the systems we look at here faced an access issue related to class and income—most starkly addressed in South Africa, though not definitively, as we will see.

Infrastructure Expansion and Upgrading

One of the most challenging issues affecting planning for change was the need to expand and upgrade the infrastructure. All of the institutions examined here were originally intended to be small elite institutions, primarily to train civil servants and meet the technical and scientific needs of the community. With the expansion of business and industry, new demands for graduates in engineering and sciences grew along with needs in agriculture and some other areas. As democratization spread, so too did the demands and expectations of the public for places for their children in higher education institutions. Few countries had either the planning or the funding to respond effectively to these demands coupled with the need for new and updated equipment to meet technology improvements once the information technology revolution began. This became part of the planning crisis in almost every case. What kinds of infrastructure would be prioritized? In Pakistan, it was in the sciences and technology; in Malawi agriculture, science, and technology. For Afghanistan, in an effort to increase the number of women students, the highest infrastructure priority in recent years was dormitories for women, whose absence was a major hurdle deterring increased enrollment of women students. As institutions grew so did the need for more classrooms, offices, laboratories, dormitories, expanded libraries, computer centers, and support facilities. In addition, buildings constructed earlier were often now in need of upgrading and repair. Some had suffered from a lack of maintenance for years. All these demands had increased costs to the institutions and the system. The problem now was to find the funding required for this repair, upgrading, and expansion.

Technology

The technological revolution of the twentieth century has been profound, given the impact of the internet, e-mail, the ability to communicate events around the world in minutes, and internationalization. While we recognized technological change as a challenge, I think Madeleine Green and I underestimated its impact in 1997. As we have seen during a number of protests, not only do information and ideas move quickly, governments are not able to stop their circulation, in spite of major efforts to do so, as we saw in Egypt and in more recent efforts to do so in Turkey and China. That has led to recognition of the growth and importance of what Castells (2012) and others have called *network societies* as facilitating change. As Castells notes, they are "movements spread by contagion in a world networked by the wireless Internet and marked by fast, viral diffusion of images and ideas" (Castells, 2012: 2). These are motivated by widespread dissatisfaction and unemployment, with mobilization sparked by some specific event that rallies people who harbor feelings of injustice for which government is held responsible. There are also the more visible externally motivated ideological drivers which use force as well, such as Al Qaeda and the Taliban in Pakistan and Afghanistan, and ISIS in Iraq, Syria, and elsewhere in the Middle East. Technology has also had a tremendous impact on costs of higher education with the need for high speed Internet and a wide range of other expensive and rapidly changing technology.

Other Issues

There are a number of other issues that made planning difficult, as we will see. They include political interference, student unrest, national and international economic crises, growing skepticism of the public about the role and cost of higher education, development needs, the ongoing demands for training and upgrading of staff, the growing problem of job placement for graduates, and finally the growing threat in several states of external interference in higher education. That became an issue especially in Madagascar at one point and was a concern periodically in Afghanistan.

Forces for Stability and Change

Forces for Stability

Clark Kerr (1994) reminded us that higher education is one of few remaining institutions that has survived over the years, along with the church, relatively unchanged throughout that time. There is something critical about its basic structure and functions that provides an amazing amount of stability and support for higher education. Part of its constancy is a result of its flexibility and adaptability over time within that framework, part to its importance as a repository of history, findings, and new knowledge, part to its socialization role in society.

One of the reasons for the stability of higher education is tradition itself. Higher education, in spite of arguments to the contrary, is very conservative, with faculty members leading that charge. Although, as faculty members, we like to think of ourselves as at the cutting edge of knowledge change, when it comes to the university as an institution we are very reluctant to support change.

The Critical Role of Strategic Planning for Change

The quality improvement changes and transformational successes we will see in some of the examples that follow did not occur by accident. All of them were the result of careful, well-thought-out strategic plans developed in each case—plans that reflected clear visions for the future, broadly shared goals in the higher education community, the ability to mobilize support and foster the often-difficult efforts required to improve institutional quality, break down deadly hierarchies, end stultifying traditions, open eyes to innovation, and encourage creativity and growth. Most of the successes involved broad participation, inclusive consultations, and often major compromises. Indeed, some of the most successful examples nearly foundered because of conflicts, stubborn insistence that past methods were the future, inability to imagine different structures and methods, and insistence on maintaining old privilege and power structures. Careful budget preparation was another hallmark of success, as we will see, tying goals to budgets and testing budget plans through risk assessment to ensure that a particular overall plan as set out was feasible. In most cases, that involved rethinking parts of the plan, goals, budget adjustments, and careful negotiations with government and donors about funding commitments. Some failed that test—and indeed their strategic plans languished or remained only partly fulfilled.

But it is not always money that is needed. We will see that many of the goals do not involve major financial costs but do require a major rethinking of basic values and strategies, commitments to change, and often hard work that sometimes does not materialize. And then there are unpredictable events that undermined success in several cases including a coup d'état, an invasion, an epidemic, and an economic crisis.

Before we look at specific cases in detail, it is useful to review what successful strategic planning involves. That process is laid out visually in figure 1.1, revised from Hayward and Ncayiyana (2003). Success usually builds on a *vision* for change in the future. That may suggest the environment to develop a comprehensive plan to build a stronger, more effective high-quality institution. Figure 1.1 reflects the direction of the process from the *vision* through the *ongoing monitoring and evaluation* with feedback both ways, as illustrated by the double-headed arrows in figure 1.1. An effective strategic plan grows out of a dynamic process of discussion, consultation, and thinking, which produces a creative and viable vision, mission, and goals for the future, shared broadly within the institution, and able to mobilize support and adequate funding, foster enthusiasm for plan implementation and a commitment to see the process through to a successful conclusion. As we will see in several cases, the vision can be a major force in mobilizing support for the strategic plan. It should also link to the mission and help define the goals for the plan.

The vision, mission, and goals define the outlines of the strategic plan (Hayward and Ncayiyana, 2003). These often come from broad

The Critical Role of High-Quality Higher Education

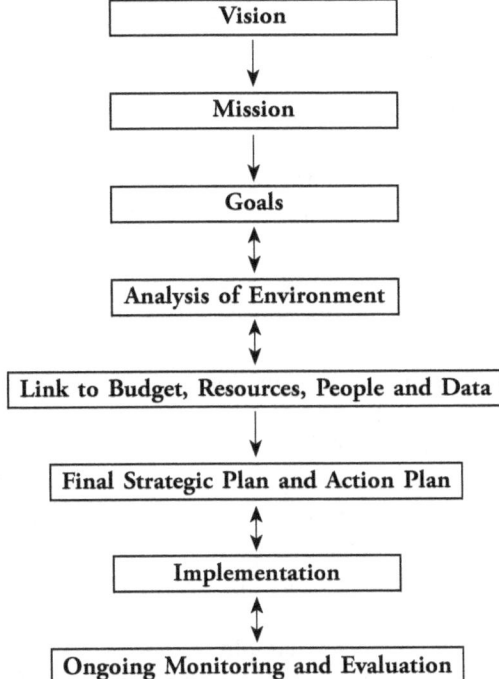

Figure 1.1. Strategic Planning Model. *Source:* Hayward, Fred M., and Daniel J. Ncayiyana, (2003), *Strategic Planning: A Guide for Higher Education Institutions,* Cape Town: Centre for Higher Education Transformation.

consultation within the university or system, especially with the faculty and staff, and in some cases the students. As Goldman and Salam suggest: "Indeed, the structure of universities requires comprehensive participation in strategic plan development" (Goldman, 2015: 4). These are tested in the context of an analysis of the environment, often called a SWOT Analysis[5]—an examination and evaluation of the goals, in which they are assessed in terms of the institutional strengths, weaknesses, the opportunities provided at the point in time, and any potential threats to success. The goals then are adjusted based on that analysis, so that there is feedback about the goals based on the SWOT analysis.

As Strike et al. (2018: 15–24) note, one of the important changes in recent years is the growing competition among universities, in part as a consequence of a number of ranking systems around the world but also of a growing concern about quality. That has pushed many institutions to do a self-assessment and start the strategic planning process.

The goals must be carefully costed and reflected in a budget that has been tested through a risk assessment to ensure that the goals can be met with available funding. Thus, there is feedback between the cost of the goals and the budget until equilibrium is achieved between goals and available funds. The budget is linked to an action plan, which details a time frame for action on each goal and defines responsibility for each goal. The implementation process must be subjected to ongoing monitoring and evaluation and adjusted when necessary if obstacles or delays emerge (as reflected in figure 1.1). Thus, there is feedback between the final strategic plan, implementation, and the ongoing monitoring and evaluation. A time line for achievement of each goal, with clearly identified responsible parties for each goal should be laid out in the action plan, which helps ensure that goals are met in a logical order, that responsibilities are clear, and that changes are made where funding proves inadequate or unexpected problems occur. Figure 1.1 provides a model planning framework.[6] Once the plan period has been completed, ideally a new strategic plan will be prepared building on the previous plan. We will see an excellent example of that in the Afghan case with a new plan for 2016–2020 prepared that builds on the *National Higher Education Strategic Plan: 2010–2014*.

Strong leadership support at every level is critical to success, especially in the fragile states such as Afghanistan, Sierra Leone, and Malawi. Where the leadership is collective at multiple levels, support is more likely to succeed. Kezar and Lester present a useful discussion of "collective leadership" in contrast to "top-down" leadership seeing it as a "dramatic departure" in the literature on leadership. We will see its importance particularly in the South African case—indeed, it proved critical to success in South Africa (Kezar & Lester, 2011: 6–7). The focus on broad participation was especially successful in a number of respects. The struggle had resulted in a tradition in which everyone got to speak at gatherings—indeed, no one could speak a second time until everyone who wanted to speak had a chance.[7] As Kezar and Contreras-McGavin (2006) were to recognize later, there was a shift to "collaboration, empowerment, multiculturalism and leadership as a collective process." As they noted, "People throughout the world connect and work together in greater frequency . . . leading to the democratization of leadership as well as to a more complex and diffuse process" (Kezar et al., 2006: 3).

Leadership that has broad experience in higher education is especially critical.[8] A particular challenge is to ensure that the changes in higher education foster greater stability and encourage national development and peace.[9] Part of the analysis of the environment involves an assessment of proposed changes to ensure that they do not have a destabilizing effect. Far too often, a focus on increased access without ensuring increased quality and relevance has long-term disruptive effects. In conflict situations in particular, including several cases examined here, that is an important issue for leadership to consider. One of the dangers, as we have seen in the Middle East, is that expanding the size of higher education, and thus the number of graduates, without increasing quality and relevance can lead to unrest and violence as growing numbers of graduates fail to meet the needs of employers, remain unemployed, and become a growing force for dissent and violence. Under those circumstances, the expansion of higher education becomes a driver of conflict. We have seen the dangers of that in Egypt and parts of the Middle East where many jobs go unfilled in spite of unemployed graduates because graduates do not meet the qualifications of employers even in their fields.[10] A recent study of unemployed young people in Egypt showed that 30 percent of them turned down jobs because they didn't think they matched their level of qualifications, while others had degrees but didn't meet employer requirements. The result of the former is what is called "luxury unemployment" in that these graduates could have job offers but feel those are beneath their dignity (Ghafar, 2016: 5). They become a growing chorus of dissatisfaction and are potentially destabilizing. A key task in planning is to ensure that higher education programs correspond to national and employer needs and that the quality of education is high enough to meet realistic employer expectations and to foster individual entrepreneurship. For that reason, we will see that quality improvement is high on the list of goals in most of the strategic planning efforts examined here.

Most successful strategic plans examined in this study followed the model laid out in figure 1.1. The University for Development Studies in Ghana and the Ministry of Higher Education in Afghanistan demonstrated the advantages of well-developed and well-thought-out goals and mission statements, which contributed significantly to their ability to mobilize support and meet most of their transformation goals. The leadership of planning in Afghanistan was goal and process-centered, highly collaborative, and context-focused. It was also transformational both in the terms of the focus on socially desirable end,[11] of the sort Burns has identified,[12] but also in terms of the magnitude of changes sought being both extensive and deep, as I discussed in the inroduction. The Higher Education Commission in Pakistan had the most elaborate and effective financial planning process with a careful ten-year risk assessment, which proved its worth when income fell below expectations after six years. It is a model of budget development and risk assessment for strategic planning. Peninsula Technikon and the University of Fort Hare developed especially effective strategic planning units, which carefully facilitated and monitored the plans, provided excellent data to planners throughout the process, and ensured that the budgets were closely linked to the strategic plan. Peninsula Technikon provided an especially effective implementation process with careful monitoring.

A large part of the successes, which we will see in the examples that follow, can be attributed to the quality of the individual strategic planning processes, the action plans and budgets they produced, and their implementation. They helped focus action on critical areas, organize people to action, mobilize support, attract funding, and foster implementation. The ongoing monitoring, as we will see in several cases, was essential to recognizing and responding to challenges along the way.

Chapter 2

Prelude to Planning in Higher Education

Overview of Case Studies

In my 2008 study of strategic planning (Hayward, 2008), I examined the planning process and its impact in three countries: Afghanistan, Pakistan, and Madagascar. The importance of excellent strategic planning was clear. In this study, I also focus on those who led the change process, the public policies at the heart of the strategic plan, and the intricacies of the change planning process itself. The roles of leaders and people at various levels in the planning process are an important part of success. What are the key characteristics of these people? What roles do leaders play in successful change? I also focus on the planning process itself. What are the key factors in successful higher education planning? What do these cases suggest about planning for higher education and higher education policy? What are the major challenges?

The Context for Strategic Planning in Higher Education in Much of the Developing World

The 1960s and 1970s saw a period of neglect and often decay in much of Africa and parts of South Asia with GDP largely stagnant in South Asia during this period, then falling (Bloom et al., 2011). In many countries there was political turmoil and loss of interest in higher education, such as in Ghana and Malawi. War and violence plagued a number of these countries, including Afghanistan and South Africa. Political turmoil was widespread. Most of Africa and much of South Asia were suffering from economic crises, which were having a profound effect on the well-being of citizens and funding for higher education.

By the late 1970s the situation of higher education in Sub-Saharan Africa had seriously deteriorated due to the convergence of falling commodity prices, trade barriers, increasing prices for imports, and political crises spawned by coups, authoritarianism, and civil unrest. Many economists at this point saw Africa as a chronic failure of growth. Indeed, the authors of *Accelerating Catch-up* suggested, "Over a 20-year period extending from the mid-1970s to the mid-1990s per capita GDP growth in SSA [Sub-Saharan Africa] was either zero or negative" (World Bank, 2009: 8). Work since that time has challenged some of those conclusions, suggesting that although African economic growth was slow, there have been periods of strong growth overlooked in earlier economic analyses. An excellent study by Jerven in 2015 noted that "I demonstrate how most African economies grew from the 1950s to the 1970s and then contracted with a debt crisis and other shocks in the 1970s." (Jerven, 2015: 5) He goes on to say: "The period from 1979 to the late 1990s can be interpreted as a vicious circle in which both economic and political conditions deteriorated. The essential point is that these are spirals, not traps—otherwise we would not have seen recurring growth" (Jerven, 2015: 94). Jerven suggests that there has been change and that "there are opportunities for further change. This is why this current period of growth should not be ignored: it should be seized upon to secure future grown on the African continent" (Jerven, 2015: 120–121).

In 2009, the World Bank and other donors concluded that development efforts in Africa should be refocused to concentrate on primary education through the program of "education for all."[1] That decision was followed by most other donors, with funding for higher education in Africa decreasing markedly after that announcement.

At that point, in Africa, higher education had lost much of its luster nationally, in contrast to the immediate postindependence period which also had negative consequences for funding. Following independence, the universities were seen with pride as part of the new order. Higher education leaders and faculty members had high prestige and were regularly called upon to serve as ministers, directors, or on national committees. In the years that followed, however, higher education began to become a source of political criticism, focused on the failures of competitive government, corruption, nepotism, and incompetence. Students, too, began to be sources of opposition and demonstrations. Higher education generally came to be seen as an expensive home for opposition. It would be tolerated but limited (as in Sierra Leone), suppressed (as in Ghana), or largely ignored and starved for funds (as in many countries). As political turmoil grew, so did the involvement of faculty members and students in these protests, and as a consequence, the anger of those in power was turned against the universities. This often resulted in increased government interference in universities' governance, as we will see in several cases that follow.

In addition, wars, coups, and other violence on campus and in the communities further hurt higher education. These factors and budget cuts drove many of the best faculty members to leave the country or undertake other pursuits. Those who stayed usually had to find second jobs to make ends meet. Thus, research declined as did attention to teaching. Many universities were on strike for long periods, further hindering higher education. In some places, such as Sierra Leone, the universities were ignored for a time. As President Siaka Stevens said to me at one point following an attack on the car of an MP who had gone up the hill to the university: "I don't go to the Fourah Bay College anymore, it is guaranteed to provoke a demonstration. At the same time, I let them alone to do what they want. Any politician who is foolish enough to go up there, deserves the trouble he gets."[2] Nonetheless, he continued to support the university, though he, too, brought politics into higher education.

As local and international economic crises spread, so too did the deterioration of higher education. The economic decline continued in most of Africa south of the Sahara until 2012, when growth rates rose to 5.3 percent, and then to 6.1 percent in 2013 (Hayward & Ncayiyana, 2014: 171). Little of this economic success was reflected in spending on higher education, however. Economic activity declined markedly in the region over the next few years and by 2015 had declined to 3.5 percent, which was the lowest in fifteen years, according to the IMF. However, Sub-Saharan African experienced modest growth of about 3.4 percent in 2018, with growth increasing in two-thirds of the countries (IMF, 2018: 1). Several countries, including Ghana, have grown 6 percent or higher, although others, including South Africa, were lagging in 2018, though showing promise as a result of recent political changes.

South Asia experienced an average growth rate per capita gross domestic product of 1.9 percent in the period 1960–1970. However, it fell "to 0.6% in the next decade, rising to 3.2 per cent for each of the next two decades, and climbing to 5.3 per cent since 2000" (Bloom, 2011: 8). By 2015, South Asia was expected to be the fastest-growing region in the world according to a World Bank press release (World Bank, 2015). Indeed, by 2018 South Asia had once again become the fastest growing region in the world, with its growth expected to increase to 6.9 percent and higher the next year (World Bank, 2018b). As one would expect, the improvements in South Asia varied by country, with Pakistan and Afghanistan among the laggards.[3] Pakistan, with a current account deficit of $18 billion and a huge budget deficit, will probably have to make a new appeal to the IMF to deal with the crisis (The Diplomat, Aug. 15, 2018).

Thus, the economic picture has been mixed for both South Asia and Sub-Saharan Africa over the past decade, with Asia looking at significant improvements by 2016 and thriving in most countries by 2018. Sub-Saharan Africa saw a period of mixed economic development but slow growth beginning in 2017 with estimated GDP growth of 2.4 percent in 2017 and encouraging growth in 2018 averaging 3.4 percent and 4.8percent, excluding Nigeria and South Africa (World Bank, 2018a: 1–3). Thus, the prospects for both regions looked encouraging in 2018.

Chapter 3

Leading Change in Pakistani Higher Education

> It is imperative that we invest massively in education, particularly in basic and applied sciences.
>
> —Professor Atta-ur-Rahman (2003), chairman, Higher Education Commission

The Context for Higher Education Change in Pakistan

Higher education in Pakistan had suffered from decades of neglect. In 2001, it was among the world's laggards with only 2.6 percent of university-age students attending higher education institutions. Only 23 percent of university faculty members had PhDs, little research took place, teaching was not emphasized, the infrastructure had deteriorated, and not a single university ranked in the top five hundred internationally. The crisis in higher education was acknowledged as early as 1947, followed by more than a dozen commissions and policy documents examining the crisis. Although there was agreement about the magnitude and seriousness of the problems, there was no consensus about what should be done or who should drive the changes—government or universities.[1] Thus, little was done other than minor expansion of the system in 1998. What was particularly galling to many leaders and concerned citizens was that India, which had been part of the same system as Pakistan in 1947, had made great strides in expanding and building high-quality higher education since independence. Indeed, the Indian higher education sector witnessed tremendous growth in the number of universities and higher education institutions following independence, growing from twenty higher education institutions in 1950 to 677 in 2014 (Govt. of India, 2016). Most importantly, many of the Indian universities were among the best in the world, including the Indian Institute of Science, Bangalore, University of Delhi, and the Indian Institute of Technology, while Pakistan had no highly rated universities.[2] This was a cause of great concern in the higher education community.

A Request for Action on Higher Education

The impetus for the transformation of higher education in Pakistan in 2002 grew out of the congruence of a number of factors. Probably most important was the general realization in the academic community that Pakistan was way behind much of the rest of the world in quality—especially its neighbor India. Added to that was the cumulative effect of a series of studies, all of which came to the same conclusion, though nothing was done in response. The critical push for change resulted from the work of Atta-ur-Rahman and the task force set up by President Musharraf, which resulted in the establishment of the Higher Education Commission and its mission to prepare a plan for major change. In 2000 Atta-ur-Rahman, the minister of science and technology, told President Musharraf that Pakistan could not make any progress in science without major changes in higher education.[3] Soon thereafter, a task force was set up to review the situation in higher education and make recommendations for reforming higher education. Their review, entitled "Science and Technology Based Industrial Vision of Pakistan's Economy and Prospects of Growth" (circa 2000), described a system in a virtual state of collapse, lacking the capacity to change. These deliberations resulted in a recommendation to create a Higher Education Commission (HEC). The chairman of the task force, Shama Kassim-Lakha, and Atta-ur-Rahman, met with the president to present the report and the recommendations for what needed to be done to improve science and higher education in general. Cabinet accepted the report in April 2002 and the Higher Education Commission was established in September 2002 as an autonomous and largely financially independent body. The president appointed Prof. Atta-ur-Rahman as the founding chairman of the HEC in October and Dr. Sohail Naqvi became its executive director.

Professor Atta-ur-Rahman was a distinguished academic with a long history of outstanding research, publications, and academic recognition for excellence in research. Dr. Sohail Naqvi was also a distinguished academic and was an expert on change management with a keen understanding of higher education finance. From the outset, the HEC began a major reform effort based on a plan that was called the *Medium Term Development Framework: 2005–10* (MTDF). It had been largely drafted under the oversight of Professor Atta-ur-Rahman by Dr. Sohail Naqvi, executive director of the HEC, and Kamran Naim, a senior staff member of the HEC. They built on an earlier piece by Professor Atta-ur-Rahman that focused on faculty development. He had been thinking about how to improve higher education since his appointment as minister of science and technology in 2000. During that period, he had launched a number of initiatives to increase funding for universities and to expand information technology infrastructure for higher education, industry, and commerce across the board. He also started work on the idea of a digital library.[4]

The plans for higher education change were laid out in the *Medium Term Development Framework*, which had four main goals: increased access (to be doubled over five years); improved quality (especially faculty master's and PhDs); infrastructure upgrading (improved teaching material, equipment, and laboratories); and a focus on relevance (concentration on key areas for development and research to meet national needs) (HEC, 2005: 5). The plan included establishing a national system of accreditation and a tenure system that would allow significant salary increases for those who qualified.

Leading the Planning Process for a Change Agenda

Professor Atta-ur-Rahman and Dr. Sohail Naqvi brought to the planning and implementation process a clear vision and goals—a strong commitment to quality improvement, a deep understanding of what a high-quality higher education system entailed, experience with first-rate research and outstanding teaching. That was coupled with a commitment to implementing the plan and the drive and talent to mobilize support. Both were actively involved in the discussion of, and planning for, the wide-ranging changes proposed. They also recognized that significant changes would require a major infusion of funds from the government and donors. As Chairman Atta-ur-Rahman noted in the *HEC Annual Report: 2002–2005*, "It is imperative that we invest massively in education, particularly in basic and applied sciences" (HEC, 2003: 6). He wanted Pakistan to develop its own knowledge society and move to the forefront of knowledge creation. He went on to say:

> This [ending dependence on the West] is only possible if we build world-class Centers of Excellence where new knowledge can be created and applied towards the development of new products and processes. We must realize that our real wealth is not the oil, minerals or other natural resources that we may possess but our children. It is only through investing in them by incorporating a challenging educational system which can unleash their creativity and by providing them the opportunities of contributing to our national development.

The commitment to high quality and an understanding of what that would entail was a critical part of the success of the implementation efforts. HEC leaders were effective at mobilizing support from government, academic leaders, and faculty members, helping them realize the primacy of quality improvement broadly if the Pakistan system of higher education was to catch up with the rest of the world and become a quality leader. The HEC moved quickly to implement faculty development through PhD training, sending the first groups of faculty members for PhD training right away, starting the process to improve facilities, allocate research funding, and provide scholarships to support faculty training in Pakistan and abroad. Executive Director Sohail Naqvi was a masterful organizer and kept the HEC staff on target with regular meetings, encouragement, support, and praise.

The Role of National Leadership in Fostering and Facilitating the National Strategic Plan Was Critical

Professor Atta-ur-Rahman was especially successful in obtaining government support. He had the ear of President Musharraf, who promulgated several decrees that facilitated the strategic planning process and the change agenda. Prof. Atta-ur-Rahman and the president were successful in dampening some of the opposition to the plan and obtaining funding. The unique autonomy of the HEC also gave it added ability to control funding and expenditures. Some of the opposition to the HEC came from the provinces, which wanted to control higher education institutions in their regions. The president helped the HEC obtain substantial increases in government funding for public higher education year after year. The successes were remarkable with the recurrent and development budget increasing 340 percent in real terms from 2001 to 2005–06. These increases restored university capacity lost over previous years. Much of the budget growth was needed to cover the costs of increased enrollment. Nonetheless, expenditures per student increased 41 percent during that period. The budget continued to increase the next year by a little more than 30 percent but remained low by international standards.

Opposition to the Plan

Many of the changes proposed in the strategic plan initially faced strong opposition from a number of chancellors and faculty leaders who saw them as a threat, an attempt to centralize power in the Higher Education Commission, and likely to weaken what faculty control existed. Thus, at the outset, the change process had many critics. Indeed, early on many of the major institutions refused to cooperate. They argued that the HEC was trampling on their autonomy, infringing on faculty authority, usurping powers delegated to the regions, and instituting changes without consultation. Indeed, the leaders of the HEC regarded a top-down approach to change as essential to success, and given previous failures to address the recognized issues and weaknesses, they were probably correct. In addition to its academic critics, HEC successes in obtaining funding resulted in criticism from several other ministries that did not fare as well in funding allocations and were jealous of its achievements and autonomy. And there were other complaints. One commentator asked:

> So why are students and professors alike worried? The chairman's many critics say the flood of money has led to corruption, plagiarism, and favouritism. Far from improving the quality of universities, they say, Mr. Rahman's financial incentives, lacking sufficient checks and balances, have led to a lowering of already abysmal academic standards. (Neelakantan, 2007: A38)

The criticism was not without merit. For example, since more than five thousand faculty members were participating in PhD programs, their replacements were usually faculty members with only bachelor's degrees.

Students resented that. Older faculty members also resented the emphasis on PhDs under the plan and were angry about the large number of new hires with foreign PhDs being accepted as faculty members.

In an effort to enhance quality, ensure faculty accountability, reward those who demonstrate excellence in teaching and research, and raise salaries to compete with many private institutions, a tenure track system was introduced which provided salaries two to three times higher than existing faculty civil service levels for those who qualified. The salary increases required a prior review, which was demanding. That too resulted in a great deal of opposition, especially from those faculty members at senior levels who felt they had already demonstrated merit, were concerned about being reviewed, and worried about the qualifications required.

The leaders of the HEC held a number of meetings with administrators and faculty members to explain the plan, with significant success. As a result, the tenure process moved forward gaining support as people began to understand it and see the benefits. The response of Quaid-i-Azam University (QAU) is typical, as reported in 2006. "Around three years back when the TTS[5] was introduced the QAU faculty had expressed its reservations over its provisions, but after lots of meetings between HEC officials and the university a final document was agreed upon." The writer went on to say that "the teachers' community was really feeling excited about the new development which would definitely help improve teaching standards" (Ghumman, 2006). This is but one example of the efforts made by the HEC staff to help people understand the plans for change, gain support, and foster implementation.

Financing the Pakistan National Strategic Plan

In developing a financial plan, Pakistan benefited from close cooperation with the World Bank. Unlike many donors, once the bank agrees to consider funding a project, it works closely with the higher education sector to develop a plan which both parties believe is feasible.[6] That usually is preceded by a Program Document for the proposed credit, as was the case for Pakistan (International Development Association, 2009). The World Bank's proposed credit was $66.9 million for the project with the rest of the funding to come from Pakistan government funds, university incomes (tuition, fees, and project income), and other donors.

From 2001 to 2005–06 the budget for higher education increased more than 450 percent, both in terms of the recurrent budget and development budget, to $270 million. In spite of these increases, bringing the total government spending to about .3 percent of GDP, its total was low in comparison to other Asian countries such as India and the Philippines at respectively .7 percent and .4 percent of GDP (World Bank, 2006:14). In 2005 recurrent expenditures in Pakistan were $770 per student whereas its global peers in Asia were at $900 (ibid.). Thus, in spite of the major increases its budget remained low in terms of other countries. The problem was that higher education in Pakistan had been woefully underfunded for decades.

A team made up of HEC staff and World Bank staff worked together to develop a long-term budget for the *Medium Term Development Framework* (MTDF). This would require an assessment of the costs of each of the goals, an estimate of potential income from the institutions, government, and donors, predictions about the state of the economy and its implications for funding the plan, and an assessment of risks involved in funding and implementation and policies that would be needed for implementation.

Putting together a budget for the plan period involved calculations related to its major components. Each of them was costed over ten years, as shown in figure 3.1 below, which illustrates the costs for

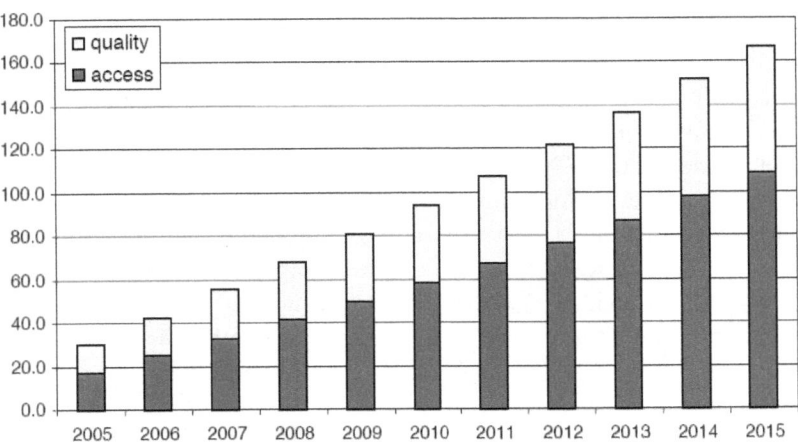

Figure 3.1. Projections of Costs Related to Increased Access and Enhanced Quality. In billions of Rupees. *Source:* World Bank, (2006), "Pakistan: An Assessment of the Medium-Term Development Framework," Washington DC: World Bank. © World Bank.https://openknowledge.World Bank.org/handle/10986/18450 License:cc BY 3.0 IGO.

access and quality assurance in the *Medium Term Development Framework*. For example, it was estimated that the cost of the quality assurance would be $37.3 million from 2005 to 2015 (World Bank, 2006: 74). After the total costs for the base year were calculated, assessments were made about enrollment growth and its implications, the additional number of faculty members needed to maintain a student faculty ratio of 19 to 1, cost of additional infrastructure, likely government subvention, income from institutions (tuition, fees, project income), and likely funding from donors. A number of scenarios were produced based on this information ranging from one using conservative assumptions to one based on optimistic assumptions including generous estimates of economic growth.

Early projections showed that the costs were too high compared to expected income even with the most optimistic assumptions about income. Thus, revisions were made and some of the assumptions changed. In the end, it was assumed that government funding would increase from 1.8 percent of GDP to 4 percent between 2006 and 2015—an increase of 6 percent per year (World Bank, 2006: 77). Assumptions about student fees now included a 5 percent increase a year (to a maximum of about $250 each per year total by 2015), university contributions to the total cost were now estimated at 21 percent of the total. Assumptions were made about increased efficiency of HEC spending, class size was increased to an average ratio of 1 to 25, which provided major savings, and other reductions in costs were made to bring the final total for the ten years to a little more than $4.8 billion over ten years (World Bank, 2006: 79). The planners were concerned about the risk that the government would not be able to increase the budget contribution as promised. They were also worried that the increases in student fees, though modest by international standards, would limit participation by the poor when coupled with other costs such as transportation, books, supplies, and clothing. The World Bank team were committed to improving the percentage of poor students in higher education, in what at that time was a system that catered primarily to middle and upper-income families.

An Assessment of Risks to Realization of the Budget and the Change Plans

The team realized that there were risks even with these changes. It was not going to be reasonable to assume that government would increase its funding beyond the 4 percent GDP level. Indeed, the risk was that it would not reach that level of funding. The team was confident that the universities could meet their commitments, since they had already demonstrated an ability to provide that level of funding. The team was also concerned that the incentives in the plan to encourage more student admissions to agriculture and the sciences might not meet the targets. That would not have a cost effect, indeed it might lower costs slightly, but the bank's team was concerned that too many graduates in the humanities and arts would lead to high levels of unemployment, dissatisfaction among graduates, and long-term instability. Similarly, too few graduates in science and technology would hinder projected economic growth and deter external and internal investment.

Overall, after the changes had been made, the team was satisfied that the revised budget plan would be sustainable, would not reduce the quality of the plan, and left the major goals in place, thus promising major improvements in access, quality, and relevance. At the same time, they recognized that additional cuts might be needed, suggesting that "[b]y somehow slowing down the pace of reforms, and prioritizing them more radically, the HEC also might find itself in a better position to rally more interest and resources into the universities and into the higher education subsector at large" (World Bank, 2006: 83). Indeed, after 2008, there was a deterioration in the financial situation in Pakistan plus growing political instability. This led to cuts in the program in later years.

A Model Budget-Making Process

The budget-making process in Pakistan is a good model of what should be done in conjunction with planning major changes in higher education. The budget goals having been identified and prioritized in the strategic plan, each of them was costed for each year of the plan. The plan in Pakistan was originally for five years, but the team chose to do a ten-year projection since that gave a better time frame to assess the benefits and to even out the costs. Once those costs were calculated, other critical factors were assessed, including: the growth in student numbers and their implications for space needs, equipment, and additional faculty members. That was factored into a target for the student to faculty ratio. As noted above, the original target of 19 to 1 proved too costly in terms of costs for additional faculty members needed at that ratio and thus it was increased to 25 to 1.

Income factors were calculated next. What were reasonable assumptions about the government subventions? Several models were tried, including no increases. That clearly would not work. Eventually, a target was agreed upon that fit in with government promises and financial projections. To that were added calculations about the contributions projected from the universities, including student fees All this was tested against concerns about how an increase in fees would affect admission of poor students. When it was determined that this level of cost to students was acceptable and would not adversely affect enrollment of students from poor areas, those increases were accepted. Finally, the cost and income figures were put together. At that point, a risk assessment was undertaken. Due to concerns in several areas about income, adjustments were made to assure a balance of costs and income that seemed reasonable, and a final budget was agree upon.

The example of Pakistan's budget planning effort during 2003–05 is a model of how planning for major changes in higher education should be carried out and put in place. It was a thoughtful and detailed process that led to some reductions in the size of the original plan but left the overall goals intact. And in the long run, the care and thought put into this effort paid off when a national budget shortfall occurred and it was able to be adjusted for higher education in a way that did not unduly affect the implementation of the changes planned and underway.

An Early Assessment of the Change Efforts

In its early assessment of the implementation the change process laid out in the *Medium Term Development Framework,* the World Bank review team noted: "Immediately after its birth, the HEC launched an unprecedented number of systemic reforms directly aimed at the worst and most immediate issues plaguing the HES [higher education sector] or, more exactly, universities" (World Bank 2006: ii–9). The report continued, noting the successes in many areas: "While the magnitude of the tasks ahead is daunting, the progress made by HEC thus far suggests that the proposed programs can result in major improvements toward the transformation of the subsector" (ibid.: 25). At the same time, the bank team expressed concern about the need to focus additional attention on governance and to include affiliated colleges which were left out of the MTDF.

Among the initial successes of the plan was the emphasis on faculty development. It was focused on the brightest young faculty members, having them compete for opportunities to study abroad, with their selection by representatives of the countries involved including Germany, the United States (through the largest Fulbright Program in the world at that time), Sweden, and others. One of the innovations of the plan was a major effort to ensure that participants returned to teach in Pakistani universities. That was facilitated by offering those with PhDs a scholarship of $100,000 a year prior to their return—payable on arrival. The scholarships included a guarantee of employment, the first year as HEC Scholars at the salary of an assistant professor, ready access to academic literature through the Digital Library, access to sophisticated instrumentation through an "Open Access" system that would provide results of data analysis within seventy-two hours at no cost to them (paid by the HEC), and positions at universities thereafter. The return rate of those sent abroad for PhDs was 97.5 percent.[7]

What motivated the development of a change strategy after so many years of inaction since 1947, in contrast to the ongoing changes in India since 1947 when each gained independence? The question is a difficult one to answer. Several commissions had laid out the problems over the years but there was no agreement about how to resolve them and so nothing was done. Part of the problem was the debate about who had the responsibility or the right to bring about the badly need changes, the central government or the provincial governments. That question opened up a long-standing debate about power in Pakistan generally, and it was not one that was easy to resolve. Part of the difficulty was that the answer would also place the costs for the changes, which were going to be substantial, on that entity—either the national government or the provinces. While the provinces wanted control, they did not have the ability to raise the funds needed, or the ability to negotiate with donors. At the same time, those in the government were not eager to take on those major costs and responsibilities. In addition, the government was so fractured that it seemed unlikely that the cabinet would agree to any of the fundamental changes needed. Thus, none were attempted or accomplished.

Part of what changed and led to the initiative to work on a change strategy starting in 2000 was the World Bank report the *Peril and the Promise* (2000), which stimulated some academic rethinking of the situation in Pakistan and contributed to the requests to set up a task force. Ms. Zobaida Jalal, the minister of education, set up the task force in 2001, encouraged by a group of academics. The task force began meeting in April 2001 with World Bank funding. Encouragement also came from Minister Atta-ur-Rahman, as noted earlier, then federal minister for science and technology. In addition, President Musharraf had given strong support for a major change initiative with promises of significant government funding. The task force reviewed the work of the previous commissions and their recommendations as well as the lack of any significant follow-up. Members talked with academics and educators around the country, with students, and consulted widely with others concerned with science and higher education.

The Task Force noted that "[n]o society has prospered without significant and sustained investment in higher education. Today, as the world becomes increasingly interconnected, higher education is considered critical for the achievement of economic progress, political stability and peace. However, in Pakistan, higher education ill-prepares the society for the challenges that lie ahead" (Ministry of Education, 2002: 2). The task force report included many findings about the failures of higher education including that it provides "an education of mediocre quality, which does not prepare them [students] to participate effectively," it has "ineffective governance," "inadequate funding," and is suffering from "politicization" (MoE, 2002: 3–7). The task force then recommended setting up an autonomous Higher Education Commission to undertake a major overhaul of higher education and provided a number of recommendations for changes in higher education including in management, finance, infrastructure, academic programs, research, recruitment, and remuneration. That served as a foundation for the preparation of the national strategic plan, the *Medium Term Development Framework*.

Thus, the stimulus for action in 2000 was the congruence of several important factors: the stimulation of the World Bank's *Higher Education in Developing Countries: Peril and the Promise* (2000), the concerns of the academic community about the poor state of higher education in Pakistan, the interest of the minister of science and technology, that of President Musharraf in improving higher education and science training in particular, and the willingness of the World Bank to fund the task force. The *Peril and the Promise* had played an important role in mobilizing awareness of the tremendous strains facing higher education in developing countries, the failure of higher education generally in the developing economies to meet the quality needed to foster development, and importantly, its suggestion that governments had an obligation to improve higher education to foster the development essential to well-being and future growth nationally.

This congruence of forces helped lay the groundwork for change by mobilizing strong sentiment for change, identifying some of the major goals for change, emphasizing the urgency of the situation, allaying fears about the funding needed to support these changes, and placing responsibility for change on the national government. That, coupled with the outcome of the task force review and its report, which was accepted by the president and cabinet, led to the establishment of the Higher Education Commission. There was the well-prepared leadership of the HEC ready to move forward with a change agenda based on the strategic plan it had developed, the *Medium Term Development Framework*.

The changes that resulted in Pakistan over the next five years in higher education were extraordinary. Almost four thousand scholars participated in programs in Pakistan during the next six years. More than nine hundred faculty members studied in foreign PhD programs. The HEC instituted major upgrades for laboratories and ICT, rehabilitated facilities, expanded research support, and developed one of the best digital libraries in the region. In the first six years, student numbers increased 210 percent, to 283,500 (HEC, 2010: 10).

The successful changes in Pakistan demonstrate the importance of a well-thought-out change plan and the ability of national and institutional leaders to gain acceptance of the plan and carry through on its implementation. Chairman Atta-ur-Rahman and Executive Director Sohail Naqvi were believers in a top-down approach and in that respect were driving forces behind the development and implementation of the plan as well as its major advocates during the early period when opposition was extensive. Watching them in action at meetings was telling, as you saw opposition melt away as they carefully and astutely explained the importance of the changes proposed, the need for higher quality, faculty development, and a new emphasis on research. The leadership also benefited from their close relationship with and support from President Musharraf who used both his political power and his persuasion to provide accommodating public policies as well as to make sure the HEC had the additional funding it needed to move forward quickly. When President Musharraf was forced to resign, his clout was lost to higher education. But by that time the policy changes were well under way and the goals widely accepted in higher education with major progress made in achieving the goals of the MTDF.

In looking at the success of the national plan in Pakistan, the importance of the leadership of both Atta-ur-Rahman and Sohail Naqvi is clear. They were also working in an environment that facilitated success with a strong president, a cabinet of technocrats who paid attention to the recommendations of the task force on higher education, and a president who helped ensure the funding that was needed to move forward with the MTDF. Both Atta-ur-Rahman and Naqvi brought a range of experience and critical skills to the process, in particular their understanding of what a quality higher education system required, coming partly through their own experience as successful academics. They complemented each other in a variety of ways. They illustrate what Northouse describes in his assessment of the skills approach to leadership as having the "knowledge and abilities [that] are needed for effective leadership" (Northouse, 2016: 43). Both had exceptional conceptual skills which complemented each other, Naqvi was especially skilled technically when it came to finance and data analysis, and they both had excellent human skills in their ability to work with people. Atta-ur-Rahman was especially good at working with other senior leaders, including President Musharraf, and Naqvi with faculty, staff, and funders. They were good organizers, understanding what was needed to gain support and how to get it. In the process, they were able to draw on their extensive knowledge of research, administration, and high-quality academic standards to make their case.

Sohail Naqvi was a master at finance, checking budget figures constantly during discussions, and understanding the intricacies of higher education budget planning. That made him especially successful with the World Bank team working with them and with other donors, since he quickly gained their confidence. Added to these two were a number of other hard-working leaders at the HEC, in the planning division, quality assurance and accreditation, research, and scholarships. Although the senior leadership was critical to success, it was a team effort and the HEC had assembled an excellent team.

Understanding the Importance of Breadth in Leadership to Help Make the Planning Process a Success

It would be misleading to suggest that strong leadership alone can achieve successful higher education change in Pakistan or anyplace else. We saw that depth of leadership in Pakistan where the HEC had an outstanding staff of professionals who helped organize the planning, establish the accreditation process, oversee faculty development, gather the data and lay the groundwork for viable planning, organize laboratory upgrades, develop the digital library, and facilitate other parts of the plan. And there were many others on university campuses who organized quality cells, helped select faculty members for study abroad, and worked to upgrade curricula.

Successes of Higher Education Change beyond 2010

Until 2002, Pakistan had done little to improve higher education since independence in 1947, in contrast to India, despite many commissions and widespread agreement about its weaknesses, as noted earlier. That began to change in 2000 when Atta-ur-Rahman became federal minister of science and technology and expressed his concerns about the weaknesses of science and higher education to the president and others. There were also growing academic demands for change. In a short period of five years, Pakistan made more progress in upgrading higher education and instituting its change strategy for 2005–10 than any other higher education system we will examine here.

As we saw, the pace of quality improvement and change moved forward smoothly and effectively for six years with little opposition to the changes, and what occurred was primarily focused on the structure of authority rather than the actual programs of the strategic plan. However, problems began for the Higher Education Commission (HEC) in 2008 when there was a change in government. President Musharraf was forced from office and with his departure a powerful ally of higher education was lost. Soon thereafter the government began to interfere with the HEC. At that point, there were several thousand scholars studying abroad funded by the HEC. Their scholarships were stopped by the government in August 2008. Chairman Atta-ur-Rahman, who still had two years left on his term, felt that both he and the HEC were being attacked, partly because of his close association with the former president. In order to protect the HEC and those studying abroad, Atta-ur-Rahman offered to resign if the government would release the funds for the scholarships. The government couldn't fire the chairman since his position was protected. They agreed to his proposal and he resigned in October 2008.[8]

Part of the new parliamentary opposition to the HEC seemed to be a reaction to the HEC's participation, ordered by the Supreme Court, in ferreting out MPs who had fake degrees. This effort grew out of the establishment of a committee in May 2005 headed by Justice (retired) Hasir Aslam Zahid to look into the issue of fake degrees in Pakistan (HEC, 2005), which put the major role for the review on the HEC. When the HEC completed the review, it was revealed that two hundred of the MPs had fake degrees, including the then minister of education. Those MPs were removed from office by the Supreme Court. However, many members of Parliament resented the HEC's role in this review. They worked to break up the HEC by putting many of the universities under the authority of the regions rather than the HEC. At this point, Atta-ur-Rahman, though no longer chairman of the HEC, determined to fight these attacks on the autonomy of the HEC and went to the Supreme Court arguing that under the Eighteenth Amendment to the Constitution, the government could not take the funding authority away from the HEC or devolve authority of the HEC to the provinces. The Court agreed, ruling that this authority belonged to the federal government and could not be changed without new legislation—legislation which Parliament was unable to pass.

While funding and authority were restored to the HEC for the universities, the attacks on the HEC continued with the focus now on the executive director, Dr. Naqvi, and the autonomy of the HEC. Dr. Naqvi was eventually forced to resign. In spite of the earlier victory in the Supreme Court, the HEC budget was cut again by about one-third from the previous year's development budget of 663 billion rupees ($7.7 billion) to 300 billion rupees. There was a further cut later in 2010, which reduced the development budget by 83 percent (Khan, 2010a). At the same time, funding for four hundred students studying abroad was suspended, which caused chaos for those students (Khan, 2010b). The government claimed that these cuts were due to the need to use this money to deal with emergencies caused by massive flooding. However, most of these cuts were made prior to the floods, and the military budget was increased substantially at the same time. Part of the reason for the cuts was no doubt due to anger of some of the members of Parliament, who, or whose colleagues, had been caught up in the review of PhDs that revealed that a number of them had bogus degrees. These cuts seemed to suggest a government that was not interested in high-quality higher education. The government argued that the institutions should offset the cuts by raising more of their own money—something they had already started to do. Nonetheless, such massive cuts could not be offset by funds raised in a short time even under ideal circumstances. At this point, the universities shut down in protest. That resulted in many of the cuts being rescinded, though some remained in place (Khan, 2010a).

In 2013, a new government was elected, headed by the Pakistan Muslim League. It acted to restore the lost authority of the HEC and increased its funding. By 2016, the HEC budget had grown to about 70 billion rupees, whereas at the end of the chairmanship of Atta-ur-Rahman in 2008 it has been about 40 billion rupees. This allowed reforms started earlier to continue. Funding now was back to reasonable levels. Nonetheless, the interim period of cuts hurt higher education and some of the best faculty members were lost, taking jobs abroad or getting other employment. Prior to the cuts, several Pakistani universities seemed to be on their way to top world rankings. That momentum was reversed, and in spite of the restoration of funds to the HEC, no Pakistani universities made it into the top ranks. Nonetheless, Pakistani higher education is now back on track to continue quality improvement and build centers of excellence as was proposed in 2002, and the quality of both science and higher education has improved significantly.

When I asked former chairman Atta-ur-Rahman if the improvements made as a result of MTDF starting in 2002 were still in place in 2016, he replied:

> I think the momentum we set up at the time was irreversible because thousands of these students sent abroad came back. So, there was a steamroller moving in spite of attempts by the previous government to disrupt the system. Things now are back on track.[9]

Indeed, that seems to be the case. In that vein, in September 2016, the minister of planning, development, and reform reported that to implement the recent roadmap for the Higher Education Commission the HEC would send ten thousand students to the United States for PhD studies starting in 2017 (Dunya News, 2016).

The implementation process of the strategic plan in Pakistan has important lessons about the critical need for careful financial planning with a risk assessment, and a willingness to reduce the scope of plans if funding is not adequate—which the HEC/World Bank team did in the early stages of the planning process. The plan was largely top-down in its implementation, and in spite of some resistance to HEC control it worked, because there was almost universal agreement about the goals and the need for major changes. Funding was available through the HEC, the leadership of the HEC was ready, effective, academic, and fair. In addition, people were exhausted by the bickering and inaction and wanted to see the long-sought-after changes put in place and sustained.

As we look at the success of the strategic plan overall, we see that it was clearly transformational. It resulted in fundamental changes in the structure and some of the major values of the system (Hayward & Babury, 2014), the system became increasingly merit-based, it fostered gender equity, became much more responsive and efficient, stimulated academic life, was clearly open to the world of ideas, enshrined academic freedom, operated in a supportive environment during most of the post-plan period, and was sustainable—all characteristics of transformed systems I laid out in the Introduction.

Especially important to long-term success, as the HEC and its planning role came under attack in 2008, was the continued strong agreement on the goals for changes, the remarkable successes that had occurred quickly under the HEC action plan for change, strong faith in the HEC, and the fact that several thousand faculty members were benefiting from the faculty development opportunities, research funding, new tenure track scheme with its substantial salary increases for those who qualified, the significant budget increases for higher education over five years in excess of 300 percent, as well as the tremendous improvements in academic programs and quality, including those stimulated by accreditation. These were powerful forces for sustainability and strong leverage against those who tried to undo some of early successes of the HEC. Furthermore, the attacks on the HEC were seen as political rather than academic in a context in which most people in Pakistan were tired of politics and the constant crises and clashes that seemed endemic to the process. When political change did occur, higher education regained much of the status lost in earlier attacks and sustained most of its implementation efforts. However, there continues to be a battle over funding in Pakistan between the HEC and the regions, though the government allocation for 2017–18 was 2.5 percent, up from 2.3 percent in 2016–17.

This is low by international standards (Tahir, 2017). Nonetheless, higher education change in Pakistan remains one of the best examples of effective strategic planning in the last several decades, resulting in transformational change in a developing economy.

Chapter 4

Afghan Higher Education

Change in a War Environment

The Context for Higher Education Change in Afghanistan

Afghan higher education was in dire straits when people began to think about the planning process in higher education in late 2001 following the defeat of the Taliban. Almost every institution was damaged, half the faculty and staff had been jailed, killed, or fled (World Bank, 2005: 48), and many institutions were closed or taken over by warlords or politicians. Afghanistan had one of the lowest percentages of higher education students in the world at that point with fewer than 1 percent of college-age students enrolled in higher education. Only 5 percent of the faculty members had PhDs and about 30 percent master's, leaving 65 percent teaching with only a bachelor's degree. The curriculum was out of date, labs were mostly destroyed, campus libraries and other facilities had been looted, and some campuses lacked water and electricity. Administrators, faculty members, and staff were dispirited due to more than thirty years of war, underfunding, and the decline of higher education. Several institutions lacked chancellors and other leaders. Replacements of some of the leaders lost were often compromised or just placeholders demonstrating no leadership.

The first task of the Ministry of Higher Education was to reopen, repair, and bring the institutions under the control of the ministry, find replacement faculty and staff, and begin the process of rehabilitation.

That was well underway under the leadership of Minister Sharif Fayez, who worked diligently from December 2001 through December 2004 in a successful effort to bring higher education back under the umbrella of the Ministry of Higher Education, start the rebuilding process, and develop policies for major changes in higher education including reorganization of governance. By the end of 2008, Minister Dadfar and Deputy Minister Babury began the process of thinking about a strategic plan. The impetus was the general recognition of the disastrous state of higher education due to the war and especially to neglect by the Taliban, as well as the exclusion of women from education generally. The effort was encouraged by potential funding from both USAID and the World Bank and the enlightened leadership of Minister Dadfar and Deputy Minister Babury. At their initiative, a steering committee was established early in 2009 to prepare a strategic plan for higher education, with about a dozen members from the MoHE, higher education institutions, several donors and NGOs participating. The World Bank was particularly active in helping get the planning process started, working closely with Minister Dadfar and Deputy Minister Babury on a weekly basis with assistance from staff at UNESCO. A number of subcommittees, which involved more than one hundred people, were established to work on different parts of the plan, facilitated through efforts of the USAID-funded Higher Education Project (HEP). After extensive work by the committees and with assistance from NGOs, by December 2009 a draft plan and budget were completed. The two main change goals of the plan were quality improvement broadly defined and increased access (but not at the expense of quality).

Increased access was a major priority given the small percentage of Afghans of college age in higher education. Yet, higher education was badly underfunded and it was clear that the demand was greater than could be funded by the state given the constitutional requirement of free higher education up to the graduate level. One part of the solution was to allow private higher education institutions, which until 2006 had been illegal. Careful rules were put in place for establishing private higher education institutions following a World Bank review carried out by the Academy for Educational Development, which suggested that private higher education be legalized (Hayward & Amiryar, 2003). Private institutions were legalized in 2006. The number of students in private institutions grew quickly as shown in figure 4.1 below.

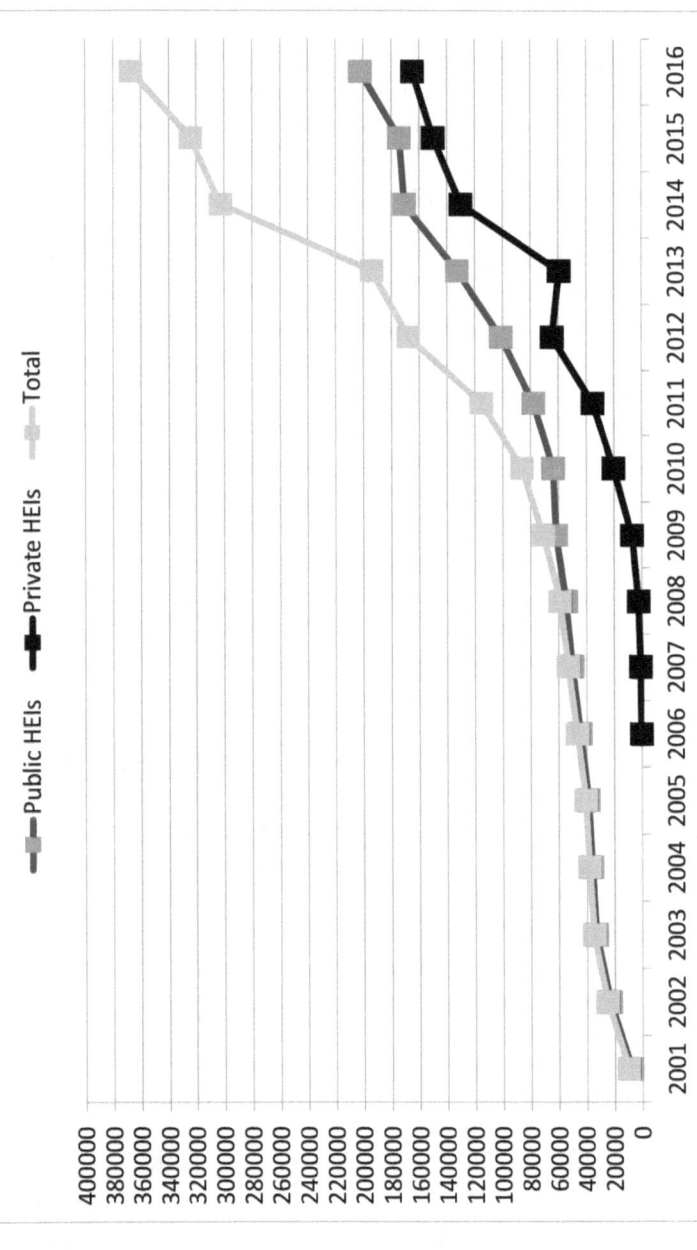

Figure 4.1. Growth of Public and Private Higher Education in Afghanistan: 2001–2016. *Source:* Ministry of Higher Education by Fred M. Hayward and Hassan Aslami. Kabul, Afghanistan.

The strategic plan was broadly welcomed in the higher education community since everyone agreed that higher education had suffered grievously due to the war and had to be improved and upgraded. The overall goals for change were transformational, aiming to change the system in fundamental ways by introducing merit hiring and promotions, accreditation, a major upgrading of the curriculum, and financial decentralization to the extent possible. The first steps to improve quality focused primarily on faculty development—bringing large numbers of faculty members to master's and PhD levels. During the plan period, more than seven hundred faculty members were sent for master's and PhD training—the PhD training to be carried out abroad since there were no PhD programs in Afghanistan at that time. The ministry also began the process of setting up an accreditation system, established a curriculum commission to encourage upgrading the curriculum, with fifty programs completely upgraded during the plan period. Another MoHE commission of faculty members and administrators was set up to develop a new framework of regulations regarding student and faculty responsibilities, plagiarism, publication expectations, sexual harassment, and faculty rights and responsibilities. That was followed soon thereafter by another group that began to work on gender issues.

Success Requires Broad Leadership at Multiple Levels

At the outset, Minister Dadfar's and Deputy Minister Babury's planning efforts suffered from a shortage of competent leaders in the ministry and in the institutions. The loss of half the faculty and staff over the years of war and political rivalries had decimated leadership at every level. Many of those who were competent and experienced were also unwilling to be involved in leadership and administration, which had become corrupt and noted for incompetence. Both Minister Dadfar and Deputy Minister Babury worked quietly to recruit outstanding faculty members to serve on national commissions[1] and to serve as directors of the various programs in the MoHE. They replaced a number of ineffective chancellors with more effective people. They also met regularly with chancellors, senior faculty members, staff, and students to get their inputs and suggestions about a wide variety of issues. Both had an open-door policy, and that paid off. When there was a crisis on a campus, Deputy Minister Babury did not hesitate to go to the campus to meet with students, staff, or whoever was aggrieved. He also was willing to meet with representatives of demonstrating students when they marched on the ministry. This had seldom been done in the past. Given the high esteem in which both men came to be held because of these efforts and the success of their campaign to clean up the corruption in admissions, people were now willing to serve on committees, commissions, and various short-term assignments. Suddenly, working with the senior leadership of the ministry became a mark of pride and respect.

Opposition to Some Proposed Changes

Not all of the change goals put forward engendered support. Indeed, early on there was substantial opposition to both accreditation and to gender equity—in the latter case forcing the drafting committee to delete some measures related to gender in the original draft of the *National Higher Education Strategic Plan: 2010–2014* (NHESP) to ensure that it would be approved. Deputy Minister Babury, Minister Dadfar, and members of the steering committee worked diligently to gain support for the changes, making some compromises along the way. They were helped by the fact that President Karzai was a strong supporter of the changes. There were a few conservative higher education leaders strongly opposed to much of the plan who argued that these were political changes to be decided by the political leaders, not the leaders of higher education. In the end that view did not prevail.

Understanding How Support for Major Change Was Built: The Challenges of Gender Equity and Private Higher Education

As in the case of Pakistan, long and careful discussion eventually led to almost universal support for the planned changes. Part of what made that possible was the fact that Deputy Minister Babury involved some of the best and brightest faculty members in the steering committee, and later on the commissions on rules and procedures, accreditation, and the curriculum. This was also true of the review boards whose faculty leadership was critical to success. These leaders, for their part, worked to convince their colleagues of the importance of the changes proposed, including accreditation, merit hiring, and promotions—in stark contrast to the old boys' network that had had primacy in both areas prior to that. Indeed, somewhat to the surprise of the leadership, the merit hiring and promotion process was implemented without objection and very few attempts were made to thwart it.

None of this would have happened without the careful leadership of Minister Dadfar and Deputy Minister Babury and their efforts to make the process participatory and transparent. Their vison for the future and the goals put forward by them and members of the Steering Committee were almost universally incorporated into the *National Higher Education Strategic Plan: 2010–2014*. The breadth of participation and the openness was critical to success. The energetic campaigning of those involved in the goals of the plan, their honesty and hard work, and their success making the case for these changes, brought the vast majority of faculty members, staff, and administrators to support the goals for change and transformation. This helped foster implementation as well.

Leaders' Ability to Gain Support Facilitated by "Moral Imperatives"

The strategic planning and implementation process was made much more difficult by the ongoing war, threats to the lives of the minister, the deputy minister, several directors, and senior faculty members who were involved in leadership of the implementation of various parts of the plan. An important part of the success of the strategic plan was the moral leadership of Minister Dadfar and Deputy Minister Babury. Both had been imprisoned for their strong beliefs, Dadfar for opposing the Russian invasion and Babury for opposing Taliban control of higher education. Both were seen as impeccably honest. Both worked hard to end corruption in the ministry and in 2007 succeeded in cleaning up corruption in the Kankor—the admissions examination. Their moral leadership had a profound impact on many faculty members and staff. They were especially impressed by the ongoing efforts and successes in ensuring that there was no corruption in the admissions process after 2007. Prior to that, for a price one could gain admission to medicine, engineering, and other preferred fields. A number of people were fired in the ministry and mechanisms were put in place to constantly monitor the admissions process. And indeed, there were periodic new schemes to thwart the admissions examination process—some of which involved armed intervention, but to no avail in the long run.

After thirty years of war, most faculty members and staff were tired of violence, corruption, and intimidation and saw both Minister Dadfar and Deputy Minister Babury as moral leaders with whom they were willing to risk a great deal. As one said to me, "I am willing to put my life on the line to bring about change, end corruption, and make major progress in higher education."[2] He then took on leadership of a review commission that received many threats against its work but moved forward to assess private higher education institutions—and in the end recommended closing eleven of them.

The one area in which the opposition was particularly strong was exemplified in efforts to prevent progress toward gender equity. While that goal made it into the text of the *National Higher Education Strategic Plan: 2010–2014* (Ministry of Higher Education, 2009: 5), all references to affirmative action had to be removed, as well as much of the language related to implementation of gender policies, in order to have the plan approved. The Ministry of Higher Education had indicated its commitment to gender equity in 2009 in the plan. Starting in 2011, in consultations with the Ministry of Women's Affairs and others, the ministry began to work quietly on efforts to improve the position of women in higher education.

At this time, in some parts of Afghanistan, strong resistance to education for women was a regular occurrence. Schools for girls were destroyed, young girls were attacked with acid on their way to schools,[3] a headmaster was killed for admitting girls to a secondary school. In 2009, at the time of the NHESP: 2010–2014, even at the MoHE only Minister Dadfar and Deputy Minister Babury and some administrators and faculty members on the plan steering committee were vocal in their commitment to improving the conditions of women in higher education.

While the top leaders in higher education were committed to gender equity and had support from some leaders in urban areas, it was not an issue that generated much interest in higher education generally (see Table 4.1 on page 60, for statistics on enrollment of women). The MoHE carried out a small study to determine the major impediments to the enrollment of more women students in higher education. That study pointed to the scarcity of accommodations for women—many fewer than for men—as the major obstacle to women's enrollment. There was a major concern for the safety of women students—that they have housing that was safe

Table 4.1. Increase in Female Students at Public Higher Education Institutions: 2001–2016

	Students						
Year	Total students	% increase	Number of females	Number of males	% female	% increase female	Increased no. female
2001	7,881		380	7,501	.5%		
2002	22,943	359%	1746	21,197	8.6%	100.0%	1,746
2003	30,121	31.3%	4462	25,659	14.8%	155.6%	2,716
2004	39,514	31.2%	8290	31,224	21.0%	85.8%	3,828
2005	39,354	–0.4%	8808	30,546	22.4%	6.2%	518
2006	39,797	1.1%	7499	32,298	18.8%	–14.9%	(1,309)
2007	49,311	23.9%	8619	40,692	17.5%	14.9%	1,120
2008	54,683	10.9%	9,991	44,692	18.3%	15.9%	1,372
2009	61,709	12.8%	12,180	49,529	19.7%	21.9%	2,189
2010	63,837	3.5%	12,465	51,372	19.5%	2.3%	285
2011	77,336	21.1%	15,025	62,311	19.4%	20.5%	2,560
2012	101,300	31.0%	19,215	82,085	19.0%	27.9%	4,190
2013	132,949	31.2%	25,206	107,743	18.9%	31.2%	5,991
2014	161,212	21.3%	29,904	131,308	18.5%	18.6%	4,698
2015	174,269	8.1%	36,959	137,310	21.2%	23.6%	7,005
2016	202,757	16.3%	45,397	157,360	22.4%	22.8%	8,438

Source: Ministry of Higher Education by Fred M. Hayward and Hassan Aslami. Kabul, Afghanistan.

and supervised, in keeping with Jane Vella's second principle for sound learning, which stresses safety,[4] both physical safety for women students and a safe learning environment for students and faculty members. In some cases that required both a change in attitudes of male faculty and students and a more open and hospitable environment on campus for women. That study also led to a call for more dormitories for women. This request was circulated in a piece by this writer as advisor to the ministry entitled "Gender Challenges in Higher Education: The Critical Need for Residence Halls for Female Students," which was widely circulated in 2012 and 2013. It was read by most donors and led to funding two women's dorms initially through the U.S. Embassy Cultural Affairs Office. Later, it generated support from France for women's dorms at Nangarhar University, from Germany at Baghlan University, from Norway at Faryab University, and from the Ministry of Counter Narcotics, which built two women's dorms, one at Ghazni University and one in Faryab University. That significantly improved the housing situation for women. In addition, the MoHE requested funding from the Kabul Donor Group for ten more dormitories for women.

The MoHE's work on a draft gender strategy was a collective effort that involved many participants over the next two years. It received a great deal of support from the Ministry of Women's Affairs, the committee on gender in parliament, the Human Rights Commission, a number of chancellors, senior female and male faculty members, and the Sharia Law Faculty at Kabul University. The Higher Education Project (HEP) and its follow-up University Support and Workforce Development Program (USWDP)—both funded by USAID)—agreed to pay for the printing of the document and assisted with preparation, translation, and overall support for the project. A final English version of the MoHE gender strategy was completed in May 2014. The final Dari version was completed and ready to be published in December 2015.

The process of preparing the gender strategy had the oral support of some male and female faculty members, students, and administrators over the years, but there was limited actual action to foster better conditions for women or to recruit more women either as students or faculty members on most campuses. However, there were some notable exceptions, institutions that made a special effort to help their campuses become more welcoming and secure for women, including: a major outdoor floodlight project to "light up the night" to enhance the safety of women at Kabul University; transportation for women students on campus, including to and from their dormitories, at Khost University; special programs to encourage women to apply to Balkh and Nangarhar Universities; and special Internet facilities for women at Kandahar. Khost University has allowed women to apply for hostel space without any preconditions; Takhar University worked with male students on a code of conduct including anti-harassment policies; several universities have set up special committees or women's councils to address issues of women's safety. In 2005–06, the institutional strategic plans of Nangarhar and Kabul University listed gender equity as long-term goals. Kabul University established a joint program with Durham University in England to provide graduate training for women faculty members. Several higher education institutions established faculty and student committees to encourage women to enroll, foster safety for women on campus, and promote gender equity.

Overall, however, the main efforts to improve conditions for women have been initiated and carried out through the Office of the Deputy Minister for Academic Affairs at the MoHE, with help from women faculty members, women administrators, and some students as well as several NGOs, donors, and the Ministry of Women's Affairs. To date, too few people in the campus communities have been willing to publicly support improved conditions for women students. Progress has also been slower than expected in hiring female faculty members, in part because of the small pool of women applying, family obligations, and hostility in some departments and programs. Progress in increasing the number of students has shown better results, with an increase in female students to 22.4 percent in 2016 from 18 percent in 2014 and near zero in 2001—attributable primarily to the addition of new dormitories for women. Thus, the number of women student numbers has grown from virtually none in 2001, to 10,016 women in 2008 (the base year for strategic planning), to 45,397 in 2016, an increase of 221 percent since 2008. As noted earlier, the Taliban had forbidden access to all levels of education to girls and women. The one exception in higher education between 1996 and 2001 was in medicine, since Taliban leaders did not want their wives and daughters to be treated by men. Thus, Kabul Medical University enrolled about 380 women medical students during that time, graduating approximately twenty-two female MDs a year.

The number of female faculty members has grown from 382 women in 2008 to 764 in 2015, comprising about 14 percent of all faculty members and representing an increase of 200 percent since the base year of 2008. The freeze on funding for new faculty hires starting in 2015 hurt the process of increasing the number of women faculty members (as well as men). A small amount of recruitment was possible to meet some of the remaining vacancies and provide replacements for faculty who were retiring or leaving higher education institutions. It is also important to acknowledge that there remain male faculty members and administrators on several campuses who are resistant to the recruitment of women.

However, the failure of women's efforts in 2013 to gain parliamentary approval of the policy "Elimination of Violence Against Women" promulgated by President Karzai in 2009 was a serious blow to gender equity when it took place. Indeed, the response of opponents to that effort was new laws and rules prepared in 2014 that make it hard for family members and any relatives to testify against abusers of women (Graham-Harrison, 2014: 1). These problems led the MoHE to delay releasing the higher education gender strategy, fearing that its premature circulation might also result in a negative and repressive response from some members of parliament, though the ministry continued its quiet efforts to increase the number of women in higher education. Nonetheless, a revised sexual harassment policy, expanding on the 2009 version, was released by the MoHE in 2015.

It was not until July 2016 that the ministry, with strong support from President Ghani, felt able to release the higher education gender strategy, even though it had been finalized two years earlier. In the meantime, the MoHE had been working quietly to implement policies to improve the status of women, such as publishing the sexual harassment strategy (MoHE, 2015), building additional dormitories for women students, and increasing the number of women students and faculty members. The reaction to the release of the higher education gender strategy has been positive. The groundwork had been well prepared for it over the previous five years.

Funding Higher Education

In spite of strong support for higher education from the presidency, funding higher education was always a challenge because of the many demands on both the national budget and donor funding. Nonetheless, the MoHE usually did better than many other areas, although not as well as primary and secondary education due to the emphasis on Education for All. The strategic plan did relatively well in acquiring two-thirds of its funding, and USAID and the World Bank continued strong support for the implementation of the strategic plan. On the other hand, the economic situation in Afghanistan deteriorated during this period, which was reflected in a decline in per capita expenditures for higher education almost every year, starting in 2011 (see table 4.2 on page 64). This reflected a general economic crisis in the country coupled with a substantial increase in unemployment from an average of 8 percent from 2006 to 2013, jumping to 25 percent in 2014, 40 percent in 2015, and 45 percent (World Bank, 2016a) in 2016 due to the loss of jobs occasioned by the downsizing of the ISAF military forces and the general economic decline in the country. This has resulted in decreases in both income tax and customs receipts. As a consequence, ordinary budget funding for higher education has also declined from $521.57 per

Table 4.2. Ordinary and Development Budgets for Higher Education: 2010–2016

	Ordinary Budget (US dollars)	Percent increase/ decrease	Development Budget (US dollars)	Percent increase/ decrease	Ordinary budget per capita
2010	$33,295,162		$10,379,000		$521.57
2011	35,000,000	5.1%	20,500,000	98%	452.57
2012	47,133,996	34.7%	57,224,514	179%	465.40
2013	64,000,000	35.8%	78,000,000	36.3%	481.39
2014	71,429,000	11.6%	82,696,472	6.0%	443.07
2015	80,868,155	13.2%	55,000,000	–33.5%	464.04
2016	70,481,953	–12.8%	60,805,165	10.6%	345.55

Source: Ministry of Higher Education by Fred M. Hayward, Kabul, Afghanistan.

capita in 2010 to $345.55 in 2016, a decline of 34 percent. That puts funding substantially below what is needed for quality higher education.

Private Higher Education

Another area that proved to be difficult in the plan implementation process was private higher education. For several years there had been a few private higher education institutions run by foreign entities, but they were not legal. The argument against them was that education was the responsibility of government, and that people could not afford private higher education. In any case, public education was free, so the Ministry of Higher Education did not see private higher education as viable. The MoHE strongly opposed private higher education, arguing that it was unnecessary for Afghanistan. Nonetheless, the World Bank set up a task force, overseen by the Academy for Educational Development (AED). It was sent to Afghanistan to examine the possibilities for private education, with the author as chief of party. The other members of the team were

Sarah Amiryar of George Washington University and Mohammed Essa of the AED Staff. Part of the push for private higher education came from the World Bank, which was encouraging private higher education in the developing world, helped by an initiative by American University to set up a university in Kabul, which the World Bank offered to help fund.

The team headed by the author spent several weeks in Afghanistan talking to leaders in the ministry and in higher education, meeting with proponents of private higher education, and visiting universities around the country. As the team traveled, it found that large numbers of families were already paying for tutoring for their children to make them computer literate and increase their proficiency in mathematics, science, and languages. They did not see private higher education as a problem and argued that Afghans were so desperate for high-quality education that they would pay whatever the cost. The team did a limited survey of private providers and found that many were charging relatively high fees for private or group courses in single subject areas. The team concluded that there was a need and that government was unable to meet it. Another major proponent of private higher education was the former minister Sharif Fayez, and his support was important to final approval of both the World Bank and the government.

The team suggested procedures for approval of private higher education institutions to ensure that they were of good quality. On that basis, the MoHE set up a committee to oversee approval of private higher education institutions—a committee that was very strict and careful at the outset. The recommendation of the review committee that private higher education should be legalized were approved in 2006.[5] Very few private institutions were approved at the outset. However, after Prof. Dadfur retired as minister, several ministers who followed allowed new private institutions of higher education to be established—through personal relationships or corruption, ignoring the admissions committee—most of which did not meet the requirements for operation. What followed was a far too rapid growth of private higher education, from no private institutions in 2005 to 128 private institutions in 2016, comprising about 130,000 students. While the initial institutions were carefully vetted, many of the later ones were not, and by 2013 the MoHE was facing a difficult problem of weeding out those below standards.[6] For the next few years the MoHE worked to eliminate the substandard institutions or force them to meet minimum quality standards but many of them had political connections and used them and other means to avoid closure. The

MoHE has continued to work to review all the private higher education institutions, close those below standards, and work with those institutions slightly below expectations to help them improve their academic programs. This has turned out to be a difficult task and sometimes has involved a struggle against corruption—often hard to prove but real in fact. Several of those involved in the review process were threatened and needed strong support from the MoHE, and in some cases the police, to carry out their duties.

Institutionalization and Sustainability of Higher Education Change in Afghanistan: 2009–2016

The *National Higher Education Strategic Plan: 2010–2014* was a remarkably successful effort, resulting in transformation of the system in major ways (as defined in the introduction), and instituting changes that fundamentally altered its structure and some of its major values.[7] The plan followed the pattern laid out in figure 1.1, with particular emphasis on analysis of the environment, which encompassed more than one hundred faculty members, administrators, and advisers. As suggested earlier, a transformed higher education system will move from a traditional hierarchical system where hiring and promotions are primarily based on who you know to one based on merit, as it did in Afghanistan. The system "enshrined gender equity" as one of the goals of the 2009 strategic plan, with substantial success achieved as the percentage of women students grew to more than 22 percent, up from near-zero at the end of the Taliban period. The system became more "knowledge-based" with an emphasis on well-trained faculty members, research, and publications. It also became much more "responsive and efficient," though decentralization efforts were only marginally successful due to opposition from the Ministry of Finance. Afghanistan "opened to the world of ideas" seeking world-class curricula. One advantage in Afghanistan was the ability of higher education to operate in an environment with a remarkably "high level of academic freedom," which allowed wide-ranging discussions about goals and procedures and thus effective planning. Another major facilitator of transformation was strong donor support through the World Bank, USAID, and several other major donors, which helped make the changes "sustainable." What has happened since the end of the plan period in 2014? Have the transformational changes been sustained? What is the current situation with the new *National Higher Education Strategic Plan: 2016–2020*? What does this suggest about the sustainability of change?

The national strategic planning process in Afghanistan was the responsibility of the Ministry of Higher Education through the Office of the Deputy Minister for Academic Affairs. He and his staff oversaw preparation of the NHESP: 2010–2014, communication about it with the institutions, governments, and funders, oversight and implementation working with the institutions. The ministry insisted that each university set up a strategic planning committee, both to develop and oversee its own five-year institutional strategic plan and to incorporate the change goals, and at a later date to incorporate the goals of the national plan into the university's own plans, rules, and procedures. The institutions had a great deal of autonomy over their own institutional plans, although the MoHE did monitor this effort and give advice when asked.

Throughout this period, implementation of the new national policy goals was emphasized at regular meetings with the chancellors of the thirty-six public higher education institutions, both in workshops in Kabul and in weekly Skype meetings. The major policy documents that related to faculty rules and procedures for recruitment, promotion, publications, quality assurance, and accreditation were circulated to all institutions and discussed at these meetings. In addition, the Curriculum Commission produced the *Curriculum Review and Development Guidelines for Review*. One of the critical successes, a sexual harassment policy that expanded the 2009 sexual harassment policies, strengthened protections and punishments for violations, and emphasized measures to improve the campus environment for women, was completed and circulated in 2015. It also applied to men. The higher education gender strategy, which had been prepared with extensive consultation, was published and released in July 2016 (MoHE, 2016a). It included an implementation plan for institutions, faculties, students, staff, faculty members, and the ministry.

Institutions had been encouraged to prepare their own institutional strategic plans, which focused on the goals and needs of each institution while incorporating the expected goals of the NHESP. The first round was prepared during 2010–12. Each plan had a budget and action plan for the institution. Twelve institutions had written institutional strategic plans under a previous World Bank project in 2005–06 and were familiar with the process. The MoHE offered a series of workshops for all the public institutions to ensure that they were familiar with the strategic planning process. In addition, the book *Strategic Planning: A Guide for*

Higher Education Institutions (Hayward & Ncayiyana, 2003) was made available to all higher education institutions in Dari and English as a base for their planning efforts,[8] which helped facilitate the strategic planning process at the institutional level.

At the MoHE, progress on the NHESP was monitored through the Office of the Deputy Minister for Academic Affairs, with reports issued approximately every six months detailing the state of the budget for the plan, progress on each of the goals of the plan, challenges and bottlenecks, and changes to be made as a consequence. The last of these reports was completed in October 2014 showing that although only 60.1 percent of the requested funding of $574,353,000 had been received by the end of the project, 72 percent of the goals had been achieved, with those eliminated being primarily infrastructure goals postponed because of lack of funding. Overall, implementation of the strategic plan was a significant success with major transformation taking place in faculty development, merit hiring and promotion, curriculum upgrading, accreditation, recruitment of women students, gender equity, and a significant start on decentralization policy (Hayward, 2015).

In May 2013, the Deputy Minister Babury and I prepared an outline for the next strategic plan—which was intended to cover the years 2015–19—to follow from the *National Higher Education Strategic Plan: 2010–2014*. The focus of the plan was to be on goals intended to continue the quality improvement underway, continue faculty development, focus on relevance of the curriculum, improvement of graduate education, employability of graduates, improved governance, increased decentralization, efficiency and transparency, improved research related to national needs, increased student contributions to their housing and food, and continued work on gender equity. This follow-up to the *National Higher Education Strategic Plan: 2010–2014* was further evidence of the institutionalization of the strategic planning process in the Office of the Deputy Minister for Academic Affairs at the MoHE.

A Breakdown in the Institutionalization of Strategic Planning in the Ministry

In late May 2013, Mujtaba Hedayet of the Higher Education Project (HEP), was at the ministry and was stopped by someone who asked if it was true that he had been involved in work on the previous national higher education strategic plan. He answered that he had worked on it but wondered why the question. He was told that a committee had been set up to work on the new strategic plan for 2013–18 and that they needed some help, wondering if he might be willing to provide that. Mujtaba asked the questioner if he had talked to Deputy Minister Babury who had led the planning effort in 2009 or to his advisor, who had facilitated it. The answer was a surprised "no." It turned out that members of the planning committee had also not read the previous national strategic plan—for if they had they would have known that it was intended to run from 2010 through 2014, not 2013. Mr. Hedayet recommended that they start their effort with a discussion with Deputy Minister Babury. The committee then met with the deputy minister and his senior advisor—the first time either the deputy minister or his staff heard from or about the committee and its efforts. How could this have happened?

In piecing together the puzzle of lack of communication and consulting, it seems these events took place in the following manner, for the following reasons. It is a lesson in how not to do national higher education strategic planning. At some point in early 2013, Minister of Higher Education Obaid met with officials from the World Bank. Among the topics discussed was the possibility of starting work on the higher education strategic plan to follow up on the existing plan. The bank promised funding for that effort and encouraged the minister to set up a committee to write the plan. The minister proceeded to do that. However, in doing so neither the minister nor World Bank employees consulted with, or contacted Deputy Minister for Academic Affairs Babury, who had overseen the highly regarded and often cited *National Higher Education Strategic Plan: 2010–2014*. The committee appointments were also made without consultation and did not include the deputy minister or any of the members of the strategic plan steering committee from 2009, which had helped prepare the previous plan. Continuity would have facilitated the process and built on the foundation that had been established by the previous plan.

This was a period during which there had been tension between the minister and the deputy minister over several actions taken by the minister that the deputy minister regarded as illegal—a conflict eventually resolved by President Karzai following the resignation of Deputy Minister Babury over these issues, a resignation the president refused to accept. That tension may have been the reason for the lack of communication. It is also probably the case that the minister wished to control the process himself, something he was certainly entitled to do. It also seems that he had advised some of the new committee members not to contact the deputy minister.

What followed was a series of missteps and failed efforts to prepare a strategic plan. None of the committee members had any significant strategic planning experience, though one had been on an institutional strategic planning committee. Several of the members had been out of the country for several years and were thus not familiar with the current state of higher education in Afghanistan. This committee had been working for three months at this point but had not achieved anything and was floundering. The main qualification of the committee members seems to have been that they were friends of the minister or someone close to him.

The committee began to prepare material for the new strategic plan, much of it based on the outline of the previous plan. They also assumed that the strategic plan was for the World Bank and should follow its directions. The deputy minister had told them that the plan was that of the ministry for the country and should be thought of in that way. Nonetheless, the discussion continued to focus on "What does the World Bank want?" rather than "What does Afghanistan need?" It also did not appear that they had very much knowledge about higher education in general, with one or two exceptions on the committee, and a very limited vision for the future. They were well paid, some as much as $8,000 a month, in contrast to the average salary for a full professor of $500 a month. The committee had a budget of about $400,000 for this work.

In October 2014, although I had retired from HEP at the end of 2013 and returned to the United States, I received an e-mail from Deputy Minister Babury asking me to read the enclosed draft national higher education strategic plan. He made no comments about what he thought of the draft. It was more than 130 pages long, yet unfinished, with many blank sections yet to be written. It appeared that when completed it would be more than 150 pages long without a budget or action plan. The previous national strategic plan had consisted of twenty-eight pages of text and twenty-three pages of the budget and action plan. I was appalled when I read the draft document. It was very badly written, some of it taken from material prepared by HEP such as the status reports about what had been achieved during the NHESP: 2010–2014 to date. Much of the text was in the form of long essays about topics like accreditation, finance, curriculum, with extensive introductions including definitions of terms—what one might expect in an academic essay from an undergraduate. Unlike the previous plan, which laid out the mission, goals, and plans clearly and concisely, this one was confusing and without a clear action plan.

The section on finance was particularly disappointing. It was very long, proposing a complicated funding formula and resulting in a budget five times the current budget for the whole ministry. That was not realistic. Finally, gender equity was treated as the last item in the plan and was not well written—at minimum, poor symbolism suggesting that gender issues were a low priority.

I immediately contacted the deputy minister and found that he too was upset and disgusted by what he had been sent, its poor quality, and the fact that it was not really a plan but a series of essays without a realistic budget. He asked if I could salvage the document. I said I would do my best and agreed to work on revising, shortening, and making the plan a reasonable and useful document. It turned out to be a major effort.

The sad lessons from this experience demonstrate the importance of continuity in the planning process, the critical need to have people involved who have knowledge about the strategic planning process, a thorough understanding of quality higher education and the importance of producing a document that clearly and concisely lays out the goals of the plan with a budget and plan of action in a tight, clear, readable document.

Now, after a year and a half, the planning process was back on track with a draft—where it should have been in the first place more than a year earlier. I returned to Afghanistan to work on an extensively revised draft with an expanded strategic planning committee including some of the original members from 2009. Work was carried out during November and December 2014, and continued into the early part of 2015, with a final document from the new steering committee by the end of February with the dates for implementation now changed to 2016–20 to reflect the realities of time lost. While it was a good strategic plan, it was still too long at eighty-six pages without a budget and action plan and was neither as well written nor as clear as the NHESP: 2010–2014, which had been prepared in nine months in 2009. The new steering committee prepared a budget and action plan. The NHESP: 2016–2020 was then circulated throughout the MoHE, to many of the chancellors, faculty members, and others, and finally approved by the new minister in March. The new minister wanted approval from both the cabinet and the president. The document was submitted to them with a few final revisions in April 2016. The cabinet wanted a few more changes and the president had several suggestions including a requirement that enrolment increases be limited to 2 percent per year. The final version then went back to the cabinet in May 2016.

Continuity Is a Key to Successful Long-Term Planning Success

While the breakdown was largely the responsibility of the minister, who was well aware of the existing process of strategic planning and the success of the previous plan, part of it also must be laid at the feet of the World Bank staff. Unlike the previous strategic planning process where bank staff worked closely with the ministry and Deputy Minister Babury on an almost daily basis, in recent years the key World Bank staff had been largely absent from the ministry and from Afghanistan, assumed they knew what was good for the country even at a distance, with local staff more interested in the prestige of meeting with the minister and senior staff than following up with the deputy minister or visiting the institutions. They preferred to stay in their offices, perhaps on the pretext of security concerns, rather than undertake the hard work of understanding and following up on the operations of the ministry, the planning process, or talking with appropriate ministry staff, chancellors, and going to the institutions to see higher education in action. In spite of promises of weekly meetings with Deputy Minister Babury, only one such meeting took place during 2013. In addition, there was very little cooperation between the bank and other donors. They seemed to prefer to operate in isolation. This was in stark contrast to their actions in 2009–10 when the bank staff worked closely with the ministry, its staff, chancellors, USAID, UNESCO, and other donors involved in strategic planning.

This is an excellent example of why continuity in planning is so important, as is the institutionalization of the strategic planning process. Fortunately, in the end the process in Afghanistan was put back on track although almost two years and more than four-hundred thousand dollars were lost, in funds that could have been used to support the strategic plan or its implementation. Fortunately for Afghanistan, Deputy Minister Babury had both the determination and the ability to put the process back on track, with the participation of a number of people who had worked on the 2010–14 strategic plan and who helped put together a credible plan for 2016–20.

President Ashraf Ghani was a strong supporter of the new strategic plan. He read the whole document, asking for several changes that were accepted, including the cap on enrollments. That was a wise decision given the financial problems besetting the country and the difficulty the government was having keeping up with the enrollment growth that had already taken place. In the interim, release of the document was held up by the new minister, Dr. Farida Momand, who was nervous about new initiatives and changes. She was later impeached by parliament for failure to spend all of her 2016 development budget, though she remained in office at the request of President Ghani for a short time.

What was it that allowed for progress in Afghanistan after the removal of the Taliban government? In part, it was the structure and the democratic symbolism, if not always the fact, of the new government led by Hamid Karzai. He was a strong supporter of rebuilding higher education. Success also had a lot to do with people who had lived with more than thirty years of war not wanting it to continue to thwart efforts to ensure that their children received some level of quality education. A key to success of the planning efforts was the emergence of a group of dedicated leaders, staff, and faculty members in higher education who were committed to upgrading and improving higher education and willing to go to extraordinary lengths, in some cases at risk to their lives, to rebuild and improve higher education in spite of the war. Some of that commitment was seen in the fight for primary and secondary education, especially for girls, often conducted under great pressure and in the face of occasional physical attacks against students—girls in particular—and school buildings. Another important factor in support of higher education change in Afghanistan was a widespread feeling among large segments of the public that all levels of education needed to be revitalized, but particularly higher education. The author and his team saw that in focus groups in 2003 in many parts of the country—an eagerness to rebuild and raise the quality of higher education. That gave strong support to those in the institutions of higher education and the ministry who were committed to making that happen. Thus, there was little opposition to the strategic planning effort, except for a small group of conservative ideologues at the outset, and they proved not to be major obstacles.[9]

Lessons Learned about Higher Education Change

The Afghanistan case demonstrates that fundamental change is possible even in a war environment. It shows that transformation can happen where there is strong, broad commitment among administrators, staff, and faculty members, some of whom are willing to put their lives on the line if needed to ensure major change. Goals regarding improved conditions for women were achieved because of the strong commitment of leadership at the ministry, supported by both President Karzai and President Ashraf Ghani. But problems remain. Ongoing funding shortages are hurting the attempts to both build high quality and increase access. Those need to be tackled by the government, institutions, and donors. A major effort needs to be made to stop the growth of private higher education, much of it conducted illegally, as noted earlier. While the MoHE has worked on this problem for the last five years, success will require the active involvement of President Ashraf Ghani. There is too much politics and corruption (along with serious threats) for it to be done by the MoHE alone. Critical to success is the continued long-term support of funders including USAID, the World Bank, Germany, and several other donors.

What is striking in the Afghan case is that in spite of war and its ongoing effects on the country as a whole, including attacks on schools and at some institutions of higher education, and in spite of a difficult economic situation, there was a core of people in higher education committed to fundamental change. They were able to mobilize the institutions, faculty members, and administrators to bring about remarkable, transformational changes during 2010–15 in that there were major changes to core values. That is a tribute to the consensus built up in higher education about the goals for the transformational change plans and the ability to put them in place even under difficult conditions, which needs to be continued and enhanced.

The current Afghan situation is somewhat different, and includes declining per capita expenditures over the last few years, as noted earlier. Nonetheless, higher education has had strong support from President Ghani, most members of parliament, and the Ministry of Finance in a difficult economic situation and a war environment. Higher education has fared better than many other ministries given the budget problems currently faced nationally in Afghanistan. In the cases of both Pakistan and Afghanistan, higher education has benefited from strong executive support as well as strong leadership in higher education able to make the case for as much funding as possible in difficult economic times. In Afghanistan, while the very effective deputy minister for academic affairs, Prof. M. O. Babury, was on leave to pursue his PhD in Germany and Afghanistan, he continued his role as adviser to the president on higher education. The president has maintained his strong support for continued improvement in higher education, and that needs to be continued and enhanced. The National Higher Education Strategic Plan: 2016–2020 has been approved by the MoHE and should provide a blueprint to continue the change process which has been so successful over the last six years.

Chapter 5

Bringing Higher Education Transformation to South Africa

The Context

Probably no country has sought to make as extensive a range of transformational changes in higher education as South Africa—changes designed to end racial inequality and gender inequities, increase access to higher education, and establish a wide range of other policies designed to make higher education more participatory and more transparent, with improved quality in all areas. This involved major changes at both national and institutional levels in South Africa, with initial efforts pursued at the institutional level even as new policies for the national level were being debated and defined. As in the case of Afghanistan, South Africa was a nation in the midst of severe conflict and violence, torn by an internal war only slightly less violent than that of Afghanistan, in this case sparked by decades of racism, violence, and the stark inequities of apartheid.

At the forefront of demands for change was outrage over apartheid education policy, which had restricted access to education for black[1] students—almost totally, in the beginning. During this period, blacks could not attend white universities.[2] The Extension of University Education Act (1959) made provision for setting up separate "tribal colleges" for black university students. Thereafter, black enrollment was limited primarily to separate historically black institutions. Nonetheless, only 9 percent of black Africans of college age were enrolled in higher education, 11 percent of coloured[3] students, and 33 percent of Indian students, while

60 percent of white students of that age cohort (Bunting, 1994: 39) were enrolled, even though they constituted only 11 percent of the population. The actual population percentages by race at that time were blacks 77 percent, whites 11 percent, coloureds 9 percent, and Indians 3 percent.

The long struggle and resultant negotiations that brought about the "dramatic transformation" in South Africa resulted in what Nelson Mandela called a "national consensus on democracy, equality and peace."[4] For higher education, part of the change process was to be the restructuring of higher education through a participatory approach, which was to be part of the movement toward greater democratization. Those involved saw it as including a culture of negotiation. While there was some tradition of negotiation among academics, it did not include staff, students, or members of the public. Indeed, academics were reluctant to negotiate with anyone outside the sphere of their fellow academics. This was far too broad a group for most of them. The notion of broad participation led to demands, especially by students and staff, for the creation of transformation forms[5] that would create a new governance and management style on campuses committed to including students, staff, faculty members, and administrators. What would this look like? Who would be in charge? How would decisions be made? What would participatory policymaking look like? How would it be done? How would it fit in with existing governance structures? The issues embodied in these questions created new tensions on many of the campuses that addressed them, and in most cases the idea of transformation forms was abandoned.

The lack of consensus about the process had its roots in apartheid. Indeed, in the old order, apartheid defined everything. The white minority had laid out the rules for higher education planning and operation for decades. The higher education structure was designed to thwart change, especially at the historically black institutions. Planning was not open to discussion by the majority. These procedures were enforced by rigid rules at every level, and when necessary, by brute force. If one wrote a novel today describing a society with such rules, no one would believe it possible. But the now somewhat forgotten reality is that in South Africa during this period, that was how things were done. There was one set of rules for white South Africans, another for Asians, another for so-called coloured South Africans, another for black South Africans. Even the black communities were divided by ethnic group. In education, each group had its own "ministry" of education, for a total of nineteen separate ministries overseen by a central ministry controlled by white civil servants. Rules and laws governed every aspect of life. For university employees, there were separate health plans for whites, Asians, coloureds, and black Africans—and the benefits were lower for women in all of the plans. Schools, job opportunities, salaries, movement inside the country, marriage, accommodations, where you could eat and with whom—every aspect of life was defined by rules related to color.

From the early 1990s during the last years of apartheid, which ended with the elections of 1994 in South Africa, a general consensus had developed about the character of the plan for higher education. There was consensus about major areas of policy such as equal access, redress for the disadvantaged, governance of the system, increased government supervision over the system, and a substantial amount of institutional autonomy (Moja & Hayward, 2001: 112). These overall goals for higher education had been laid out in a number of policy documents developed in the pre-1994 period. While it is not my intention to go through an analysis of apartheid here, it is important to understand the context and its consequences for the change process.

The Policymaking Process

In developing new public policy for the post-apartheid period, planners focused particularly on those features of the system that could be changed quickly, as well as those that had been the most offensive aspects of higher education policy during the apartheid period. Policies had to be put in place that would help reverse this discrimination, provide access to quality education for black students, and ensure that the disadvantaged would have access to funds to assist with their education. Policymakers recognized the need for a differentiated system containing a diverse range of institutions. Differentiation was not to be based on race but rather on missions. As planning continued into the later 1990s, rectifying these inequities became a major focus in the preparation of public policy regarding higher education (Moja & Hayward, 2005).

The path to the development of a national plan for South African higher education was a long and highly participatory process that had started years earlier within the overall struggle against apartheid. It was built on a strong commitment to openness and broad participation. The struggle for equality included a long history of conflict, suffering, and violence dating back decades before the elections in 1994 and involving many different groups in addition to the African National Congress—efforts with multiple leaders in a context in which if any of them were to have claimed leadership of the higher education project it would have eliminated any chance of having a leadership role. It was truly a collective effort with collective leadership.[6] There were a number of people leading these groups, but the process was one that was collective with loose coordination among the groups involved.

Development of a Framework for the New Order

One of the major factors leading to the success of this effort at the institutional level was that years of discussion during the struggle against apartheid had led to a general consensus among the opponents of apartheid about goals for higher education change as the struggle progressed, focused especially on the promise to establish a nonsexist, nonracist society. The system was to be built around the principles of equality, justice, accountability, and high quality. While these goals had broad support, in spite of the fact that it was clear the old order was coming to an end, there were many people who were still proponents of apartheid and were preparing to do their best to thwart any transformation in higher education. That complicated the way forward.

Discussion about a framework for national higher education prior to 1994 was facilitated by several organizations including the National Education Policy Investigation (NEPI), the policy forum of the Union of Democratic University Staff Associations (UDUSA), and the Centre for Educational Policy development (CEPD). The African National Congress's committee on higher education had been involved in education policy discussions over many years in an effort facilitated by Dr. Blade Nzimande and others who were part of the ANC's preparation for action after the struggle ended in what was called Post-Apartheid South Africa (PASA).[7] These efforts demonstrated how complicated the transformation was to be in spite of the general agreement on basic goals. In February 1994, the CEPD set up a higher education task team, which was to prepare draft terms of reference for a proposed commission on higher education (Moja & Hayward, 1999: 338).

The Consultation Process for a National Plan

The development of higher education policy was to be the responsibility of the National Commission on Higher Education (NCHE). Probably no country took the analysis of the education environment more seriously than South Africa. Building on the work done previously, they began a long consultation process open to everyone. This involved visits to various parts of the country, travel abroad to look at other systems, public forums, publication of subcommittee reports reviewed by both local and international specialists, extensive use of the internet to collect comments on various drafts from the public, consultations with higher education institutions, faculty members, staff, and students. A remarkable part of this consultation was the formal effort to include external expertise and an amazing openness to their suggestions.

Even the terms of reference for the NCHE came under challenge during this process by members of the old order, acting in their own capacity, who sought to protect white privilege and derail many of the change efforts. Appointments to the commission were open, with nominations requested from twenty stakeholder organizations. Those appointed to the commission represented a broad range of views among the stakeholders. All of them had backgrounds in higher education but had diverse political views, including a few who had been supporters of apartheid. The ability to put drafts on the Web and request feedback gave them regular input from a broad range of the public. The open meetings they held around the country were often raucous affairs and hard to control given the range of views expressed, but they gave everyone a chance to be heard. The consultations provided important input to the work of the commission and helped lead to consensus about the plan in the long run. One remarkable aspect of the process was agreement that it should be open, even to defenders of the old order.

There were major differences about specific goals among members of the commission, especially over the issue of a single coordinated system versus a decentralized one and about the issue of redress[8] funding. Dissents by some commission members were also published. After a great deal of discussion of a draft document and major revisions of some parts of it, the final plan of the National Commission on Higher Education was produced and sent to the Department of Education in July 1996. It spelled out major principles for the higher education system, including:

equity in the allocation of resources and opportunities; redress of historical inequities; democratic, representative, and participatory governance; balanced development of material and human resources; high standards of quality; academic freedom; institutional autonomy; and increased efficiency and productivity (NCHE, 1996: 4). Its major goals were adopted by the Ministry of Education in its Green Paper, which emphasized that the changes in higher education should be based on fundamental principles that "ensured equity of access, and the possibility of success . . . irrespective of race, colour, gender, creed, age, or class" (NCHE, 1996: 52).

Outcomes of the South African Transformation Efforts Nationally

The goals for change in higher education were spelled out in a document entitled *National Commission on Higher Education: A Framework for Transformation, the White Paper on Education and Training* (Department of Education, 1996), and the Higher Education Act of 1997, and were designed in particular to "restructure and transform higher education," provide "redress," and "contribute to the advancement of all forms of knowledge and scholarship" (Department of Education, 1997: 3). They were designed to bring far-reaching changes to higher education in South Africa through major policy changes. These documents and legislation were designed to establish a single coordinated system of higher education, change the funding system to foster greater equity, allocate 27 million rands for redress funding for the historically underprivileged institutions, encourage stakeholder participation in governance, foster a "non-racist, non-sexist democracy," encourage modernization and quality improvement, protect academic freedom, increase access of majority students to higher education, encourage gender equity, and foster broad international cooperation.[9] Indeed, these were major accomplishments, especially when coupled with the end of apartheid nationally and the tremendous social and economic progress that began with that success.

Understanding the Success of the Change Process

The consultation process in South Africa that led to these changes was among the most remarkable experienced anywhere. It followed from an abiding concern for openness, a rejection of secrecy, elite control, and racial injustice, and recognition of public demands for input into the process. Consultation was a major factor in the success of the final strategic plan and its implementation. Major efforts were made to involve students and staff in the deliberations—efforts that were later to prove critical to the success of the plan. Given the violence and rampant inequality under the apartheid government, the process had to clearly demonstrate transparency, openness, and toleration of differences when they occurred. Yet, to their credit, those who had been defenders of much of the apartheid policy at the outset came to support the overall plan in the end, and where they continued to disagree, they were allowed to include, in an appendix, their dissenting views. As we will see, these commitments to openness and consultation continued to be essential to the implementation process nationally, to the legitimacy of the strategic plan, as well as to the process of governance and change at the institutional levels.

Collective Leadership of the Process was a Key to Its Success

What was important for success was the general agreement on the process—agreement in which the collective leadership recognized that the process must be open and transparent, without exception, and showed a willingness to consider a broad range of ideas before preparing a final version of the plan. That agreement on the process proved to be essential to many of the individual university's efforts to prepare their own strategic plans, in an environment often torn by disagreement about how to achieve the agreed-upon goals, priorities, and the implementation process itself. We will return to these issues later.

Implementation: Successes and Failures

The ability to implement the broad changes put forth in the national plan was remarkable. The changes were transformational in that they represented major changes in the basic values behind the structure and organization of higher education, were extensive in that they covered all higher education, and resulted in fundamental changes in the nature of higher education in South Africa ranging from the abolition of racial and gender division, efforts to increase funding for the historically black institutions, and a commitment to equality.

Part of the key to the success of the process was the broad participation that was encouraged and facilitated at both the national and institutional levels. The struggle had emphasized the importance of individual participation and contributions. It had built up a tradition in which everyone got to speak at gatherings—indeed, no one could speak a second time until everyone who wanted to speak had had a chance.[10] This effectively thwarted those who occasionally tried to take over such meetings and steer the process in their own direction. This helped foster the kind of collective leadership that developed and remained at the helm of the process and ensured that all voices were heard. That is not to say that there were no leaders or organizers of the process, but they were never totally at the forefront and always showed a deference to those who wished to present their views, to a degree that was remarkable. This often meant that meetings were long and sometimes tedious, but at this juncture in South Africa's history that was essential. At the same time, as the process moved forward, actual leadership of the process shifted to the National Commission on Higher Education (NCHE). Yet even here, the formal leadership under Prof. Jairam Reddy was nominal, with the actual leadership being collective in the commission members and staff influenced by continued input from the other groups involved, and later the staff of the Ministry of Education and the minister, Sibusiso Bengu. The importance of the ongoing broad participation, openness, and cooperative leadership was critical in South Africa to institutional strategic planning.

What was particularly striking about this process was the collective nature of the leadership and the continuing close relationship between participants and those writing the plan. This is in marked contrast to much of the writing on leadership traditionally where people have looked for charismatic or heroic leaders who would be at the forefront of the process. While Nelson Mandela performed some of those functions, it was not a process led by a heroic leader but one in which his calm thoughtful demeanor and openness helped smooth the way for an effective planning process for higher education in South Africa. When he intervened, it was to ensure openness and inclusion. As Kezar, Carducci, and Contreras-McGavin (2006) were to recognize later, there was a shift to "collaboration, empowerment, multiculturalism, and leadership as a collective process." As they noted, "People throughout the world connect and work together in greater frequency . . . leading to the democratization of leadership as well as to a more complex and diffuse process" (Kezar et al. 2006: 3). And that process was very complex with so many groups and individuals involved, strong resistance from the old order, and impatience among the young for a rapid transformation that was not to be and probably not possible.

It Is Important to Think about Leadership as not Just the Province of One Person, but of Many

The case of South Africa helps us understand the importance of collective leadership. Estela Bensimon and Anna Neumann put it well when they wrote: "[A]s the world grows more complex . . . it is likely that we will stop thinking of leadership as the property or quality of just one person. We will begin to think of it in its collective form: leadership as occurring among and through a group of people who think and act together" (Bensimon & Neumann, 1994: 2)." That is exactly what happened in South Africa—to good effect. And it proved to be a model that has had tremendous staying power there. It reflected the realities of the political situation at the moment, but also made it possible for a very complex and difficult situation for higher education transformation to be undertaken in a way that facilitated planning and change.

Failures of the Change Process: The Issues of Redress

One of the major goals of the plan for the transformation of higher education was provision of redress funding to make up for years of underfunding of the historically black institutions. In spite of the strong support for redress by Minister Bengu and the vice chancellors and rectors of the historically disadvantaged institutions, and initial funding of 150 million rands allocated by the Ministry of Education in 1997 (Moja & Hayward, 2005) for redress, there was little redress funding forthcoming thereafter, largely because of opposition from some senior officials in the ministry (though Minister Bengu was strongly supportive) and the minister of finance. To make matters worse, the funding formula included a "penalty for failure" that was unchanged from the national funding formula of the apartheid period and had tremendous unexpected consequences for those institutions admitting large numbers of black students with poor educational backgrounds—primarily the historically black institutions.[11]

The policy had been designed to encourage institutions to admit students who would be likely to succeed, but had the consequence of penalizing those institutions that admitted large numbers of black students, since most of them came from poor quality secondary schools (a consequence of apartheid funding and lack of support for those institutions) and thus needed a great deal of remedial work to reach the level needed for success. A high percentage of them failed in their first year.

It soon became clear that there was a high cost to historically black institutions such as Peninsula Technikon for taking in large numbers of underprivileged students. The American Council on Education and the Centre for Higher Education Transformation Pilot Project, with four higher education institutions (Peninsula Technikon, M. L. Sultan Technikon, University of Natal, and University of Durban Westville), undertook a study to try to identify the magnitude of these costs, what was called the "cost of failure." That study showed that the funding formula was deducting 50 percent of the subsidy for each student that failed. These penalties fell primarily on those institutions that took in large numbers of disadvantaged black students, most of them historically black institutions. The University of Natal, a historically white institution that also took in large numbers of disadvantaged students, was also affected by this policy. However, it had sufficient funds to help disadvantage students make up for their poor preparation, which partly offset the penalty. The historically black institutions had no such funding, though redress funding was intended to assist with this process, but it proved insufficient. A large percentage of these disadvantaged students failed in year one. Some dropped out; many repeated the year. This penalty for failure greatly hurts institutions admitting substantial numbers of black students from poor educational backgrounds. As can be seen in the table below, the costs to all of them were substantial. This was a powerful incentive to many institutions to avoid taking in these students. Yet, they were the natural clientele for the historically black institutions. For some institutions, including the historically white University of Natal, such admissions were essential to their commitment to work to overcome the consequences of apartheid. We can see the cost of this effort for the University of Natal, M. L. Sultan, and Peninsula Technikon in table 5.1. Adding the first-year dropout rate, which was about 10 percent, to the average first-year failure rates in 2008 and 2009 shows a loss of about 45 percent of first-year students at Peninsula Technikon and M. L. Sultan with the institutions receiving only 50 percent of the support rate for those students—a loss

Table 5.1. Funding Formula "Cost of Failure" for Peninsula Technikon, M. L. Sultan Technikon, and the University of Natal in 2008 and 2009

Institution	Year	Rand	Dollars
Peninsula Technikon	1998	5,584,316	$1,581,478
	1999	10,613,727	$3,005,807
M. L. Sultan Technikon	1998	5,564,901	$1,575,980
	1999	5,562,188	$1,575,212
University of Natal	1998	15,305,000	$4,334,376
	1999	14,215,000	$4,025,688

Source: Pilot Project Consortium, (2001), Implications of the New Higher Education Framework, Cape Town: Cape Town: Centre for Higher Education Transformation, p. 54.

of a little more than 5 percent of their total subsidy funding. The cost to the University of Natal was substantially higher since the number of students was higher. They had some success in lowering the numbers due to their remedial programs funded by outside funds, which allowed them to establish a professional academic development program. Nonetheless, the cost to all of these institutions was substantial, as can be seen in table 5.1.[12] This penalty for student failure, plus the limited amount of redress funding, hurt the efforts of the historically black institutions to overcome the effects of years of underfunding, and led them to continue to be second-level institutions in spite of their successes in improving faculty training, the quality of the curriculum, and their publications record. It remains a contentious issue to this day.

An Assessment of South African Higher Education Transformation and Reform

South Africa made major progress in transforming both institutional and national higher education over the next ten years. In terms of my definition of transformation, higher education moved from a hierarchical structure under apartheid to one that was open and merit-based, dismantling separate salary scales by race, differential health benefits by race and gender, and a whole host of other areas of discrimination. Major efforts were made to upgrade the qualifications of faculty members, improve the curriculum, and provide at least some redress funding to historically black institutions.

Especially important was the effort to ensure that people of all ethnicities had equal access to higher education. From the outset, gender equity was enshrined in the goal of a nonracist and nonsexist society where women students outnumbered male students by 2018, though women were still underrepresented in higher education administration. Academic freedom for all was guaranteed with a major emphasis on support for high quality, checked by accreditation, and new broad and widespread research and publications support. Although funding per capita has declined in recent years, government support remains substantial. As we have seen, changing attitudes is a difficult task, but great strides were made in that regard in higher education during this period, although the struggle to change attitudes is a long and difficult one.

There were major improvements in ending racism nationally in all levels of education, though problems with the quality of primary and secondary schools in predominantly black areas continued to be a problem for higher education in that the level of preparation of most of these students was inadequate and bringing the students up to proper levels required a great deal of supplemental assistance.

The implementation of the policy plan for higher education, the *National Commission on Higher Education: A Framework for Transformation*, resulted in major progress in achieving its fundamental goals. It resulted in significant increases in the number and percentage of black students in higher education and increases in the number of women as well. Indeed, the percentage of black students in higher education as a head count increased from 27 percent in 1986 to 62 percent by 2005, as shown in figure 5.1 (Cloete, 2009). Women students increased from about 45 percent in 2004, with numbers doubling by 2004 and growing to 58 percent of the total enrollment in 2013 with 573,598 women students (Phosa, 2015:4). The improvement in the numbers of women students however, was not reflected in a major increase in the number of women faculty members or senior administrators, as noted earlier (Moodie, 2010).

In many respects, the progress in numbers is deceptive in that most of that increase took place early in the period from 1990 to 1994 due to institutional efforts, especially at the previously historically black institutions, which experienced major increases in enrollment. As impressive as the increases are, as Cloete notes, "the real measure of equity is not the colour of the student population on campus, but the participation rate of the different population groups. Surprisingly, it shows that not

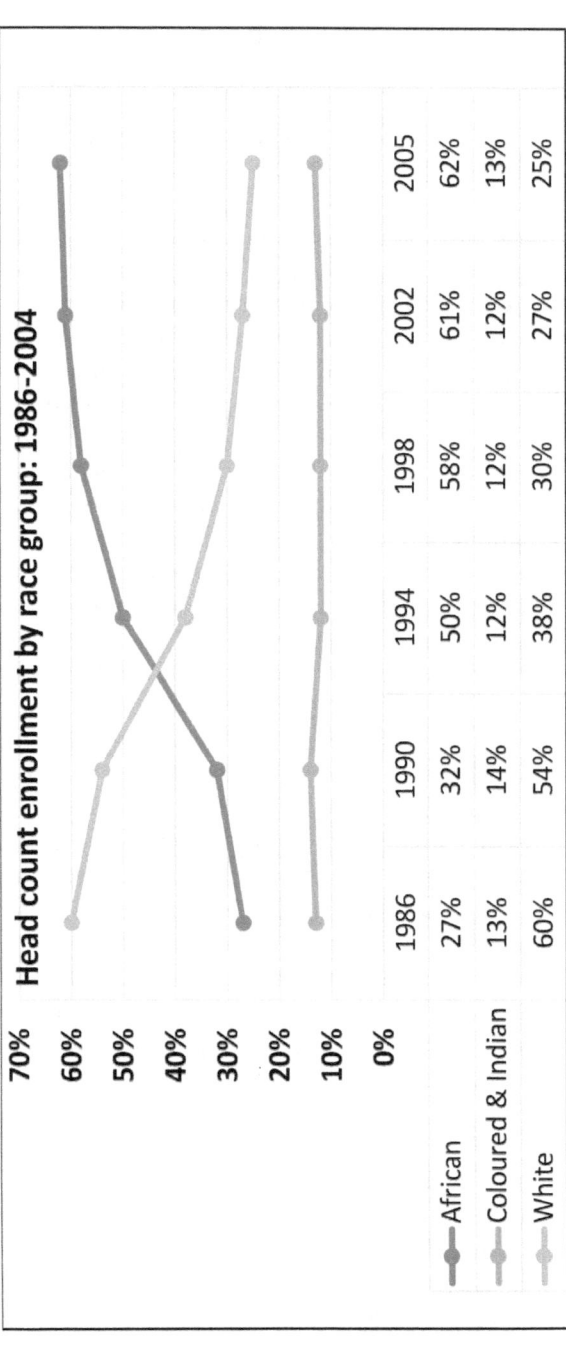

Figure 5.1. South African Higher Enrollment by Race. *Source:* Ian Bunting and Nico Cloete, (2007), Governing Access, Cape Town: Centre for Higher Education Transformation.

much has changed" (Cloete, 2009: 3). That can be seen clearly in figure 5.2 by Bunting and Cloete. The gross participation rate for African students grew only from 5 percent in 1986 to 12 percent in 2005. The white percentage of the population remained rather steady at about 60 percent, and only the Indian population made a major increase, from 32 to 51 percent.

Much of the problem is a consequence of the inequity in pass rates, with black students failing at a high rate because of the inferior education provided at most primary and secondary schools. But it was also exacerbated by the failure of the Department of Education and the treasury to allocate the promised redress funding that would have allowed the historically black institutions to provide a greater value added to students by allowing more institutions to add a preliminary year and provide other redress education. Added to that was the poor labor market for school graduates, which tended to discourage enrollment. More importantly, in recent years, funding for higher education has continued to decrease while student fees have gone up (Langa, 2016)—a further disincentive for black students, who have seen student debt increase substantially with the increase in student fees.

The situation has been further hampered by the deteriorating economic situation in South Africa and the discord within the ANC governing party, which has not shown great concern for either higher education or unemployment during the Zuma years, in contrast to those concerns at its origins. Thus, the great promise for education from the ANC during the early years not only disappeared in the face of poor governance and corruption within the ANC, but the public became very discouraged by its poor performance as demonstrated by its loss of support in the elections of August 2016. While the ANC managed to barely squeeze by with 54 percent of the total vote, it lost in several major cities and was humiliated nationally (Norimitsu, 2016). The forced resignation of President Zuma and the appointment of Cyril Ramaphosa as president brought hope for reform in 2018.

What does the case of South Africa have to teach us about higher education change and transformation? In spite of the recent problems, the transformation of higher education is an amazing example of what can be done through a collaborative process, democratic leadership, and an open participatory national change planning process. Major changes took place in higher education in regard to race, though not as completely as people had hoped. Nonetheless, there has been an amazing change in

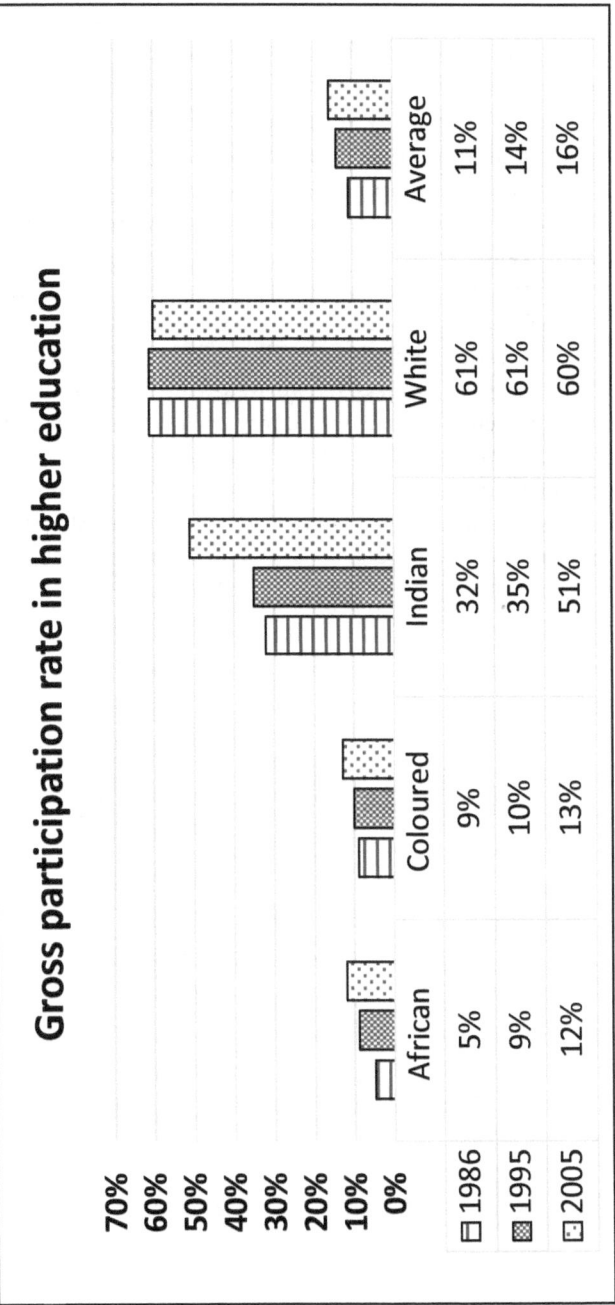

Figure 5.2. Participation Rate in Higher Education South Africa: 1986–2005. *Source*: Bunting and Cloete, Governing Access (2007).

attitudes, opportunities, and access since 1994. Though the Zuma government cut funding to higher education, on the positive side, there was a very active opposition with vocal critics both in higher education, in the ANC, and in society generally. In addition, higher education leaders are both articulate and vocal in their concerns about the weakness of some government efforts and its failures to adequately support higher education financially. Many of the major changes and improvements that flowed from the national and institutional strategic planning efforts remain in place and were not threatened. Those changes were indeed transformational for the majority population. What has been lost is the forward momentum of the earlier period—one that had served as a model for many other emerging economies. Yet, many of the institutions on their own, even with somewhat limited funding, continue to move forward in the spirit of the change efforts of the strategic plans and the overall goals of justice and equal opportunity. South Africa remains a model of what can be done to change higher education, especially through a collaborative, participatory process.

Chapter 6

Three Cases of Institutional Transformation in South Africa

Strategic Planning at the University of Fort Hare, University of the North, and Peninsula Technikon

> The idea of strategic planning became a very useful instrument for pulling together diverse groups of people in an institution that was thinking about its future.
>
> —Sipho Pityana, former strategic planner, University of Fort Hare

While work on the national strategic plan was underway, a major effort to undertake institutional strategic planning took place at twelve historically black institutions in South Africa. In this chapter we will look at three of these cases that are especially interesting examples of the apartheid struggles at the individual university level—the institutional change processes at the University of Fort Hare, one of the oldest black institutions in South Africa, at the University of the North, one of the early "hot spots" among the historically disadvantaged institutions (HDIs), and Peninsula Technikon, an early participant in strategic planning in South Africa. They are particularly noteworthy examples of how institutions faced the challenges of strategic planning at the end of the apartheid era.

Transformation at Fort Hare

The impetus for strategic planning at the University of Fort Hare came from the Kellogg Foundation, which worked with leaders there in 2002 to initiate a strategic plan. That effort failed, partly because it was a top-down process. During 2003, the leaders of historically black institutions met with the leaders of the American Council on Education (ACE) and the Ford Foundation to talk about what they needed to begin their change agenda to end the legacies of apartheid. The consensus was assistance with strategic planning. Each wanted an American university president as a mentor for the process. The Ford Foundation agreed to fund the effort for five HDIs, including the three discussed in this chapter. ACE then provided a list of American university presidents willing to serve as mentors, from which they could choose. Each president would visit twice a year for at least two weeks for two years. In the meantime, ACE would set up a team of strategic planning specialists to work with them on an ongoing basis in South Africa. That project continued from 1993 to 1997, with USAID joining during the latter part of the effort allowing the program to be expanded to thirteen HDIs, including the University of Namibia.

The major challenges to strategic planning at the University of Fort Hare were primarily about process—how one should operate strategic planning, manage the campus, and bring about the desired goals. They were also affected by two challenges resulting from the implementation of majority rule, the reduction of Ciskei funding (which had been about 55 percent higher under the Ciskei government) and the loss of some of their best students to the historically white institutions which were busy recruiting black students now that apartheid was official ended (Cloete et al., 2017: 3).

There was some campus opposition to strategic planning. While some of the opposition to the strategic plan was symbolic, the inability to find a way to move forward with planning at the outset of discussions at the University of Fort Hare seemed to be unresolvable. One of the important lessons from this case comes from the recognition that sometimes conflict can create the conditions for progress. As one writer puts it so well, "Only when we have leaders who understand healthy conflict in its inevitability and its productivity will we begin to develop the skills to mine it well" (Walsh, 2006: 24). That is what happened at the University of Fort Hare.

While apartheid theoretically came to an end with the election victory of the ANC and President Mandela, the attitudes and assumptions about the process remained a major negative force for many people for years to come. These had to be dealt with at each institution if any progress was to be made toward equality, justice, and quality education for all. Yet at the institutional level, especially at the historically black institutions, there was little or no experience among black staff or students with policymaking or planning and no mechanisms were in place to tap the talents of the education community since broad participation had not been part of the apartheid order.

Background of the University of Fort Hare

The establishment of a college in Alice grew out of efforts of South African Christians, several churches including the United Free Church of Scotland, the Presbyterians, the YMCA, and black and white liberals that led to the establishment in 1916 of the South African Native College, which eventually became the University of Fort Hare. It was an autonomous institution with high standards. It was subject to racial laws but took in a broad range of students from other African states and from the black, Indian, and coloured communities of South Africa. In 1958, with the Extension of University Education Act, it came under control of the apartheid government and was made a Xhosa-only institution. It had a majority white staff with several black academics. In 1980, it was put under the jurisdiction of the Ciskei Bantustan, one of a series of attempts to set up black mini-states within South Africa.

There was strong student resistance to apartheid, with a number of student organizations active on campus over the years, the most prominent of which was the Black Consciousness Movement, associated with the South African Students' Organization. Student resistance was quickly and brutally suppressed by the Ciskei government with support from the South African government. The university boasted many distinguished graduates, including Nelson Mandela, Oliver Tambo, Govan Mbeki, Robert Mugabe, and Dennis Brutus. With the victory of the ANC, the University of Fort Hare was once again semiautonomous, with Sibusiso Bengu as its first black vice chancellor.

Planning for Major Transformation at the University of Fort Hare

The strategic planning effort at the University of Fort Hare was led by Prof. S. M. E. Bengu, vice chancellor, and Sipho Pityana, strategic planner and registrar. A first draft of a strategic plan had been prepared with support from the Kellogg Foundation in 2002. It was a top-down project that was strongly resisted by faculty members and many senior administrators and was soon dropped. The University of Fort Hare was a troubled campus at the time Prof. Bengu became vice chancellor in 2001, with very active politicized students as well as a vigorous and unhappy staff association. The institution had been torn by violence and struggles. Part of the problem was an old guard of white administrators, faculty members, and staff who were deeply steeped in the ideology of apartheid with strong hostility to dissenting staff and student activists.

A Renewed Effort to Prepare for Major Changes at Fort Hare

From 1993 through 1997, the American Council on Education (ACE) facilitated the South Africa Project, to foster and implement major changes in higher education institutions, begun at Fort Hare. As a result of this project, the strategic planning process was restarted at Fort Hare, this time with a broad participatory framework and regular consultation from the ACE project staff,[1] with assistance from Josephine Davis, president of York College, CUNY, in the United States, who was the senior associate[2] to the University of Fort Hare. Both Vice Chancellor Bengu and Sipho Pityana had a good deal of experience as leaders, with Sibusiso Bengu having been secretary general of the Inkatha Freedom Party, a professor and director of student affairs at the University of Zululand, and then secretary of the Lutheran World Foundation in Switzerland, before he became vice chancellor. Sipho Pityana had administrative experience at Fort Hare before he became head of strategic planning.

Professor Sibusiso Bengu took over as vice chancellor at a particularly difficult time, with the university in turmoil, dominated by faculty members wedded to the old order and strongly committed to apartheid, as was his deputy vice chancellor. The University of Fort Hare, with an active black student body, was often at odds with the Bantustan government of Ciskei and the local police. On one occasion, Vice Chancellor Bengu confronted the Ciskei Police, literally standing in front of them at the entrance to campus to keep them out of the university, where he feared they were going to harass and possibly harm students. He managed to keep them out and prevent violence.

The vice chancellor was a master at dealing with the tensions on campus. On the one hand, he was a strong supporter of the ANC and close to its leaders, while at the same time he was committed to bringing peace and justice to South Africa and to integrating all parties into the university community. During his leadership, there were two attempts to assassinate him, probably by Inkatha supporters.[3] His courage was greatly admired by students and staff and helped create an excellent relationship with them. He involved the university community broadly from the beginning in the institutional strategic planning process and supported student and staff efforts to be involved in negotiation of a new order in university governance. As Pityana noted several years later:

> One advantage that the institution had was the legitimacy of its leadership. The members of the Fort Hare Council and the institution's leadership had impeccable credentials as community leaders—from Bishop Tutu to Oliver Tambo and Vice Chancellor Bengu, they had outstanding reputations as anti-apartheid and human rights activists These leaders helped establish a culture that promoted tolerance and celebrated differences. That helped turn around an institution that was tearing itself apart. (Pityana, 1997: 7)

Pityana himself was an outstanding organizer with charismatic qualities. He worked hard to make negotiations work in a context that was not very promising at the outset. That was not an easy task, since on one side were those who thought the apartheid system should be maintained. Some of them saw the ANC and students as traitors and refused to work with them. At the other extreme were some activists, including students, some faculty and staff, who believed that with the election of President Mandela, change would come quickly and they, in particular, deserved to benefit from the victory, given their years of suffering. Many of the students had developed a sense of entitlement with unrealistic expectations about what was possible—such as the abolition of tuition and other fees. It was also hard to break their accustomed role as opposition to the university administration—a continuing problem even with the ANC in control nationally and strong supporters, including Vice Chancellor Bengu and members of the council in leadership positions at the University of Fort Hare.

Understanding the Conflicts over Goals at Fort Hare

As a practical matter, there were two sets of goals on the table at the university: on the one hand, those inherited from apartheid, based on a top-down notion of governance and white supremacy, and on the other, those growing out of the struggle against apartheid, which were participatory, bottom-up, and transparent. Thus, the dilemma was, on the one hand, the drive for transformation based on what we might call the ethical justice paradigm[4] versus, on the other, a worldview based on apartheid with its elaborate justification of racial hierarchy and differentiation—the total opposite of ethical justice. Thus, at the outset, it was very difficult to have any dialogue with some administrators, faculty members, and staff on one side and other administrators, faculty, staff, and most students on the other. Yet, observing the vice chancellor and strategic planner operate in those early meetings, it was amazing to see how well they negotiated the differences and worked to create conditions for dialogue. Sipho Pityana and I often talked late into the night about strategies to bring the different groups to the table and to make the process a success. He and the chancellor also spent many hours working together on ways to allow the university to move forward with change plans.

As Pityana noted in 1997, thinking back to these events: "First, the idea of strategic planning became a very useful instrument for pulling together diverse groups of people in an institution that was thinking about its future. At Fort Hare, these people ranged from those who opposed the previous administration to newcomers, all of whom had their own ideas about what the institutions should be like" (Pityana, 1997: 7). In addition there was the old guard that was resentful of the changes, hostile to the new leadership, and eager to do what they could to sabotage the process. Pityana went on to say: "I found that very difficult to deal with, because it indicated to me that people who had a valuable contribution to make were not doing so." Nonetheless, both Vice Chancellor Bengu and Pityana worked to bridge the gap, and, as Pityana noted some years later:

> In retrospect, I think these difficulties were empowering for students and teachers alike. One of the strong critics of strategic planning was appointed to the post of deputy vice chancellor. When he got the post, he called me to ask for advice on how to proceed and build on the process already in motion, because he felt it was very important to the institutions. That was an

indication that he had confidence in what we produced. I may have been coordinating the process, but the plans that emerged through the participatory nature of the process, were produced by the entire institution. (Pityana, 1997: 7)

On the other side of the divide were the activist students and members of the staff association. Again, Pityana recognized the need to bring them to the table. He noted:

Another lesson I learned—and I think it was a lesson for the entire country—was that in our heated political environment, we had to include in our work the highly politicized student and staff associations, both of which felt entitled to certain benefits because they had played a role in the downfall of the previous administration. Because their leaders were accustomed to being the "opposition," it was difficult for them to make the transition to more constructive approaches. We had to get this group of very important stakeholders to look beyond themselves and examine their roles as participants and key actors in the context of the challenges that faced the country. While it was very difficult, I think it is fair to say that we managed to do that, especially with the students and workers. (Pityana, 1997: 7)

Between the two of them, Bengu and Pityana were able to bring most of the old guard around to understand that a new order was in place—one based on justice, equality, and democratic values. They worked hard to dismantle the structures of apartheid on campus, including a health and pay system that differentiated by race and gender. Both men, and many faculty members and other staff who worked with them, had a clear vision of a multiracial future for South Africa and for the institution. While there was very strong opposition to the strategic planning transformation efforts at the outset by the old order, the strategic plan was eventually approved at the university with few dissenting voices. Indeed, Vice Chancellor Bengu's success in bringing about peace and understanding led several faculty members, who had been strong advocates of apartheid, to go to him to apologize for their racism and ask his forgiveness. I talked with several of those involved and was struck by both their contrition and their efforts to make amends.

The goals for change spelled out in the Fort Hare Strategic Plan included distance education, bridging programs (with a fourth year for students who needed it), a focus on agriculture and science, shrinking biblical studies (which was the largest major), expanding public administration, and biological science. The short-term goals included:

> A major new initiative 1) to improve the quality of the faculty, including staff development to enhance teaching and research capacity; 2) to focus attention on academic development with the aim of short term improvements in output and a long-term restructuring of academic development for all students; 3) to complete the priority setting effort . . . ; 4) to review the self-studies of each of the units and their priorities culminating in a discussion of final priorities by the Senate; 5) to link these priorities to the budget making process and have them reflected in the 1996 budget; 6) to lay out a clear five-year plan for Fort Hare linked to the institutional budget planning process provided by Cambridge Associates; 7) to begin the implementation process for the major objectives of the strategic plan for Fort Hare; 8) to continue the ongoing institutional strategic planning process focusing on academic and program reviews, leadership training, and academic planning. (University of Fort Hare, 1994: 1–2)

These efforts moved forward over the next few years under the leadership of the new vice chancellor, M. Y. Mzamane, who replaced Prof. Bengu, who was named minister of higher education in 1994 by Nelson Mandela and the ANC government.

Fort Hare and the Merger

From 2003 to 2005, Minister Kader Asmal began a process of mergers of South African universities and technikons to bring about what he thought would be greater efficiency, higher quality, improved administration, and removal of the major legacies of apartheid. After a great deal of dispute about what would happen to the University of Fort Hare, including a plan to totally merge it with Rhodes University, it was decided to preserve Fort Hare but to merge part of Rhodes University—its campus in East London—with it. Fort Hare was largely a comprehensive residential institution, while the Rhodes campus in East London was made up mostly of part-time working students from urban areas. It had a smaller curriculum than Fort Hare. The merger was slow to be implemented in part because of the very different cultures at the two institutions, partly because of the dissimilar nature of its students and staff. There was a need to reconcile those differences. Both institutions survived the merger, but even by 2015 it was not yet a complete success, demonstrating how difficult it is to change campus cultures, especially when student backgrounds and experiences are so different. Sadly, this later period brought a great deal of corruption to Fort Hare, which was eventually put into receivership by the government, with outside financial advisers and control.[5] On the positive side, the university developed a new institutional strategic plan in 2009 increasing the focus on research and knowledge development. That was very successful with publications increasing from fifty-four in 2005 to 142 in 2014—then ranked ninth in South Africa in terms of publications. There was concern, however, that some of these were in predatory journals,[6] and that hurt the reputation of Fort Hare. The university also tried to strengthen its programs in science and technology with some success, with 25 percent of its student in STEM fields in 2016 (Cloete et al., 2017: 17).

Conclusions and Lessons Learned at the University of Fort Hare

The institutional strategic planning process at Fort Hare was one of the early successes in South Africa, and its strategic plan (2004) served as a model for several other institutions. Under the leadership of Vice Chancellor Sibusiso Bengu and Planner Sipho Pityana a badly divided campus with totally divergent goals and ideas about higher education and how it should be changed was brought together within the framework of a new strategic plan. Over two years, they developed a highly participatory approach to change, with a "culture of planning" where one did not exist before. In a conflict situation, their determined yet calm leadership of the process, with a clear commitment to justice, equality, and democratization, helped foster the agreement and understanding needed for success. Vice Chancellor Bengu managed to neutralize the Bantustan mentality of Ciskei to gain the Bantustan government's cooperation and begin to break down the hostility that had been built up between the Ciskei government and the university. Those involved in the planning also recognized that change planning is an ongoing process that needs continued review, assessment, and agreement over a long period of time and set up a strategic planning office and a process designed to ensure that it happened and was sustainable.

Both Vice Chancellor Bengu and Strategic Planner Pityana, used the "moral imperative" of equality to good effect in a quiet, nonthreatening way that changed minds and even engendered support from previous apartheid supporters. Yet equality required very major changes in attitude and behavior for many people on campus—and for the most part the changes were successful and endured. The courage of Vice Chancellor Bengu amid threats and attempts on his life strengthened support for the proposed changes. The goals and objectives of the plan were accepted broadly at the institution and were able to be implemented and sustained. The broadly participatory process and transformation served as a strong basis for the long-term successes of the university in dealing with a variety of challenges, including declining enrollments, publications scandals, merger difficulties, and corruption.

Part of the success of the change effort at Fort Hare was that it took place in an environment in which the change goals for higher education generally were agreed upon. That was a powerful force for successful change. Part of the success on campus was the democratic nature of the process. That, as suggested in the introduction, was a critical part of the success of the strategic planning effort. At the outset, that was hard for some of the anti-apartheid activists and other participants to understand in practice. Yet success required encouraging broad participation, quieting some would-be leaders who wanted to take control—not unlike those running the apartheid-era institution—and listening to those who were concerned not only about control of higher education but about building a community in higher education that focused broadly on the well-being and equal opportunities for everyone regardless of race or gender, and that would improve the quality of life for everyone in higher education and the broader community (Castells & Himanen, 2014: 12–19). The changes put in place at the University of Fort Hare were seen not only as changes at the institution, but part of the broader transformation that was taking place in South African society as a whole. That was what the struggle was all about—equality, justice, and opportunities for everyone—a process in which the University of Fort Hare played an early and a pivotal role. A major lesson was the importance of a broad participatory process in mobilizing support for transformation and bringing others who had doubts about it, on board.

While the reputation of the university was somewhat damaged by later corruption, the intervention by the ministry cleaned that up, and after a period of receivership the University of Fort Hare was back on track. The university continues to benefit from its long and distinguished history, including its attraction of some of the best students from around Africa, including people such as Nelson Mandela (South Africa), Robert Mugabe (Zimbabwe), Yusuf Lule (Uganda), Seretse Kama (Botswana), Julius Nyerere (Tanzania), and Kenneth Kaunda (Zambia), who attended the university. It also had been a center of student organization against apartheid, although it suffered from several government crackdowns as a consequence of those efforts. With the end of apartheid, it had to compete with the best historically white institutions for the outstanding students, and as a result its entering undergraduates were down 16 percent after 1995 (Cloete, 2017). It also struggled to reassert its identity. It succeeded to some extent in that effort, and by emphasizing research and funding it became one of the most published universities in South Africa, although, as I noted, the quality of some of that was called into question (Cloete et. al., 2017: 11). In 2016, it decided to open enrollment to students from around Africa. Its staff also became a majority non–South African, as did its graduate enrollment (Cloete et al., 2017: 7). After a period of difficulty, it seems to be back on track in 2019.

Higher Education Transformation at the University of the North—Creating a Shared Understanding

> The strategic plan, at the University of the North, was in the true sense of the expression, an act of liberation.
>
> —Njabulo Ndebele, former vice chancellor,
> University of the North

THE CONTEXT OF HIGHER EDUCATION CHANGE AT THE UNIVERSITY OF THE NORTH

The University of the North was another of the institutions established as part of the ethnically based apartheid policy in South Africa for African students. It was built at Turfloop Farm, north of Pietersburg, and was intended to serve as a model of separate development to show visitors, but because of underfunding and strongly enforced racist policies, it experienced years of student unrest and was occupied by the military most of the time from 1960 through the 1980s. It was merged with the Medical University of Southern Africa in 2005 to form the University of Limpopo, as part of an effort to cut the number of institutions, reduce the effects of separate racial institutions, and increase efficiency—a process that produced an unhappy and troubled union that was eventually scrapped.[7]

The Change Process Begins at the University of the North Starting in 1993

The apartheid-era administration of the University of the North was largely intended to make sure the students were kept under control rather than foster educational development. The quality of higher education was low, and students understood and resented that. Thus, when apartheid came to an end, the challenges confronting those seeking to change the university in keeping with the goals of the freedom movement, equality, and national plans, were fraught with difficulties. Its institutional strategic plan was being developed at the same time as the national plan.

Indeed, the first effort at the University of the North had been a confused failure, with an initial planning coordinating committee unable to function effectively with a disastrous top-down approach, lack of a planner, or agreement about a process (Marcum & Kamba, 1997: 6). It was clear that a whole new relationship was needed between students, faculty, administrators, and staff if plans for change were to be successful. In that context, planning was an extremely difficult task. There were no traditions to build on, no consensus about process—just very strong feelings about what people did not want by way of process. Let's look at this case as it demonstrates, *in extemis,* the problems faced in putting a new order in place in much of South African higher education, especially its historically black institutions.

Creating a "Shared Understanding"

After the first failed attempt at strategic planning, Chancellor Ndebele saw the ACE project as a good opportunity to start the process properly and asked to join the project. This process began in 1993 with an effort to create agreement among all the participants about the planning process—an endeavor that was often long and tedious. Having attended a number of these meetings when the planning process began, I was struck by the level of participation of the students, the care they took in putting forth proposals, the thoughtful negotiations, their acceptance of differing views, and the progress that was made over a two-year period on the strategic plan. Indeed, the students were often more helpful and accommodating than some of the deans, who still saw the previous order as far preferable to the current one and were doing their best to undercut progress. Yet progress was made.

The early goals of planning for change focused on: hiring a senior management planner to help with the planning; reorganizing human resources and hiring new high-quality faculty members; reorganizing the finance section to bring it in line with the strategic plan needs; making progress in student development, including student financial services working with the SRC (Student Representative Council) and involving students more fully in the institutional strategic planning process; improving the quality of instruction; working to make the campus more student-centered; and preparing a five-year budget for the plan (University of the North, 1994: 1-2). All this was to be in the context of the new national focus on equality, redress, and transparency.

This effort finally resulted in a period of progress and peace at the University of the North for the next two years. Much of its success is owed to those who worked so diligently to build a framework and a process for discussion that allowed a strategic plan to be developed and agreed upon. As Vice Chancellor Ndebele noted in reflecting on the process in 2007, several years after it was completed:

> A strategic plan that places emphasis on achieving shared understanding in the first instance and then a programme of action in a later instance underscores the need for the non-participant majority to own its future through universal participation. The strategic plan, at the University of the North, was in the true sense of the expression, an act of liberation not just a plan or framework for action. That is why some sixty people comprising the university executive, academic staff, professional and service staff, and student organisations participated in creating it. In this way, a strife-torn campus, was to enjoy some peace for a couple of years while determining the best way of marshalling action toward identified goals.

The entire experience was fraught with imperfections, but the imperfections paradoxically became a source for new ideas.[8]

There was also the problem of the rapid turnover of leadership at the historically black institutions as the new Mandela government tapped these institutions for national leadership positions in government. At the five institutions involved in the initial South Africa Project in 1993, only one vice chancellor remained in place in 1995, Vice Chancellor Ndebele, and he had been in office only eighteen months (Hayward, Moja, & Cloete, 1995 :7).

Starting a New Institutional Change Planning Process

New vice chancellors had been appointed at almost all of the historically black colleges and universities by the new government, but their task was to be Herculean. Njabulo Ndebele was appointed vice chancellor of the University of the North. He wrote of the encouraging start of that period, stating:

> I was Vice-Chancellor of the University of the North when freedom came in 1994. I remember the sudden, almost euphoric lull that descended on an otherwise rumbustious campus. Adam Kahane, writer and facilitator of dialogues on "tough problems," facilitated a historic campus dialogue over three days. The dialogue brought together a cross section of teachers, students, and workers to envision together the future of the campus. It was an extraordinary, tightrope walking experience that seemed to work for a while. It was an attempt at public transparency, trust and visioning as foundations for sustainable solidarity on an otherwise fractious campus. There were to be no protest songs on campus for a while, but plenty of tough interactions. (Ndebele, nd circa 2016)

Indeed, that began a period of major campus efforts to put together a strategic plan for change at the University of the North.[9] It was a difficult process. As Vice Chancellor Ndebele noted several years later, "The University of the North was a site of intense struggle by students and workers against the apartheid system and its symbols on campus.

Institutional authority was seen in the main to be one such symbol. The minority that governed the university mirrored the minority that governed the country. The majority that was governed by force, was a non-participant target of government actions."[10]

Newly appointed Vice Chancellor Ndebele and other administrators had to work to change that perception, to show that the "new order" operated in an open, transparent, and participative manner. Yet, even that was in a context in which many of the administrators and faculty members, steeped in the apartheid traditions, had trouble operating in that way. This put tremendous pressure on the vice chancellor and others working on the change agenda. To make progress, the dialogue had to be changed from a tradition of top-down policymaking to one of open participation in the process, negotiation, listening to and understanding the demands of students—in particular for "change from below." The students expected change now—the fruits of their victory against apartheid. Yet, no one could provide such instant gratification. Thus, the challenge at the outset was to end the polarization and tension that existed at the University of the North. How were policy decisions to be made in the "new South Africa"? In the context of the HDIs, and their faculty and administrators, who were mostly white and in many cases still immersed in the ideology of apartheid, this posed major challenges. For the students and some of the staff, there was confusion between what they hoped for in terms of representative democracy and what others saw as the continuing need for top-down management. And then there were the practicalities of running a university. Agreement on the process was essential if the institutional change and transformation was to be carried out at all within the framework of the national policy, focusing on equity (redress), financial resources for the HDIs, democratic governance at the institutions, and increased effectiveness and improved quality of the higher education system.

A PERIOD OF NEGOTIATION

What followed was a long period of negotiations, daily student demonstrations, and periodic confrontations between some members of staff, some administrators, and the students in particular. Vice Chancellor Ndebele worked diligently to bridge the gaps and work out an agreement on the processes to be followed. There was no history of policy planning at the institution. The only processes were those developed by the vice chancellor, suggestions provided by the ACE Strategic Planning Project, and those of U.S. university president Delores Cross who was serving as senior sssociate[11] for the project at the university.

There was major resistance to the process from many of the deans, some faculty members, and a few administrators. On the other side were the students, who wanted quick action on a number of demands ranging from an end to tuition for students, participation in every area of decision making at the university, and improvements in the quality of teaching.

I was on campus during much of this period, working with the vice chancellor and others. We were regularly interrupted in his office by student demonstrators. We then proceeded to have very good discussions with them about the current issues. This was an almost daily occurrence, which became increasingly friendly and productive over time. The students were never kept out of the vice chancellor's office. The daily demonstrations started with a *toyi toyi*[12] while shouting slogans and demands. We could hear them coming from across the campus. Once in the office of the vice chancellor they were orderly, polite, and usually constructive. Indeed, over time these encounters began to lay the groundwork for more formal discussion in a strategic planning committee, set up and composed of about sixty members, including a number of students, staff, faculty members, and administrators. The initial effort was to agree on a process for planning the strategic plan. As Vice Chancellor Ndebele wrote me some years later:

> I learned at the University of the North that a strategic plan is far more than a list of things to be done to take the university to the next phase of development in its history. More fundamentally it is also about ensuring institutional conditions for the list of things to be done. At a certain stage in the life of the university those conditions might be far more important than a programme of action. From this perspective, the programme of action is best seen providing a frame for the possible, while the enabling institutional conditions are the source of institutional energy that will drive the change.
>
> The most important institutional condition to achieve is arriving at "shared understanding." This becomes the basis on which the roles of various institutional partners are

discovered and embraced rather than assigned. Intervention for change has a greater chance of being self-motivated and self-directed, either at the level of individuals or at the level of organizational units. (Ndebele, 2007)

SHARED UNDERSTANDING UNDONE

The Strategic Planning Process for the University of the North

What Vice Chancellor Ndebele both understood and has articulated so clearly is that a critical requirement for successful change is to understand the need for a shared understanding among the many different views within the university community and how that creates the conditions for progress. He saw how agreement on process, in this case, allowed people to move on to discuss, to encourage broad participation, and in the long run to agree on what was to be changed and the major change goals for the strategic plan for the University of the North. Particularly importantly, he and others recognized that while the experience "was fraught with imperfections," in many ways those paved the way for shared understanding.

The broad consensus achieved during the institutional strategic planning process was to be tested and put under great strain in 2005 with the decision by the government to cut the number of higher education institutions from thirty-six to twenty-two by merging a number of them, including the University of the North and Medunsa, the medical university on the outskirts of Pretoria, which were combined to form the University of Limpopo. The merger was an unusual one in that the two institutions were very different and had very dissimilar cultures, one a comprehensive university, the other a medical school, with the merger forced on the institutions by the Ministry of Higher Education. The merger process never really succeeded, though some of its structures were put in place by an interim council. The institutions were three hundred kilometers apart, had very different histories, and in spite of some science programs in common, had very different goals and curricula. The unions protested the merger from the outset, as did the students with major demonstrations in 2015 which led to closure of the university. The effects of the merger on the medical profession were negative according to the minister of health. The number of students in the medical school declined because of the merger (Makhubu, 2014), and staff and students were extremely unhappy with the process. A review in 2010 confirmed the failure of the merger, which had been especially strongly resisted by Medunsa, with many of its best senior faculty members resigning and taking jobs elsewhere (Hall, 2015: 156). In 2011 the minister appointed a task team to review the merger. They concluded that "the merger had not been successful and should be undone" (Hall, 2015: 156). With the end of the merger, the university rebounded and moved on with the implementation of the strategic plan.

What does this case teach us about higher education? Most importantly, it demonstrates that overall the change process succeeds when it is highly participatory, democratic, public, and inclusive. As former vice chancellor Ndebele noted, the strategic planning effort succeeded because of a "shared understanding" that was carefully built over a long period of discussion and negotiations. That shared understanding was destroyed when the ministry of education tried to force a merger on two unwilling partners—a merger that lacked a compelling reason for taking place other than the wish of the minster. There was no shared understanding outside the ministry about the merger, with both institutions opposed to it and little progress made during the interim period for that reason. What was important in all the South African cases, for the students and staff in particular, was that institutional changes were related to their concerns about national and local change—creating a system that fostered human development, equality, and affirmed individual dignity—change that overcame the injustices of the apartheid past. Success required recognition that higher education institutions were part of a wider society that also required changes. While the university community might be at the forefront of change, it was part and parcel of the nation as a whole. That understanding fell apart with the forced merger of Medunsa and the University of the North, bringing to an end ten years of disruption, student strikes, and police shootings, and in October 2015 finally bringing about the dissolution of the merger. This experience demonstrated once again at both Medunsa and the University of the North that successful change requires agreement on goals and a shared understanding of the benefits of the proposed changes. Both institutions had that agreement with their own strategic plans, which were being successfully implemented—a campus agreement that was undone by the forced merger by the ministry. Now that the merger has been scrapped, the two institutions are able to move forward productively.

Building Change at Peninsula Technikon

> Plans are nothing: planning is everything.
>
> —Dwight D. Eisenhower

Context of Peninsula Technikon

Peninsula Technikon was established in 1962 under the government apartheid system as an institution for coloured students. It moved to Bellville in 1967 and became a College of Advanced Technical Education in the 1970s, and was renamed Peninsula Technikon. The institution opened its doors to all races in 1987 and offered degree programs starting in the 1990s with faculties of engineering, business, and science. As part of the mergers organized by Minister Kader Asmal in 2001, it was merged into the Cape University of Technology, which, after difficult negotiations that continued for years, finally came into being in 2005.

Planning for Change at Peninsula Technikon

The strategic planning change process was led by Rector Brian Figaji from the outset. He was among the first to start work with the American Council on Education (ACE) and was an enthusiastic supporter of the project, inspired by the ACE meeting with rectors and vice chancellors of historically disadvantaged institutions. There was some experience with strategic planning at Peninsula Technikon, though no plan, so the process already had a bit of a base there.

Rector Figaji was a well-liked, hard-working, and experienced administrator who was active in technikon leadership nationally as well as a dedicated leader of Peninsula Technikon, a graduate of University of the Western Cape with a master's in education from Harvard University. He was assisted by David Bleazard, the strategic planner, who was an energetic and hard-working member of the faculty. The institution had established a strategic planning group prior to the South Africa Project that would meet each year to make plans for the year ahead but had no written strategic plan. The group had produced a "Mission, Vision, and Values" statement for the institution. That served as an important source for the strategic planning process when it began in 1993.

The strategic planning process at Peninsula Technikon was part of the American Council on Education's South Africa Project, involving thirteen historically black institutions in South Africa and Namibia from 1993 to 1997. The project funded a full-time strategic planner, provided workshops and training by planning professionals and some equipment for planning, and brought together the leaders of these projects in periodic meetings on various of the institution's campuses. The project provided a senior associate—an American university president—to work as a mentor with the rectors or vice chancellors and strategic planning team at each institution. The university president and senior associate for Peninsula Technikon was William DeLauder, president of Delaware State University.

From the outset, Rector Figaji wanted to move quickly on the change process, to be built on the foundation already laid out with their "Mission, Vision, and Values" statement, and to get to work writing a plan. The first thing the committee did was to publish the "Mission, Vision, and Values" and post them in every program office at the Technikon. The basic parameters and goals for higher education nationally, focusing on equity, had been worked out over the preceding years and were broadly accepted by the historically disadvantaged universities and technikons, progressives, and apartheid opponents, although the national strategic plan itself was still being developed, as noted earlier. Unlike the situations at the University of the North and the University of Fort Hare, there were neither major disagreements between students and administrators, among faculty or staff members, nor did the institution have a history of racial tension of the sort that had existed at the University of the North and Fort Hare. That made the planning process much easier. Similarly, since there was already a strategic planning committee made up of senior administrators and faculty members, processes for planning were already in place and accepted.

Publicizing the Goals of the Strategic Plan Widely Is Important to Successful Implementation

The committee immediately set out major goals for the change process, with measurable objectives that could be monitored. The overall objective was to ensure equity for all students admitted to the university and to give them strong support. The major goals focused on: student success and development, research, quality improvement, expanded science and technology, and staff development (Figaji, 2007). The strategic planning committee urged departments to link their own goals to those of the institution and to monitor them regularly. At the same time, they worked with the rector and finance people on a budget for the plan. The committee also made the decision that "any new initiative that any staff member wants to initiate or any new partnership or collaboration with the institutions must be aimed at satisfying at least one of the institutional objectives" (Figaji, 2007). Thus, when negotiating with USAID and the European Union during this period on two programs, they were able to modify these initiatives so that they fit the goals of their strategic plan. This became very important as it helped "shape the support we got from both these programmes so that the funding contributed to the activities we had envisaged in each of our strategic objectives" (Figaji, 2007: 5). Too often in the past institutions had agreed to donor goals that were not priorities of their own.

A Strategic Planning Unit

Peninsula Technikon set up a planning unit at the outset, with several full-time staff members to assist the strategic planning processes. It became an ongoing part of the institutional structure and provided a focal point for planning, implementation, monitoring, and identification of problems when they occurred. It kept track of the plan budget and monitored expenses and income on an ongoing basis. It also became a repository of the history of the institution's planning over the years. Those institutions without such a resource, which have carried out strategic planning on an ad hoc basis, find themselves repeating mistakes, duplicating processes tried before, forgetting decisions made earlier (often very painfully), and fostering inefficiencies because there is no history of earlier planning processes. Peninsula Technikon avoided that problem with its very efficient and active strategic planning unit, which became an integral part of the administrative structure of the institution.

Implementation of the Change Strategy

Peninsula Technikon worked carefully on the implementation of the change plan and monitored it regularly. Let's look at each of their major goals.

An Implementation Process Is Only as Good as Its Goals for Change

Student Success and Development

The Strategic Planning Committee was concerned about the low pass rate of students, concluding that the failure rate was at unacceptably high levels of 35 percent for first-year students and, after that, 35 percent for all students up to graduation (CHET, 2001: 20). The failure rate for first-year students would increase to 42 percent by 1996, because access had been opened to all disadvantaged students (black, coloured, Asian), and the addition of these students, who collectively came from poorer secondary schools, raised the failure rate. After examining the data and identifying the departments with serious problems, the planning committee met with staff to assess the nature of the problems and try to find solutions. The programs identified had tried various approaches previously including mentoring, peer tutors, and other special assistance, but with limited success. After the review, the committee decided to design a foundation program for these students based on what they learned in the review.[13] This foundation program was so successful in cutting the failure rate that it was eventually adopted by the ministry for all Technikons and funded by government.

Research

The goal was to increase the amount of research carried out at the institution and improve on the number of publications and papers written by faculty members. To support this effort, the institution significantly increased the funding available to the research committee,[14] improved the institution's relationship with the National Research Foundation, and appointed coordinators in each faculty to mentor the process (Figaji, 2007:6). These efforts resulted in an increased publication rate.

Quality Improvement

The goal was to develop measures of quality improvement for every activity at the institution, from teaching to the gardens. A position of quality manager was established to oversee this process, with a team to design the process. Later, this effort included the accreditation process developed through the ministry. Monetary prizes were given for the best academic and nonacademic performance each year. Those programs found to be below par were given warning letters and instructed to improve (Figaji, 2007: 6).

Science and Technology

The strategic plan had identified science and technology as a major area on which to focus in order to distinguish Peninsula Technikon from other institutions. That meant that the majority of students should be concentrated in the science and technology curricula, notwithstanding that at the time the plan was devised the majority were in business and the humanities. A moratorium was put into effect on the growth in enrollments of business students since it was the largest program. This had the short-term negative consequences of income lost as these enrollments declined. In the long run, however, the plan worked, and science and technology became the largest academic areas of the institution. Funds were allocated to encourage women to study engineering—traditionally an area entered by few women.

Staff Development

Staff development focused on improving the training and qualifications of faculty members. It was administered by a committee that reviewed applications for funding set aside for this purpose. The funds covered the fees for programs and for special leave costs for staff involved in development efforts. Staff were also allowed to receive study leave in advance of their eligibility for it if they were involved in staff development. Under this program, leave could also be used to develop or improve teaching material. This project was especially successful.

Other Achievements

The institution set up what were called an Earmarked Fund and an Innovation Fund, to which departments could apply for special one-time projects. Proposals were judged competitively. The program entitled departments to buy equipment and do things they would not have been able to do otherwise, such as purchase computers, which were then in short supply. It had the unintended effect of differentiating the active departments from those that were not doing much (Figaji, 2007).

A Successful Implementation Plan Will Be One That Is Carefully Monitored

What distinguished the implementation process at Peninsula Technikon from that of many other institutions was its formality, clear goals, ongoing budget and program monitoring, and overall success. The institution benefited from having both an active strategic planning office with several staff members, a quality manager, and a number of committees set up to deal with different aspects of the plan such as faculty development. The process was also carefully monitored by the strategic planning committee, which met monthly, as well as ongoing oversight by the strategic planner and the rector. The whole approach of the institution was clear, pragmatic, fair, and constantly monitored by the strategic planning committee. If things were not going well in one area, adjustments were made. Where things went well, the successes were publicized. The whole process was widely publicized throughout the campus during the course of the five-year project. This implementation process, from the outset, is a model of how to organize, oversee, and monitor an implementation of the change strategy—to good effect. The project was organized in a way to ensure strict adherence to its goals, its budget, and to ensure that there was no unintended deviation along the way.

Incentive Funding Can Play an Important Role in Plan Success

The project was also noteworthy because it was carefully tied to the budget, with funds clearly allocated for each of the goals. In addition, and uniquely, funds were set aside to reward those who did especially well in the implementation process—incentive funding, which served as a bonus for success.

A Plan That Actively Involves the Whole Campus Is Especially Likely to Succeed

The strategic plan at Peninsula Technikon involved the whole campus—students, staff, faculty members, and administrators. Wherever you went on campus you saw evidence of that, from the Mission, Vision, and Value statements in every program office and around the campus, to signs about various goals posted on campus. The process helped develop a new sense of pride in the institution and a public commitment to high quality.

Upgrading, Beautifying, and Keeping the Grounds Clean at an Institution Can Create an Important Sense of Pride That Helps Foster Successful Change

One striking result over the course of the planning period was that the campus environment improved. A major effort was organized to keep the campus clean—one that was amazingly effective. Bishop Tutu used to chastise students around the country for throwing their garbage in the street, lawns, and bushes, and talked about how one could tell where students had been by all the trash caught on the barbed wire fences or in the trees. There was no trash on the campus of Peninsula Technikon. Even a walk across the campus with the rector would find him bending over to pick up any trash he saw. What was amazing, however, was that unlike the first year, in later years one would be hard pressed to find any trash anywhere on the campus. And the staff too worked hard to make the gardens, lawns, and grounds beautiful—and they were. That helped set a tone for the whole campus of quality, pride, and respect, and helped raise the image and reputation of the institution. As the rector commented after the planning project came to an end, "This was a wonderful period in our institutional history and the ACE project gave us a new meaning to strategic planning which we embraced fully for the benefit of the institution" (Figaji, 2007: 10).

Strong Support from the Institution's Leader from the Outset Is Essential to Successful Agreement on Goals and Plan Implementation

The role of the institutional leadership in the change planning effort was critical to its success at Peninsula Technikon. Rector Figaji was someone with a long history of successful leadership in education, in the community, and nationally. He was an engineer by training and had worked in that area before his academic career. He had been head of the engineering department at Peninsula Technikon, vice-rector at Peninsula Technikon, and then rector, starting in 1994. He had the respect of students, staff, the board, and members of the community for his leadership, honesty, hard work, and fairness. He was a visionary in a very pragmatic way with an eagerness to get things done. His campus did not have the kinds of problems with students or staff associations that plagued some other institutions. He had a direct style and a no-nonsense way of operating. Yet at the same time he was charismatic and a leader among the vice chancellors and rectors of the historically disadvantaged institutions. He was an expert at relationship-oriented leadership—at ease with and interested in people. As a result, he was named as one of the thirteen members of the National Commission on Higher Education (NCHE), which began working on the national higher education strategic plan in 2005. When problems did occur on campus, as with union negotiations, he moved quickly to meet with people to work out a solution. His skills, the respect people had for him, and his ability to mediate conflicts led to a peaceful campus and contributed to the success of the strategic plan at Peninsula Technikon.

Once the decision was made to move forward with a strategic plan, Rector Figaji was one hundred percent committed, and so were those who worked with him on the plan. Thus, the writing was completed quickly, the goals were discussed widely on campus until agreement was reached, and the implementation started right away. He worked closely with his strategic planner and committee members to ensure that progress was being made each year to meet the targets that had been set. And they were largely successful. While their efforts were hindered to some extent by the lack of promised redress funding from the ministry, the rector and his finance people were able to carve out enough funding from their regular budget and donor funding to move forward with their plan without major difficulties. They were the most successful of the thirteen participating institutions in linking the plan and budget and providing the funding needed for implementation. This is a model case for implementation of a change strategy, with strong leadership and long-term success.

Financing the Strategic Plan

Too often, strategic plans are written without a budget. That turns out to be a fairly useless effort. A plan without a budget is destined to fail. A good strategic plan serves as a blueprint and source document for the operational financial plan and defines the budget process (Hayward &

Ncayiyana, 2003: 19). The budget should also reflect reasonable expectations about funding for the plan. That is frequently not the case. One draft institutional strategic plan from an Afghan university had a budget that was five times higher than the total budget for the Ministry of Higher Education with thirty-six institutions. Not only is that not reasonable, but any donor who reads such a plan will not take it seriously. Peninsula Technikon was a model of good budgeting practices, with each goal tied to a carefully costed budget section and monitored regularly. While preparing the plan for change, the strategic planning committee reviewed the existing budget of the institution and made changes that ensured that the change goals were all funded. The addition of incentive funding for innovative projects in keeping with the change plans was a unique and successful idea that helped motivate successful change. In recent years, Cape University of Technology (formerly Peninsula Technikon) has managed to improve its funding situation with some exciting cooperative efforts, with the private sector recently leading an effort to set up the fifth Institute of the Pan African University.

Lessons Learned from Peninsula Technikon

Strategic Planning

The higher education change effort through the strategic plan at Peninsula Technikon was among the most successful of the thirteen institutions involved in the South Africa Project. Much of that success can be attributed to the sense of community that already existed at Peninsula Tecknikon at the time the change process began[15]—which facilitated the discussion of goals for change and their implementation. There was already agreement on the process for change based on the work of the existing institutional strategic planning committee, and the goals were in keeping with those discussed over the years as part of the national anti-apartheid effort. Peninsula Tecknikon had also been spared the long history of tension between students and administration. Indeed, Rector Figaji had a long history of successful leadership at Peninsula Technikon, as noted earlier. Thus, the institution did not face the jarring administrative changes that took place at many of the historically black universities, as we have seen. That leadership played a major role in facilitating the change process, as I have shown in the preceding pages. Peninsula Technikon had the advantage of carrying out the change process from administrative and faculty positions held for years by a leadership that was united about the changes needed.

By 2015, we saw a decline both in financial support for higher education and in the political stability of the country, as noted in the previous chapter on South Africa. However, the budget situation of Peninsula Technikon was somewhat better than that of several other historically black institutions, though it too was affected by the "penalty for failure" charge in the South African higher education funding formula that we examined in chapter 5.

The implementation of the strategic planning process at Peninsula Technikon was facilitated by having one of the most effective strategic planning units among the higher education institutions in South Africa. The careful monitoring of the change effort on an ongoing basis, willingness to make changes when needed, and careful control of the budget also contributed substantially to successes. Most importantly, no campus community so enthusiastically embraced the change process as did the campus community at Peninsula Technikon, as could be seen in the wide range of successful changes implemented there, ranging from faculty development to beautification of the campus grounds. Pride in the institution and its change process grew during this five-year effort in ways that made it a model for other institutions.

Merger and Its Consequences

The merger plans announced in 2002 by Minister Kader Asmal were opposed by Peninsula Technikon from the outset—first, the suggestion that it be merged with the University of the Western Cape to form a comprehensive university, and then a plan to be consolidated with Cape Technikon to form the Cape Peninsula University of Technology (Hall, 2015: 150). The opposition by Peninsula Technikon staff and administrators stalled the merger, leading eventually to the resignation of Rector Figaji of Peninsula Technikon and the decline in quality of that institution, partly because of the distance between the two institutions (Peninsula Technikon and Cape Technikon), their very different cultures, a less effective administration of the merged institutions, and the loss of careful financial oversight that had marked the leadership of the previous two rectors of Peninsula Technikon. In addition, this merger did little to undo the legacies of apartheid since both institutions were its products and were primarily composed of black students. The quality of education and opportunities for students at Peninsula Technikon at best remained the same rather than improving, and the sense of community that had developed at Peninsula Technikon was undermined. Now, however, the situation of Peninsula Technikon, after a long period of uncertainty and resistance following the forced merger that created the Cape University of Technology, looks good. The institution has built on its planning successes with an expanded engineering department and a promising cutting-edge space program, which launched its second satellite in 2019.

The overall results of this merger were "at best neutral" (Hall, 2015: 170), and their effectiveness in bringing an end to segregated campuses and economic inequalities was minimal or negative. There were no cost savings; indeed, the mergers proved to be more costly, with salaries, for example, raised to those of the highest paid at the merged partners.

For Peninsula Technikon, the overall result was negative based on the loss of community, the loss of financial control, and the sense of purpose that the strategic planning effort had created among students, faculty members, and administrators. In the long run, however, the excellent policy planning structure, the well-run strategic planning unit which had been put in place and had monitored the institutional strategic plan, helped get the university back on track. It expanded its engineering school, with a special focus on satellite technology.

During 2018, final preparations were being made for the Cape Peninsula University of Technology to host the fifth Institute of the Pan African University, set up by the OAU, focusing on space sciences, with several other universities in South Africa. Its institutional headquarters were at Cape Peninsula University of Technology. It is set to open in 2019.[16] The institute has excellent facilities including up-to-date laboratories and strong cooperation from the ministry and other South Africa universities. Its prospects look excellent. All this builds on the excellent foundation developed over the years through high-quality strategic planning.

Chapter 7

Challenges for Higher Education Change in Sierra Leone

The Context

Sierra Leone is among the poorest countries in Africa. Its economy had been sustained over the years by the export of diamonds, iron ore, and several other minerals. At one time, it was an exporter of rice, but in recent years has imported rice. In March 1967, Sierra Leone became one of the first Sub-Saharan African countries to achieve a peaceful transfer of political power when Siaka Stevens and the All People's Congress defeated then–prime minister Albert Margai and the Sierra Leone People's Party. However, shortly after he was sworn in as prime minister, both Siaka Stevens and the governor general were put under arrest in a coup organized by now–previous prime minister Albert Margai and the head of the army, General Lansana. Military rule lasted only a year, and in April 1968, Stevens was once again sworn in as prime minister. The economy during this period deteriorated, in part due to poor budget controls but also as a consequence of the decline in mineral exports. During the Stevens period, the country became a one-party state, with Stevens as president. At the end of his term, Stevens was replaced by Joseph Momoh, who had insisted on campaigning in the election even though he was the only candidate for President. Momoh would later move the country back to a multiparty system.

Fourah Bay College (FBC), the oldest university in Sub-Saharan Africa, was founded in 1827. It had an excellent reputation for providing a high-quality education. It attracted students from many other parts of West Africa but especially Nigeria and the Gambia. Njala University College (NUC), founded as an agriculture college in 1964, also provided a good quality undergraduate education. There were no graduate programs at either college.

At this time, Sierra Leone suffered from 85 percent illiteracy and a very poor health system. Infant and maternal mortality were among the highest in the world. Support to higher education from the government, the Ford Foundation, and USAID had allowed both FBC and NUC to provide a quality education. However, by 1970 both foundation support and government funding were in decline.

Planning for Change in Higher Education

The funding crises continued to grow and the quality of higher education continued to decline in the 1970s. Both Fourah Bay College and Njala University College, which had become part of the University of Sierra Leone, showed the effects of inadequate funding. The infrastructure at both institutions had begun to deteriorate due to lack of funding, the economic crises, and a long period of neglect by the previous government and loss of most donor support. This was the impetus for a request for help with strategic planning. At this point, the president, Joseph Saidu Momoh, asked the Midwest Universities Consortium for International Activities (MUCIA) to come to Sierra Leone to assess the needs of the University of Sierra Leone and consider what might be done to bring substantial change and improvement to the university. The president was made aware of MUCIA by its earlier work in Africa and an earlier visit by his deputy to several MUCIA campuses in the United States. MUCIA sent a team[1] during October and November 1989 to carry out a site visit and make recommendations to reverse the declines of the institutions. The team met with leaders of the country and the universities, faculty members, students, and others interested in higher education.

The site visit team was distressed by what it found. As their report noted, the team was "shocked by the decay of the infrastructure of Fourah Bay College and Njala College in particular. The problems range from little or no water, limited and irregular electricity, to decaying buildings, classrooms without seats, labs without equipment, libraries without much up-to-date material." But the reviewers also emphasized that "we are convinced that Fourah Bay College and Njala can and should be upgraded to be among the best in Africa (as they have been in the past), to help give Sierra Leone the tools to deal with current economic and social problems, including badly needed research, advice, and trained personnel to assist those in positions of power in Sierra Leone. We have concluded that Fourah Bay College and Njala can and should be rehabilitated if Sierra Leone is to solve its mammoth economic and social problems—in particular, if it is to be competitive in an increasingly technological and complex world" (Riodan et al., 1990: 1–2).

Background of the Project

The early days of Fourah Bay College (FBC) were heady ones. It was one of the leading institutions of higher education in West Africa, with half of its students coming from neighboring countries, especially Nigeria and Gambia. It was well funded by the government[2] and attracted additional funding from a variety of donors, including the Ford Foundation and a number of donor countries, which helped construct additional buildings, support the library, establish an African Studies Center and program, upgrade laboratories, and get a number of research projects underway. Njala College was established in 1964 with support from USAID to focus primarily on agriculture, and in 1967 became part of the University of Sierra Leone. Njala College was also well funded at the outset and had a number of staff members from United States universities, especially the land grant institutions after which it was modeled. The University of Sierra Leone was expanded to include a College of Medicine and Allied Health Sciences and several institutes. The country had done well financially for many years after achieving its independence in 1961, with impressive economic growth and a gross domestic product that increased by about 5 percent a year. Foreign exchange earnings and public revenues were at reasonable levels, the consumer price index was relatively stable, and external debt low. Earnings from diamond mining, iron ore mining, and other exports were good. This was reflected in substantial support for higher education and the growth of the university.

Deterioration of Higher Education

By the 1970s, however, the situation had changed, and both institutions had deteriorated markedly. This was in large part due to the economic decline in the country. Revenue from diamond mining had fallen and the iron mines at Marampa were closed. Iron exports had been the second-largest foreign exchange earner after diamonds. There was the shock of the oil price hikes, which tripled the cost of fuel, in the early 1970s. Cocoa and coffee earnings also declined. The fall of the international diamond prices in 1980 hurt diamond exports as did the government's failure to work out a deal for kimberlite mining, which would have been an additional major foreign currency earner. Added to these problems was the impact of the general international economic decline in the region. The government chose to deal with these problems by deficit financing, which caused additional long-term problems. In addition, the government incurred a large debt by hosting a meeting of the Organization of African Unity (OAU), brought about by the major costs of building an "OAU Village" to house the delegates in 1979–80. Its development expenditures jumped 146 percent because of these costs. State policies also discouraged agricultural production by controlling prices for rice and other food prices. All this was accompanied by a growing rate of inflation with the Leone moving from Le 1 = $1 in 1980 to Le 175 to $1 on the black market by January 1990 (Riodan et al., 1990: 5). These problems had a negative effect on funding for higher education. There was little money for upkeep of the facilities and they began to deteriorate. At the same time, national shortages in electricity and water developed, which also had an effect on both institutions, as did the increases in oil prices.

All this led to the deterioration of the whole education sector, such that Sierra Leone had the lowest rate of literacy in Africa, at 15 percent.[3] When the MUCIA team arrived in Sierra Leone, they found both major higher education institutions "in such a state of deterioration that they can make little contribution to developing the Nation, returning the economy to solvency, let alone to buoyancy and eventual prosperity" (Riodan et al., 1990: 6).

Efforts to Upgrade and Change Higher Education in Sierra Leone

The review team met with President Joseph Momoh, his chief of staff Dr. Abdul Karim Turay, who was also professor of Linguistics at FBC, the vice chancellor of the university, Prof. Kosonike Koso Thomas, and his staff, the principal of FBC, Prof. Cyril P. Foray, and Dr. Abu Sesay, acting principal of Njala University, and a number of deans and faculty members, as well as students. The team was asked to put together a "Project to Revitalize the University of Sierra Leone" and work with donors on its feasibility. The team was impressed by the commitment of the president to upgrade and strengthen higher education. He had given the need for improvement a great deal of thought and, with his chief of staff, promised to provide the government responses necessary to move forward with the project and to attract donor support. In their visits to the campuses, the team also found the heads of the institutions and their staffs eager to work on the project and committed to improving the state of their institutions.

The MUCIA team agreed that the critical problem was "to revitalize the core of the University of Sierra Leone—Fourah Bay College and Njala University College . . . so that its faculty, students and staff can make the vital contributions to Sierra Leone they have the capacity to make and to orient the future of higher education toward development needs" (Riodan, 1990: 7). This would be achieved by restoring critical parts of the infrastructure, realigning programs in higher education to match emerging needs, improving the situation at the institutions to reverse the morale problems at both institutions, and making a number of changes in academic programs. In addition, the government agreed to pay its arrears of $7 million owed to the World Bank, focus higher education funding on the substantial base that already existed rather than new programs, and increase its base budget to a level that ensured that improvements and developments by donors would be sustainable. It was also agreed that student fees would be increased modestly and that student numbers would not be increased beyond the percentage of the population increase for the country. The upper limit for students at Njala would be nine hundred, and at Fourah Bay it would be capped at 1,500 (Riodan et al., 1990: 8–9).

The estimated minimum cost of the program was $17,203,000, of which 60 percent would be focused on improvement of the infrastructure. However, the team believed that the overall need was actually between $20 and $30 million, with the former amount the absolute minimum needed to get the institutions back to reasonable levels. Programs that required support would include improvement of the water system at FBC and NUC, a standby generator, a study to evaluate whether or not FBC should set up its own electricity generation capacity, rehabilitation of the electric system at NUC, completion of the library block at FBC, including replacement of the central cooling system, construction of a library for NUC, service and scientific equipment for both institutions (including small computers), construction of four student dormitories at NUC and a student union, reconditioning and refurbishing existing buildings at FBC, including dormitories. Additional laboratory space was proposed for NUC for teaching science and for staff and postgraduate work, as well as additional space for mechanical engineering at FBC, a new agriculture building at NUC, expansion of the arts faculty at FBC, and development of the farm at NUC.

There was general agreement that, overall, the academic programs at NUC and FBC were excellent, reflecting high standards, good depth and breadth of the curriculum. The need was to upgrade facilities and equipment to sustain them. The team suggested that two additional academic programs were needed, computer science and a program in management and business, plus elimination of bottlenecks in existing curriculum areas involving chemistry, biology, language, and other laboratories (Riodan et al., 1990: 11). The team urged the institutions to put greater emphasis on those areas in which students were actually finding employment, as well as on computer literacy for all students. The team recommended that the faculty be encouraged to carry out more research work at both institutions.

Meetings with faculty, administrators, staff, and students at every level resulted in agreement that improving the infrastructure was the highest priority. The team believed that implementing these programs would be relatively easy and that the additional programs could be covered by the addition of no more than eight new faculty members and a small number of additional staff. The team was impressed by the high quality of faculty members at both institutions, but stressed the need for faculty development, especially for faculty members without PhDs.

The report emphasized that "[t]he decay and deterioration of Fourah Bay College and Njala University College are at such dangerous levels that steps must be taken immediately if Sierra Leone is to avoid the collapse of the higher education and intellectual resources it currently has available." It concluded with the admonition: "Steps must be taken quickly if Sierra Leone is to avoid major losses of quality faculty, as well as preserve and build this vital national resource. The costs at this juncture are within reason. The price of inaction will be far too high" (Riodan et al., 1990: 28).

Following the site visit to Sierra Leone and additional discussions with the president, senior University of Sierra Leone officials, university leaders, faculty, staff, and students, at the request of the government two of the team members met with officials of the African Development Bank in Abidjan, Ivory Coast. The meeting was positive. In mid-1990 a final version of the report and plan was submitted to the office of the president, the vice-chancellor of the University of Sierra Leone, and the principals of the Fourah Bay College and Njala University College. They expressed their appreciation for the report and promised to work to meet the conditions imposed by the World Bank, the conditions noted in the plan, and to cooperate to attract the funding needed to implement the plan. First steps were taken in Sierra Leone to move forward with the plan.

Liberalization of Politics in Sierra Leone

At the same time, President Momoh was working to change the country from a one-party state to a multiparty democracy. He had pushed for free and fair elections from the start of his term, even in the context of the existing one-party state—a system he deplored. He devoted major attention during 1990–91 to moving the country toward a multiparty system and the legalization of political parties other than his All People's Congress. He also made major progress in addressing the economic problems in the country and took steps that led to the reopening of talks on funding from the World Bank and IMF, which had been suspended under his predecessor, Siaka Stevens. These activities were very popular and involved many people in politics as well as many faculty members at FBC, in particular those on some of the committees responsible for making recommendations about constitutional revisions, a multiparty system, and other efforts at liberalization (Hayward, 1995). In August 1991, a new multiparty constitution was put to the voters and overwhelmingly approved. Political parties were allowed to register, and seven had done so by early 1992 (Hayward, 1998: B146). Plans for the election later that year were underway. That diverted efforts from the strategic plan for higher education, but it was still in the works at this time.

Disasters Strike Sierra Leone

On March 23, 1991, soldiers from the Revolutionary United Front (RUF),[4] supported by Charles Taylor's National Patriotic Front of Liberia

(NPFL), invaded Sierra Leone from Liberia. The NPFL was one of the major protagonists in the Liberian civil war. It saw Sierra Leone as a potential financial lifeline with its diamonds and gold. By early 1992, about one-third of the country was either under rebel control or outside government control. The rebel forces were brutal, cutting off the hands of people they regarded as enemies, taking young men and women prisoners and using the men as bearers, or forcing them to fight, and the women as sex slaves. There were brutal killings of civilians in the areas they controlled. The Sierra Leone army, with help from Nigerian, Ghanaian, and Guinean troops enjoyed some successes in 1992, but the war continued, becoming all-consuming for the government. In addition, the nation had to deal with hundreds of refugees, both from Liberia and from the fighting in Sierra Leone, many of them maimed and wounded. In spite of help from Nigeria, Ghana, and Guinea, large sections of southern and eastern Sierra Leone continued to be held under rebel control. As a result, President Momoh reluctantly decided to postpone the elections, fearing that the fighting would unfairly disadvantage political parties with strength in those areas. Ironically, these were areas in which the SLPP and other opposition parties were strongest and elections at that time would have advantaged the governing APC. The decision to postpone the elections led to growing mistrust of the government among some of the parties, including the president's own APC, which wanted to hold elections while they were advantaged (Hayward, 1998: B152).

In early April 1992, a foreign embassy with troops in Sierra Leone warned a senior advisor to President Momoh that their intelligence had picked up talk of a coup among some of his troops. The president discounted that warning. Alarmed, this senior embassy official came to me and asked that I warn the president, saying, "I know he will believe you." I confirmed the authenticity of the sources[5] and then called the president at home and asked to speak to him urgently. We met upstairs in his study, while scores of supporters waited to see him in the large living room downstairs. I told him that Embassy X had received information that Valentine Strasser and several other young officers were planning a coup very soon. He said he could not believe Strasser would do that, that Strasser was indebted to the president because when Strasser had been wounded the president had sent his personal helicopter to the north to bring him back to Freetown for treatment. Nonetheless, I urged him to take the threat seriously and put in place measures to counter that possibility in case the information was correct. He assured me that he had the full support of the army and noted that he had sent the armored car guarding his compound to the front at the request of senior military officers. I urged him, in spite of his confidence in the army, to take precautions to prevent a possible coup. He assured me he would do so. I was to leave the country a few days later on a scheduled leave.

On April 29, 1992, President Momoh was overthrown in a coup led by Valentine Strasser and military rule was instituted. President Momoh had not taken any countermeasures. However, he was able to escape to Guinea by air with help from the Nigerian embassy and army. Some months later he called me at home in the United States from Guinea, saying, among other things: "You were right; I should have listened to you."[6] The coup ushered in a long period of ongoing disasters for the country and for higher education. The financial situation of the University of Sierra Leone continued to decline under military rule. So too did the freedoms so necessary for effective university education. Plans that had begun were suspended and all planning efforts came to an end. Higher education went into a long period of what might be called suspended animation and decline.

Further Deterioration in Sierra Leone

Sierra Leone's higher education change efforts started out with a thoughtful plan and modest budget put together by a joint team from the Midwestern Universities Consortium (MUCIA) and higher education leaders in Sierra Leone. They had strong support from the country's president. The plan had a well-prepared budget, with each item in the plan costed. The next step would have been to work with donors on a more detailed budget, carry out a risk assessment, and lay out an action plan by year. Unfortunately, the coup d'état ended the government of President Momoh, which, along with leaders at the University of Sierra Leone, had initiated the higher education rehabilitation and development effort. That resulted in a period of more than fourteen years of instability, corruption, fighting, war refugees, disease, and neglect of education in general, leaving the country with a broken higher education system. There was little initiative from leaders in higher education to improve conditions as people sought merely to survive this terrible period of war, corrupt government, and violence. Then, just as it looked as if democratic governance had returned, the country was hit with the Ebola epidemic, from which it was still struggling to recover in 2016. While there is now talk about reviving the University of Sierra Leone, the conditions at the university have deteriorated further and the economic situation of the country remains difficult. While there is some hope of recovery, early in 2018 there did not appear to be the kind of active leadership in higher education or government needed to restart the process of strategic planning and upgrading.

Strategic Plans and Processes Have to Survive Any Changes in Government or Leadership

Following the coup that overthrew the elected government of President Joseph Momoh in 1992, a long period of civil strife, poor government, corruption, and misrule began. It is not my intention to detail the whole period of military and civilian rule here, but merely to give a sense of what followed. The overthrow of the government of President Joseph Momoh resulted in a long period of further decline for higher education as a consequence of the war itself and government neglect. This period also saw the loss of many of the best faculty members, starting in the 1980s and gaining momentum in the 1990s, who left both institutions because of the conflict and deteriorating conditions.[7] The ruling military had little interest in higher education[8] other than that the students keep quiet. Njala College was eventually closed due to the fighting, and later reestablished in Freetown. There was a second coup in January 1996, which brought to power Brigadier Julius Maada Bio. New elections were held in March 1996. They were won by the Sierra Leone People's Party, with Ahmad Tejan Kabbah elected as President. Kabbah ushered in a reign of corruption unparalleled in Sierra Leone history.[9] Education at all levels was ignored, including higher education (Hayward & Kandeh, 2001). There was another coup in 1997 led by Johnny Paul Koroma, which removed the Kabbah government briefly, only for it to return in 1998, although rebel fighters took over Freetown during part of that period. British and Ecomog troops[10] joined in the effort to defeat the rebel forces, with the war finally ending in 2002, and Kabbah returned to power. His rule continued to be rapacious and corrupt.

In elections that followed in 2007, Earnest Koroma and the All Peoples Congress (APC) won overwhelmingly, supported by a population fed up with corruption, incompetence, and greed (Kandeh, 2008). Sadly, the Koroma government proved to be more corrupt than its predecessors. In addition, they soon faced the Ebola epidemic which began in Sierra Leone in December 2014 and had a devastating effect for almost two years, with an estimated death toll of about four thousand and many more suffering, with limited capacity to work, their lives blighted by homelessness, and little hope for the future (Reuters, 2012).

The sad truth at this point is that higher education has deteriorated beyond calculation from what the MUCIA team saw during its site visit to Sierra Leone during 1979–80 to work on a plan to rebuild the University of Sierra Leone. Examples of the further decline of higher education abound. As one writer commented in 2014 about Fourah Bay College, "The university itself has slid into apparently irreversible decline. Material conditions have atrophied almost continuously since the civil war ended in 2002, and campus accommodation is now uninhabitable to the extent that even students from the farthest provinces are denied lodging" (Gardner, 2014: 2). Another writer, in 2015, noted: "The entire infrastructure is completely decrepit. You name them—the buildings are completely dilapidated, with no renovation for a long time now; and the library is a mini pool during the rainy season" (Dandy, 2015: 2–3). One writer commented that students have to scramble for chairs and tables, which are in short supply, the road up the hill to campus has deteriorated badly, and all the dorms are closed and continue to deteriorate. He pointed out that the promised rehabilitation with funds from the Arab Bank for Economic Development in Africa (BADEA) had not been realized even five years after the agreement was signed and suggests that in the best case work wouldn't start until mid-2016 in order to be completed in 2020 (Dandy, 2015: 4–5). That did not happen.

During the intervening years, some discussions other than the BADEA proposal had taken place about rehabilitating higher education. In 2007 there was the "Sierra Leone Education Sector Plan: A Roadmap to a Better Future," by the Ministry of Education, Science, and Technology,[11] though nothing came of the plan. There was a two-day retreat in 2012 at Njala to discuss a new strategic plan for the university for 2013–17 (Lebbie, 2012: 1). At that time a committee was set up to formalize a strategic plan, again with little result. There was also "The Agenda for Prosperity: Sierra Leone's Third Generation Poverty Reduction Strategy Paper (2013–2018)" compiled by the Government of Sierra Leone, prepared with assistance from the United Nations Development Program (Government of Sierra Leone, 2012), with only one page on higher education and that focused on revising the curriculum to meet demands, private-public partnership, and improving quality. The war, the coups, and the rampant corruption crushed the spirit of higher education leaders, faculty members, and students at FBC and Njala, with survival becoming their watchword. In the meantime, the institutions continued to deteriorate.

The tragedy of the Sierra Leone case is that although there was a major push to improve the University of Sierra Leone following the initiative under President Momoh with MUCIA assistance in 1989–90, there was no real, concerted effort by the government or University of Sierra Leone to fund such a plan following the coup of 1992. The interruptions of the elections in 1991, and the coup that ended the Momoh government, brought that effort to an end. During this whole period there was no government commitment either to provide the needed funding for infrastructure repair and upgrading, to rebuild the institutions, or to strengthen the academic programs. Perhaps the BADEA proposal served as a smokescreen for inaction. In any case, the situation continued to deteriorate. In 2018, thanks to a Saudi loan, efforts were underway to rebuild Fourah Bay College, with the contract going to a brother of former president Ernest Koroma. Sierra Leone also received $172 million in new loan funds from the IMF[12] to help with development. We will see if any of that goes to higher education. The task ahead is now gigantic. As the MUCIA team warned in their report in 1990 (Riodan et al., 1990): "The costs at this juncture are within reason. The price of inaction will be far too high." That is certainly now the case. There is need for leadership at both the higher education institutional level and at the national government level to put the necessary resources behind a plan to rebuild both Njala University College and Fourah Bay College at the University of Sierra Leone. A plan without support or resources is of little or no use at all.

The continuing misfortune for Sierra Leone is that there does not seem to exist either the will or the higher education leadership to make any significant move to bring about improvement to higher education in Sierra Leone. Part of that seems to be the consequence of political interference, which has limited both institutional and public criticism of inaction, corruption, and lack of leadership—problems that worsened under the Koroma government. After a long history of excellence in higher education, it is puzzling that there does not seem to by any leadership in higher education today, within the community of graduates, politicians, or ordinary citizens, with the interest, drive, or energy to organize the rebuilding of higher education. Yet, as all the evidence demonstrates, no nation without a high-quality higher education system moves into the realm of developing nations. Sierra Leone could have done that some years ago. There is currently some talk of free higher education,[13] but that would require a major increase in government support, which, as we have seen elsewhere, runs the risk of further weakening the quality of higher education.

No Nation without a High-Quality Higher Education System Moves into the Realm of Developing Nations

Until strong leadership and support for rebuilding higher education appears, it seems that the inaction of the past decades will continue. Sierra Leone has little to teach us about higher education change other than the importance of higher education leadership and the need for strong public and national political support—both of which the country lacks.

Chapter 8

Fostering Higher Education Change in Uganda

The Context for Change in Higher Education in Uganda

Enrollment in higher education in Uganda grew from about 5,000 students in the 1970s to 124,313 in 2005. By the 1980s and 1990s, Ugandan higher education had a reputation as one of the best systems in East Africa (Hyuha, 2017: 1). The system was dominated by Makerere University but included a total of twenty-seven universities in 2005, with four of them public and the rest private institutions. There were more than 130 other tertiary institutions offering a range of programs from teacher education to hotels and tourism, as well as technical subjects. There was no allowance for transfers between institutions and, unlike Afghanistan, it was not an integrated system (NCHE, 2015: 7–8).

The mechanism for bringing about higher education change in Uganda in 2003 was seen to be the National Council for Higher Education (NCHE). It was established in 2001 under the Universities and Other Tertiary Institutions Act (UOTIA) and charged with regulating higher education in Uganda, which at that time comprised more than one hundred tertiary institutions[1] of various types. It began staffing in 2002 but did not become fully active until 2003, when its executive director and council members were appointed. The council consisted of twenty members (later reduced to eighteen) chosen to represent a broad range of stakeholders, including representatives of each major type of tertiary institution—universities, technical colleges, teachers' colleges, agricultural colleges, medical training institutions—as well as two student members, the chairman of the NCHE, and a representative from each of the public and private university senates.

The council was designed to regulate and guide the establishment and management of the institutions of higher learning and to monitor the quality of higher education, review qualifications, and advise the government and the Ministry of Education on higher education issues, including any changes that were needed. It was in that context that the NCHE decided to prepare a national higher education strategic plan. The main driver of that effort was its director, A. B. K. Kasozi, and the NCHE.

The major functions of the council were to set up and administer an accreditation system, look into complaints, evaluate national manpower needs, set admissions standards, ensure that institutions had adequate physical and education facilities, deal with transfer of credits, oversee policy formation, and conduct a wide range of other duties (Kasozi, 2004). It existed separately from the Ministry of Higher Education and Sports but worked closely with it. The council had decided that it needed a strategic plan to lay out its change agenda, and scheduled a workshop for 2004 to review a draft strategic plan with leaders of higher education institutions and other interested parties, including several specialists on strategic planning recommended by the World Bank.

In 2004, the NCHE was a relatively new institution, still getting organized and working to train its members in their duties and responsibilities. The workshop was held in July 2004 for training and to review the strategic plan. The NCHE faced a number of challenges at that time including its lack of adequate funding, the very diverse character of its membership, the wide range of different goals of the institutions that were under its supervision, ambiguity about its authority, and the possibility of conflicts and overlapping responsibilities between the NCHE and the Ministry of Education and Sports.

The NCHE secretariat set up a number of individual departments as it grew, beginning with accreditation and quality assurance, established in 2003. Accreditation was further elaborated in legislation in 2008. The secretariat also had units responsible for research, finance, development and documentation, legal affairs, and human resources (Bailey, 2014: 13).

From the outset, the leadership of the secretariat was concerned about a number of critical issues and their ability to deal with them effectively. These included the rapid growth in student numbers without a comparable increase in the budget, low salaries for faculty members, the rapid change in the needs of business, government, and other employers, deteriorating infrastructure due to lack of maintenance, the small number of women students compared to men (about 30 percent female), inadequately trained administrative staff, and regional imbalances.[2] The limited funding made it difficult to carry out all of its functions. As the retired executive director noted some years later, "[I]ts initial underfunding caused a number of problems to the institution. First the NCHE failed to perform a number of its functions as stipulated by the Act because of failure to recruit sufficient, experienced and highly qualified staff. Secondly, the NCHE could not purchase appropriate equipment and other inputs for use in ensuring the delivery of quality higher education or build an office structure that was appropriate to its image and functions" (Kasozi, 2016: 63).

The quality assurance functions had become a major part of the work of the NCHE at the outset and included licensing of institutions, and accreditation of public and private programs. This was expanded to professional programs in 2006. These functions entailed major tasks, including assessment visits to the institutions. These efforts strained the NCHE's limited human and financial resources and were sometimes not fully operational. According to one report, by 2014 the accreditation aspect of the program was still not completely in place and the monitoring function was only 20 percent complete (Bailey 2014: 19).

While the NCHE enjoyed a remarkable level of autonomy, its funding came through the Ministry of Education and Sports and it reported to the minister there. There was also some confusion about overlapping functions. However, the major problem limiting the effectiveness of the NCHE was its limited funding, which affected both staffing and its ability to carry out its functions effectively. For example, the staff numbers for the licensing and accrediting functions were far too limited to cover the required reviews, and there was a shortage of transportation resources affecting site visits and other quality assurance activities. One of its strong points was its high level of autonomy in its decisions over licensing and accreditation, including its ability to close institutions, which it had done, and to shut down programs it found had failed to meet NCHE standards.

Starting the Change Process: The Uganda Strategic Plan for Higher Education 2003–2015

The strategic planning effort began in 2003, with an ambitious draft plan for change in higher education, which began the national higher education plan: The Uganda Strategic Plan for Higher Education: 2003–2015.

The mission of the system was stated as follows:

> The Mission of higher education is to provide quality higher education through teaching and research using modern technologies. This will be achieved by creating a diversified, integrated and flexible higher education sector capable of managing the required curricula changes. (Ministry of Higher Education and Sports, 2003: 3)

The mission statement was clear and defined reasonable goals, including improving quality broadly defined and an emphasis on "modern technologies." It envisioned the higher education sector as diversified, integrated, and flexible (Hayward 2004: 28–31).

The major goals of the plan were organized around five themes:

- Enhancing quality and relevance
- Increasing equity and access
- Achieving efficiency and effectiveness
- Improving governance
- Preventing HIV/AIDS

Each of the themes was then broken down into listings of the changes that would have to be made to meet the goals—activities such as reformed financing, curriculum reform, increased science enrollments. Finally, key performance indicators were spelled out, to allow people to measure implementation success. These included implementation of science programs in the first year, revision of the curricula at a number of institutions, and development of sustainable research funding (Hayward, 2004). Let's look briefly at each theme.

Enhancing Quality and Relevance

Raising and sustaining quality, in part through reform of the curriculum, was the central theme for change under the strategic plan. That was seen as key to tertiary education's being able to provide the teaching, research, and service necessary to fulfilling higher education's central role in development. Part of that effort was a commitment to expanded ICT—essential to quality given the wealth of resources available on the Internet. The changes focused on an expanded role for ICT in teaching, improved access to the Internet for faculty members and students, and the enhanced efficiencies ICT might produce for the whole academic community.

Another critical area was to establish quality assurance and accreditation. To assure high standards and to protect students against unscrupulous providers, it was essential to develop a formal quality assurance process. This had worked well in other parts of Africa and needed to be established in Uganda. Establishing an effective accreditation system was a major new effort that was seen as essential for higher education.

Increasing Equity and Access

The provision of gender equity, along with access for students from poor backgrounds and students with disabilities, was an important part of the strategic plan. The activities proposed, such as affirmative action and facilities for the disadvantaged, were major changes and were seen as central to success. The plan's target was the admission of 51 percent women students by 2015. They came close to that goal by 2017 with 45 percent (Hyuha, 2017: 1).

Achieving Efficiency and Effectiveness

This section of the plan was more about funding than anything else, suggesting that "[h]igher education requires adequate resources, and especially financial resources, to make it efficient and effective" (Hayward, 2004: 12). The changes proposed would require more physical facilities, more staff, and expanded libraries, laboratories, and other facilities. A major part of this section focused on the recognition that the costs of higher education changes must be borne by all stakeholders—that there would need to be "multiple funding sources for higher education," though government was still seen to be the largest contributor. The plan suggested that a higher education grants committee should be established to allocate and source funds. It called for government scholarships for strategic disciplines in public and private institutions. It suggested that each institution should set up a research fund equal to 5 percent of salaries. The plan also suggested that the private sector should be given more incentives to finance higher education. This section emphasized the need to get away from a sole dependence on government for funding.

The document encouraged the private sector to participate more actively in funding tertiary education. That was an important goal but one that is often difficult to realize in fact, as it was not clear what the incentives would be to encourage increased private sector funding. It would involve working with the private sector to show people the stake they have in higher education and to convince them they have an obligation to help and will benefit from it in the long run. The kind of cooperation between public and private higher education institutions suggested that it was a useful ideal but it was not clear how that would be realized. This goal would be especially difficult to achieve given the very different methods of funding between public and private higher education institutions—the one based largely on tuition as the major source of revenue versus government funding and low tuitions for public institutions.

Improving Governance

The strategic plan suggested major changes in tertiary sector governance to better link institutions—to "harmonize" (Hayward, 2004: 14) the roles of higher education institutions, strengthen the national council, guarantee autonomy, and allow non-university tertiary institutions greater freedom within the framework set out in the plan. It also recommended creation of a data base management system at the NCHE. Among the goals was greater horizontal integration among universities of the same type. An especially important suggestion related to the articulation of credits—developing a system in which comparable student course work at one tertiary institution could be transferred to another. That would require establishment of a credit hour system that was uniform (even if the actual number of credits were not). These were recommendations for major changes, though little was said about how they were to be implemented.

Preventing HIV/AIDS

Uganda has had significant success in stemming the HIV/AIDS pandemic, as the authors note, but "[T]here has been no deliberate effort to manage the scourge in higher education institutions" (Hayward, 2004: 15). The losses of students and staff to HIV/AIDS were high and the effects on higher education significant. The proposals included an NCHE committee on HIV/AIDS, development of higher education guidelines to prevent and control HIV/AIDS, and additional activities to prevent and control the disease. In several countries, tertiary institutions provided treatment for students and staff who were HIV positive or had AIDS (such as UNIMA in Malawi) with help from the donor community. Uganda became successful in this effort thanks to donor assistance and their own well-developed policies.

Financing the Strategic Plan

Part of the discussion of financing involved rethinking how tertiary institutions are funded. The section of the strategic plan on costing suggested several different models for financing higher education—among them one based on student numbers (calculated as full-time equivalents, or FTEs) rather than block grants. It appears that some costs, such as infrastructure and capital, would be funded by block grants of some kind adjusted for student numbers in a very general sense (Hayward, 2004: 17). It was not clear what this shift to student numbers (FTE) as a basis for funding would mean for different disciplines, and there was no evidence that these options had been explored at the outset, though they were at a later date. For example, would the funding for one FTE science student carry a different monetary value than one FTE humanities student (as was the case in South Africa, for example)?

One concern about the discussion of funding was the assumption that the private sector would assume more of the costs, thus producing savings. For example, "The plan further assumes that the private sector will take up the welfare component of the student in the tertiary sector" (Hayward, 2004: 17). My experience is that the private sector is often unwilling or unable to take on the load expected of it. A second concern related to the expected savings from private sector participation. As noted earlier, it was not clear how this would happen. Not surprisingly, there was little success in obtaining this funding in the long run. Indeed, funding for higher education became a continuing problem for the NCHE. State funding declined throughout most of the period from 2002 to 2012 (Kasozi, 2016: 91).

The section of the strategic plan devoted to financing included a budget with assumptions about growth, costs, budget increases over time. It covered the plan period from 2003 to 2015. This was an excellent start on budgeting—rare in my experience with strategic planning, where far too often there is no budget at all. The assumptions used were presented clearly in a way anyone could examine. At this point, there was no prioritization of the budget items. A risk analysis was also needed of the type described in the Pakistan strategic plan. That did not happen either. Nonetheless, the NCHE was constantly trying to improve its funding situation, mostly with no success. Only in 2010 did it begin to have increases in government funding, which allowed it to expand its activities and better meet its mandate. However, as the former executive director noted in 2016, "[I]ncreased income also led to increased conflicts as staff struggled to access resources." To avoid that, the executive director recommended that the NCHE should adopt "performance-based work" (Kasozi, 2016: 268). I think a better solution would have been to create a more detailed budget that had been through a careful risk analysis of the type carried out in Pakistan and then worked out with the Ministry of Finance.

In the long run, an effective strategic plan is one that combines a careful assessment of the current conditions with a well-reasoned discussion of the budget that will allow the goals to be met. For most of higher education that budget includes many sources of funding: government, donors, businesses, students, grants, and income from other sources (e.g., sale of university farm produce, short courses, night classes). Often, as was the case here, the budget is based on certain assumptions about what government will do, about the private sector, and about other donors. The Uganda strategic plan included some of this discussion under the heading "Options for the Implementation of the Strategic Plan." Yet, as noted earlier, there was no unanimity about the funding strategies within the higher education community, with the education sector review seeing one set of options as the most implementable and realistic while the vice-chancellor's forum recommended different, more expansive options. As time went on, the problem for the council was that appropriate levels of funding were not forthcoming, in part due to the lack of agreement between the major leadership groups. In the long run, its operations were regularly impeded by inadequate funding. Thus, while the discussion of funding got off to a good start, it was not followed up with the kind of careful analysis and planning we saw in the Pakistan example or similar to that carried out by Peninsula Technikon in South Africa. Thus, in the long run, funding was insufficient to meet plan goals, but there seemed to be faith that the funding would eventually come from somewhere. It did not. In addition, the lack of agreement on a funding strategy made the kind of lobbying needed to get the funding required difficult.

Problems for Implementation of the Strategic Plan

The major problem for implementing the desired changes was insufficient funding. The government sector continued to underfund higher education, and this made it very difficult to implement much of the strategic plan. Executive director Prof. Kasozi worked diligently to gain increased government support as well as to attract donor funding to support the strategic plan. Some funding was received from the Rockefeller Foundation for the initial planning efforts. But overall, little help from donors was forthcoming at the outset. There was some discussion with the World Bank in 2004,[3] but that requires a direct government request to the bank from the Ministry of Education and Sports through the government including the Ministry of Finance. That does not appear to have happened.

As a consequence, adequate funding for strategic plan implementation was not forthcoming in 2005. As the NCHE emphasized in its 2005 review of the year:

> The implementation of academic programmes has been hampered by financial constraints, out dated curricula, institutional inability to recruit and retain qualified staff, the lack of adequate and appropriate instruction materials and inadequate physical facilities. Programmes that require practical training lack laboratory materials and equipment. Most science and technology students find it difficult to complete their programmes and receive a lot more theoretical than practical training. Unless the financing of the sub-sector is addressed, the quality of higher education will continue to deteriorate. (NCHE, 2005)

The report noted various attempts to acquire more funding, including requests to the legislature. None of these had great success. As a result, the NCHE ended its report with the following suggestion:

> The first strategy would be to gradually raise fees to cover the cost of educating students in a period of three years. . . . This scenario would just buy good higher education but not the best. (NCHE, 2005: 55)

Overall, the situation has not improved much in the years that have followed. As later reports continue to emphasize, funding has remained in crisis, the best faculty members have been leaving to go to other institutions elsewhere in Africa and abroad where salaries and conditions were better, and the situation has become dire. A report in 2011 continued:

> Since 2006 when NCHE first published "The State of Higher Education and Training" the Ugandan higher education sub-sector has continued to expand in terms of student enrolments and the number of institutions. These increases, however, have occurred in the face of declining or stagnant unit cost funding for education facilities, infrastructure and academic staff. The state and other stakeholders must address the problem of funding higher education before standards are severely compromised. On a positive note, there have been improvements in female access to higher education, computer access and use, as well as enrolment in science and technology. However, these latter enrolments are largely in computer-related areas rather than in basic, mathematical or other technical sciences. The unfortunate decline in the production of middle level technicians from technical institutions has continued. (NCHE, 2011: 1)

Oversight of Tertiary Education Change Needs to Come with the Ability to Prioritize Its Focus, Giving Its Leaders the Ability to Build Quality in Areas that Foster National Development

Progress was made in realizing some of the change goals for higher education. The accreditation process initiated early in the NCHE years had its framework further spelled out in law in 2008 (NCHE: Statutory Instrument, 2008). By 2007, it had accredited 1,088 programs provisionally, but since 2009, "75 percent of university programmes have remained illegal, having not been accredited" (Kasozi, 2016: 66). This was due to the funding shortfall as well as limited staffing.

During the period following the establishment of the NCHE, student numbers continued to increase, from 80,000 in 2002 to 198,000 in 2010–11 (Kasozi, 2016: 79), though not with the hoped-for shift to the sciences. Funding did not keep up with student growth, and shortfalls remained a critical problem. Thus, what was an excellent plan for higher education change remained largely unrealized, and higher education continued to languish except for some individual successes at places such as Makerere University which managed to attract its own funding in a variety of ways from both donors and fees.

The improvements at Makerere were quite remarkable, especially in spite of shortfalls in government funding. Though well-regarded, like other institutions Makerere suffered from lack of funding, with government funding falling from 100 percent of its total budget in 2000 to 41 percent by 2005 (Kasozi, 2016: 104). Given its growth in student numbers, even with fees for some students and other outside sources of funding, its financial situation was difficult. Nonetheless, through the creativity of its faculty and leaders it was able to attract enough funding to significantly improve to the point that it was regarded as the second-best university in Sub-Saharan Africa, just behind the University of Cape Town in terms of knowledge production in a CHET study. In that 2014 analysis they did very well in meeting CHET's high-level performance indicators including production of graduates at the master's and PhD level, research publications, academic staff with PhDs, and permanent academic staff by 2011.[4] Its doctoral enrollments increased by 8 percent a year, growing from 26 in 2001 to 563 in 2011—as Bunting et al. note, "a 2165% increase during that period." Part of its success was due to the fact that it capped enrolment increases in 2007 at about 34,000 total students, kept its graduate student to faculty ratio at 3:1 (as did Cape Town), with graduate programs led by senior faculty members at the full professor and associate professor levels (Bunting et al., 2014: 25–30). Its growth rate was kept at about 2 percent a year (ibid.: 8).

Part of the problem of funding for change in Uganda was that the NCHE mandate was very broad, with only limited ability to focus its change agenda on a particular sector of tertiary education. Unlike the Ministry of Higher Education in Afghanistan, which regulates both public and private higher education but focuses funding on public higher education and can differentiate by type of institution, or the

Higher Education Commission in Pakistan, which focuses on the public university sector and science and technology, the NCHE covered a very broad range of institutions including universities, teacher training, technical colleges, colleges of commerce, forestry, hotels and tourism, as well as medical training institutes. Because its mandate was so broad and funding limited it could not cover all areas. It also seemed to lack the will or ability to focus on one or two areas, such as quality assurance, or on one or two levels of tertiary education as a priority. That left higher education overall seriously underserved, underfunded, and limited in its quality improvements. Some of the problem was related to confusion about the role of the NCHE versus that of the ministry and various of its departments. That too may have hurt funding efforts or wasted funding. Thus, higher education was unable to prioritize in a way that focused on critical priority areas. Overall, the funding question was not given the attention by government, especially prior to 2010, that was necessary for success. Higher education has suffered as a consequence in its inability to significantly improve quality, coordinate activities, realize many of the change goals of its strategic plan, or meet many of its current needs.

The university sector was also hindered by rigid rules that restricted its ability to raise funds and spend them in the ways it thought most important. Kasozi argues that part of the problem, even for the best universities, was state interference, with rules and regulations that hampered their ability to raise funding and imposed a "lack of autonomy in raising and spending money as well as managing their affairs" (Kasozi, 2016: xxv). He makes a strong case for that argument.

Lessons Learned

A successful higher education change process is invariably complex with many parts that need to fit together, as we see from the experience of the Uganda plans. The efforts to bring about higher education change in Uganda were not without major successes, though not to the extent desired in the long run. What was missing? Their efforts combined a well-thought-out set of goals for change, a thoughtful assessment of the current conditions, and a well-reasoned discussion of a budget that would allow the goals to be met. There was an implementation plan and a structure to oversee the implementation process in the NCHE. The planners expected most of the funding to come from government, though they also thought other funding would be forthcoming from private higher education, donors, businesses, grants, and perhaps from other sources such as night classes. This supplemental funding did not materialize to the extent expected.

As time went on, the major problem for the National Council for Higher Education was that expected donor funding was not forthcoming, no doubt in part due to the lack of agreement between the major leadership groups as well as the ministries of finance and higher education. As it was, funding proved insufficient to meet many of the plan's goals, and the change agenda was thus less successful than it might have been. I am not suggesting that a risk assessment and inclusion of the ministries of finance and higher education would have solved the problems, but surely such an effort would have made the problems clear and suggested a need to revise the change goals to meet available funding or seek additional funding. It might well have leveraged more funding. Instead, in retrospect, there was hope that the World Bank or some other funders would come to the rescue of the change plan at that last moment. That did not happen, which suggests that a more complete financial planning and risk analysis might have changed the situation.

As a recent discussion of Ugandan higher education by Hyuha noted, the funding shortages began in the 1990s following a long period of strong excellent support: "Uganda's quality of education at all levels used to be the best in Eastern Africa. The sound quality of education was sustained by a highly qualified team of instructors, well-equipped and well-funded institutions, adequate supporting service and staff, and good governance at all institutions." Hyuha went on to say: "After that, the situation changed for the worse—mainly due to serious underfunding" (Hyuha, 2017: 2–3).

The situation of higher education in Uganda remains mixed. While the economy has been one of the fastest growing in Sub-Saharan Africa, its GDP growth has slowed to about 5 percent and its future growth may be marred by a recent unsuccessful government development plan. While government accountability has improved, the situation remains fragile and that is not good for higher education, already suffering from underfunding as noted earlier. On the other hand, the percentage of the population suffering from poverty (defined as living on less than $1.25 per day) has dropped from 56.4 percent in 2003 to 19.7 percent in 2013 (World Bank, 2016f: 1–2). The trend line for the economy is somewhat positive, but political problems and a fragile economy are at the mercy of the weather, given the country's dependence on agriculture and the recurring threat of drought, making the prospects of major funding increases for higher education limited.

Overall, however, it is important to emphasize that the NCHE strategic plan was a very good plan for higher education change. In addition, a number of the institutions, especially Makerere, were quite successful in fundraising and quality improvement on their own. Indeed, a great deal of change was accomplished in Uganda in improved quality, accreditation, training for faculty leaders, and in thinking ahead about the needs of higher education even under great financial stress and facing the ecosystem problems noted above. The NCHE did a very good job of supervising the growth of higher education over more than a decade including overseeing expansion of the number of institutions, growth of the student population, and expansion of the curriculum. However, in the long run they were never able to overcome the ongoing funding shortfalls. The lesson from this case is the need for careful assessment and assurance of commitment of the funding needs, to revision of the strategic plan to correspond to expected funding. In retrospect, in Uganda some of that stress might have been avoided and more of the change goals achieved with a little more focus on finances, as well as better articulation of the needs and risks at the outset.

Chapter 9

Madagascar

Higher Education Change Efforts Thwarted

Background to Higher Education in Madagascar

Higher education in Madagascar was established in the 1950s as part of the French colonial Institut des Hautes Etudes. The University of Antananarivo evolved from this base in 1961. It began with an enrollment of 723 students and fifty-two faculty members, of whom nine were Malagasy. At the beginning, it focused on law, medicine, pharmacy, science, and the arts. By 1970, it had grown in enrollment to more than four thousand students. The condition of higher education in Madagascar in 2006 was poor, in spite of recent increases in budgetary allocations for higher education. Funding for higher education remained low, less than 3 percent of GDP, and expenditure per student was among the lowest among developing nations. In 2004, it amounted to only $233 (less than Afghanistan at $238, Ethiopia at $470, and Uganda at $1,200). Funding for higher education was increased substantially in 2005, bringing the total expenditure per student to $390, still far below what was needed for quality education. The budget for the universities in 2005 was 159,639,374,353 Ariary (approximately $80 million): salaries comprised 64 percent of total budget, scholarships were 25 percent, operation and infrastructure 11 percent.

Only slightly more than 2 percent of college-age students were admitted to the universities—among the lowest percentages in the world. About 44 percent of students who applied were admitted. There were six public universities (Antananarivo, Antsiranana, Fianarantsoa, Mahajanga, Toamasina, and Toliara) and forty-five private higher education institutions authorized by the government by 2005. At least another twenty nonrecognized private higher education institutions existed.

The strategic planning process grew out of discussions with the World Bank and Minister Haja Nirina Razafinjatovo in Washington, which resulted in bank funding to start a strategic planning project, including the assistance of a consultant.[1] The reform agenda, which started in 2005, faced many challenges. Among the most difficult to overcome was the effort to stem the major losses of students between secondary school and college graduation. Of the almost 57,000 secondary students who took it at the end of secondary school, only 44 percent passed the baccalaureate examination, which makes them eligible to take university entrance examinations. Of those who passed the baccalaureate examination, only about half (13,503 of 25,049 students or 53.91 percent) were admitted in 2005. An unacceptably high percentage (35 percent) failed during their first year of studies and 18 percent of those repeated the year. This high failure rate had devastating consequences for students and represented a huge waste of government resources. Of those who made it to the second year, 83 percent received a diploma, about 42 percent of those admitted. Part of the problem was inadequate preparation in secondary school (especially in the rural areas); in part it was a function of the fact that many students went to universities because that was the expectation, though they had no idea what they wanted to do with their education.[2]

In 2006, higher education was beginning to revive after a long period of neglect, underfunding, and inaction. This improvement was led by Minister of Education Haja Nirina Razafinjatovo and his staff. He was a well-liked leader with a clear vision about the improvements needed in higher education and strong leadership skills, and was greatly respected in the academic community. He had the ear of President Ravalomanana, whose campaign he had helped organize, and worked well with other ministers having been minister of telecommunications previously. The president had major goals for rebuilding the economy of Madagascar after years of misrule and corruption and had largely succeeded in making gains in both areas. The president had overseen preparation of a national master plan for the nation, the Madagascar Action Plan 2006. This plan focused on rebuilding the country, repairing its roads, improving governance, investing in education, fostering economic growth, and broadening access to foreign investors. The ministry was preparing its own strategic plan through its task team of ministry and higher education staff, called the Groupe de Réflection, to work on the plan, and a Groupe de Pensée of public university presidents to prepare the final plan. By the end of 2006, they had developed a clear outline for the plan. The ministry staff leadership was a talented group of hard-working directors, many drawn from the universities, with clear goals for improvement of higher and secondary education.

The initial reaction to the draft plan among higher education institutions was mixed, with some lukewarm or actually opposed to the plan. There was a widespread view that nothing needed to change, that things were all right as they were. It took time to help this very isolated island community understand that they were far behind even their African counterparts, whom they tended to look down on. The private higher education sector was especially resistant. Their attitude was, "Let the market decide." Yet, the ordinary citizen was not in a position to make knowledgeable judgments about the quality of these institutions. The minister recognized the poor performance and low level of quality of many of the education institutions and would periodically drop in unannounced at an institution, public or private, to carry out a brief inspection. In many cases, what he saw was depressing, with faculty members absent, facilities in poor condition, laboratories poorly equipped, and students often on their own. When such conditions were found, the institution was put on notice to improve.

By the end of 2007, attitudes of higher education leaders had changed substantially, in part due to prodding by the minister. There was general recognition of the need to improve and upgrade higher education with widespread agreement on goals for the strategic plan. The best of the private higher education institutions were eager for accreditation to get underway, as they saw that it would be a good public indicator of their quality and differentiate them from other institutions of lower quality.

The draft of the plan for major changes in higher and secondary education, the *Document de Strategie: Réforme de l'Enseignement Post Fondamental*, was completed in 2008. It set forth more than fifty goals for higher education, including establishment of a system for quality assurance and accreditation, general improvement of the curriculum, increased access to higher education, growth of faculty numbers following a freeze of more than a dozen years, expansion of research, a start on distance education, faculty development especially at the PhD level, work on mechanisms to raise faculty salaries, improved relevance of the curriculum, enhanced governance, an increase in the number of women faculty members, and work to improve the quality of private higher education (Ministry of National Education and Scientific Research, 2008). Most of the private higher education institutions were of very low quality, with a few notable exceptions including the excellent Institut Catholique de Madagascar.

The strategy of the minister was to work on finalizing the change plan while starting to implement it at the same time. He continued to meet regularly with the presidents and the two committees working on the strategic plan. Support for the plan grew markedly as leaders began to see how far behind Madagascar was in comparison to Mauritius and its neighboring countries in Africa as well as those in Asia. The low-key manner of the minister and his senior staff and the logic of his arguments worked to shift attitudes. He also traveled around the country to make his goals clear and foster support for the changes needed to improve higher education. Meetings were held in the rural areas and several presidents were actively involved in presenting the strategic plan to the public. Strong support from the World Bank and several external advisors also helped change attitudes. The president was an active advocate for change and improvements in higher education and regularly made that clear to the press and in meetings around the country.

The implementation process began with quality assurance and accreditation. The policies and standards for accreditation were completed in May 2007 and the process was established by decree. Workshops and training began shortly thereafter. After a long freeze in hiring, work began on faculty recruitment. The ministry established a digital library for faculty and students, with help from a consultant from Pakistan who was involved in establishing the digital library in Pakistan, building on the experience of the Higher Education Commission there. That work was undertaken during 2006, with the library in place during 2007 assisted by The Programme for the Enhancement of Research Information (PERI) in London.

The overall plan for change in higher education was well written, clear, and detailed, but far too ambitious for five years. Parts of it were too complex, with many new initiatives with separate committees running each of them. There were not enough qualified people to staff all these committees. Similarly, the plans for reform of the ministry itself were too extensive to be completed in five years, though they were a good start on what needed to be done. While the problems were identified, not enough thought had gone into solving them. The ideas for financial reform too were excellent, but not developed. For example, a student loan program was proposed without recognizing how complicated such programs are or the history of their substantial failure in most of Africa (Gasikara, 2015). Those issues should have been taken into account in considering the possibility of a successful scheme in Madagascar.

One important step proposed to improve the financial condition of universities was to change the law so that universities could keep the funds they raised. At that time, they were required to turn these funds over to the Ministry of Finance and thus lost them. This was a powerful disincentive to being entrepreneurial. That rule needed to be changed. The idea of an innovation fund was an excellent one but again it was not clear where the funds would come from. Nonetheless, the ministry moved forward in a number of these areas at the same time that the committees worked to resolve the problems and complete the overall plan for higher and secondary education. Another committee of the ministry was working on a separate strategic plan for primary education. Donor support for these efforts was provided by the World Bank.

Catastrophe Strikes Madagascar

Fostered by opposition parties and encouraged by the French community and government,[3] in early 2009 protests against President Ravalomanana's government became a regular event. The protests were the outcome of a personal vendetta by Andry Rajoelina, who was angry about government closure of his television station, and were abetted by French interests arguing that the president favored his own businesses at the expense of the French, as well as opposition by French businesses to his having opened the market to encourage external investment, especially by investors from Germany, the United States, and Canada, and to his introduction of English as the third national language, along with Malagasy and French, in 2006. This latter move, in particular, outraged the French, who still regarded Madagascar as an integral part of the French orbit.[4]

The leader of this opposition to the president, Andry Rajoelina, was the mayor of the capital city, Antananarivo. His TV station was closed by the government after he aired an interview with Ratsiraka Rajoelina, a former politician who had gone to France after serious political problems in Madagascar. Rajoelina organized daily demonstrations. He and his French supporters were paying many of the demonstrators and buying support from the military, with whom he maintained close contacts (Palmares, 2014).

Rajoelina's almost-daily rallies, where he was a very persuasive speaker, succeeded in mobilizing large groups. In February 2009, he urged them to attack the presidential palace. When the demonstrators tried to tear down the fence at the palace, the guards, having exhausted their supply of tear gas, used live ammunition, shooting in the air originally but later into the crowd.[5] By the end of the attack on the palace there were many dead (Dewar et al., 2013: 5). Once people were killed, popular anger grew and the fate of the president was sealed. The situation was complicated by the fact that the government had recently given the police a raise, but not the army, and that angered the military. It was also clear that the French were angry with the president and encouraged the military to step in. Whether they helped organize the coup is not clear, but they certainly supported it. They had also been paying some of the units involved in the coup (Deltombe, 2012: 5). When the situation became untenable, the president turned the government over to the leaders of the army and left for exile in South Africa. The military then turned over the presidency to Rajoelina. He deemed himself president of the *Haute Autorité de la Transition* (HAT) since he was too young to meet the constitutional requirements to be president.

The aftermath for the people of Madagascar was devastating. The immediate response to the coup was chaotic. The World Bank, IMF, USAID, British Aid, and other funders cut off all funding to Madagascar because of the coup. The violent demonstrations and the coup led to an almost total decline of tourism, a major foreign exchange earner. Many other markets were disrupted and lost customers, some never to be regained. Investors pulled out, or sat on the sidelines, and the uncertainty caused widespread confusion throughout the country, which also hurt the economy. Growth fell from 7 percent in 2008 to .6 percent in 2009 (Deltombe, 2013: 7). The withdrawal of humanitarian aid was a major blow since it had constituted 75 percent of government spending. The UK suspended debt relief and a number of businesses closed due to the chaos, rising crime, and insecurity. Because of the political uncertainty and the refusal of the international community to recognize the government of Andry Rajoelina, the economy continued to suffer, tourists and investors stayed away, and the economic and political situation remained unstable. As one report noted: "[P]overty has increased significantly since the 2009 crisis, reaching 77% of households in 2010, the highest in Africa, with an estimated average income of $400 per capita" (Deltombe, 2013: 10).

All this left higher education in deep trouble too. With the economy deteriorating, the higher education system suffered from a shortage of funds, many staff members went unpaid for long periods of time, recruitment stalled, and implementation of most of the goals of the strategic plan came to a halt or made only limited progress. A future that was looking so bright at the beginning of 2009 continued to dim, with no prospect of improvement in sight. While the political situation was somewhat stabilized by the elections of 2013, that did little to improve the economy. Although the new president Rajaonarimampianina promised to move to restore democracy and improve the economy as well as follow the plans developed by the Southern African Development Community in 2011, there was little improvement. Corruption, which had been greatly reduced under President Ravalomanana, began to skyrocket once again, as did crime and the breakdown of law and order. The improvements that were beginning to be made in higher education stalled with little hope of improvement any time soon. As was the case with the coup in Sierra Leone, higher education was largely forgotten and in some cases the reforms undertaken earlier were reversed by the Rajoelina regime, especially the use of English in instruction, as well as some of the curriculum reforms seen to be Anglo Saxon and not French by a government that once again moved closer to France.

Institutionalization of the Plan

The planning process for change was housed in the Ministry of National Education and Scientific Research through its staff and the two committees, one of presidents, the other made up of staff and vice presidents (which did the actual ongoing oversight). Both were very active committees. The process of laying out the plans for change in the strategic plan, which started in 2005, was an ongoing one through these two committees and ministry staff, and in that sense was institutionalized. Everyone agreed on the process, unlike the case in South Africa. The contestation initially was about goals and there was no disagreement about process. The differences about the plan's goals, however, represented more contentment with the current state of higher education than opposition to any specific parts of the plan or any goals. There was some opposition to accreditation from several private institutions, but that was primarily based on their fear of being closed down. Their concerns were answered in meetings with them, and they agreed to the process during the early months of discussions. A few public institutions thought they shouldn't have to go through accreditation since they were authorized by government. That idea, however, was soon dispelled by the minister and others.

A good example of institutionalization of the strategic plan was the accreditation process. Work first began on accreditation in May 2005. Standards and criteria for accreditation had been written, discussed, revised, and finalized. After that, the minister and his team met with public and private tertiary institutions in a number of meetings to discuss the process, held workshops on accreditation and self-assessment, selected a pool of fifty peer reviewers to carry out site visits for candidacy for accreditation, and at a later date, for accreditation. The staff was hired for the accreditation process, now called the System d'Accréditation and d'Assurance Qualité (SAAQ). They participated in several two-day training sessions and worked with the national and international consultants on accreditation for several months.

Lessons Learned

The proper functioning of the education system is dependent on many things, but continued political stability is key among them. That was lost in Madagascar after the coup of 2009 and with it a breakdown of law and order. There was a rapid increase in crime, some of it undertaken by the military, now in a position of power, and still resentful of the failure of the previous government to raise salaries. Military personnel now took it upon themselves to get what they felt they deserved by taking vehicles, televisions, and other goods from the public. The loss of humanitarian aid left the government with a shortage of funding even to pay salaries, and the loss of tourist income and income from exports compounded that loss. All this weakened the education system at every level. There was no funding for new initiatives, and even paying salaries was often delayed, sometimes for months. In an effort to curry favor with the French, the new government of Rajoelina also reversed some of the new policies in education, especially those related to language. Many of the best Ministry of Education staff left and took jobs elsewhere in Madagascar or outside of the country. Most of the reform efforts stalled and even the accreditation process seemed to have become inactive, with no institutions accredited by 2016.[6] All this was a major setback for quality higher education in Madagascar. While there had been widespread support for the major changes proposed and some of them implemented, that support was not strong enough to reverse the effects of the coup and the breakdown in law and order, coupled with the financial crisis which followed.

The coup, coupled with the fact that some of the changes were associated with the previous government, which was felt to be too West-oriented and anti-French, led to dropping some of the changes that were already underway. Added to that was the fact that higher education was no longer a priority of government as it had been under the previous government. Those then appointed to senior positions in the ministry were not academics or specialists in higher education, and so higher education suffered. Once again, we see the devastating effect of military intervention on the country as a whole and on higher education. While a few of the changes remain in place in theory, such as accreditation, there has been little or no action to continue the process. Higher education in Madagascar, which was making good progress in improving quality is now once again on a downward slide. In spite of recent elections, higher education remains a low priority.

Chapter 10

Ghana

Building Transformational Change at the University for Development Studies

Background to Change at the University for Development Studies

The University for Development Studies (UDS) is in the north of Ghana, an area that had been systematically neglected during colonial times and suffered from continued neglect after independence. Indeed, those few students from the north who were sent to secondary school in the south during the colonial period, when they returned to the north for holidays, had to take off their uniforms and store them until their return trip when they crossed on the Yeji Ferry over the Volta river into the north so that they would not unduly influence the young people in that area. The north is the poorest part of Ghana, with a malnutrition level in 2009 over 35 percent. The largest percentage of the poor were women, who also had lower levels of literacy than men. Its agriculture was underdeveloped, and in recent years has seen a decline in output (Kaburise, 2003). The literacy rate for Ghana was 58 percent but in the north it was as low as 12 percent in Gushiegu-Karaga and only 43 percent in Tamale, the largest city (Worldreader, 2015).

The Ghanaian legislature, concerned about the lack of development in the north, created the University for Development Studies (UDS) in 1992, with a charge that it "blend the academic world with that of the community in order to provide constructive interaction between the two for the total development of Northern Ghana in particular and the country as a whole" (Kaburise, 2003). Although UDS was established in 1992, it was never sufficiently funded to develop its facilities and infrastructure adequately. Nonetheless, a great deal of progress was achieved by using buildings re-leased to it, land obtained from the local community in Wa, and facilities from the regional administration and other government agencies, and by being very creative within the context of an extremely limited budget in a poor part of the country (Hayward, 2002: 3).

Building the Change Agenda at UDS

It was in that context that the leaders and faculty members of the university began to set forth what they regarded as a major change agenda through their strategic plan for the institution with a radically new approach. This became the impetus for their strategic plan over the next months. Their change plans were based on a "pro-poor" philosophy, an emphasis on student learning, a major effort to involve more women in higher education, and a unique and innovative Third Trimester Field Practical Programme (TTFPP) with student teams working each year to carry out a development project in a rural area developed by the students and the local community. The UDS strategic plan was built on wide consultations on campus, in the communities, with traditional leaders, and in the northern region generally. Indeed, the input, and later support, from traditional councils, local chiefs, and the public was essential to the success of the change plans. The public input is widely quoted in the plan document.[1]

An Innovative, Far-Reaching Plan, Requiring Radical Changes, Can Be Put in Place if Its Leadership Can Mobilize Strong Support for the Plan and Its Implementation

The strategic planning effort was led by Vice Chancellor John B. K. Kaburise, who had previously been a senior administrator and vice chancellor in South Africa, and the UDS pro-vice chancellor, Prof. Saa Dittoh, a distinguished scholar. Both leaders had clear goals and a vision for the university and worked together on the efforts to set out a strategic plan. Both men wanted to create a new kind of learning environment in

Ghana, what Vice Chancellor Kaburise called an "alternative approach to tertiary education" with a focus on rural areas, with an academic emphasis on health, agriculture, and development studies (Kaburise, 2003: 1). Prof. Dittoh oversaw the day-to-day operation of the strategic planning committee, chairing its meetings, and overseeing its activities. As the work progressed, the major goals of the strategic plan were: to improve

Table 10.1. UDS Strategic Plan: Inputs from Stakeholders and Constituents (2003)

- There should be more involvement of stakeholders in UDS matters and in effective cost sharing (especially in kind).

- Course and research programmes should originate partly from the communities.

- Considering the fact that University education has favoured privileged persons and is expensive, special effort should be made to reach the poor and marginalized groups (especially women, persons with disabilities, and others).

- The programmes of UDS are unique, broad, and complex and hence require special attention, resources, support and political commitment.

- UDS should be proactive in advocacy issues that relate to the regions, and the people who have a weaker political voice.

- Platforms should be organized regularly to give an opportunity for interactions among stakeholders as well as build public policy engagement.

- Frequent interactions between the University's Faculties, Departments and Units and stakeholders should be encouraged and a mechanism put in place for such interactions.

- Faculties and campuses should be expanded in order to reach all the four constituencies of the University.

- Introduction of new programmes such as Business, Law, Education, French, and post-graduate studies should be given priority.

- The internal University community should reach out to its external communities with the view to influencing gender advocacy.

Source: University for Development Study Strategic Plan, Tamale, Ghana: UDS Planning Committee, p. 16.

institutional funding; to expand interaction with rural communities by contributing to their development through the tri-semester program; to improve science and clinical programs at the university's medical school; to mainstream gender equity; to improve IT; to enhance academic performance; to increase access; to assure quality improvement; to expand the infrastructure; and to improve efficiency (UDS, 2003: 18–23). The planning process was assisted by a grant from the Carnegie Corporation, which included some strategic planning technical assistance.[2]

The tri-semester field program[3] consisted of student teams, with faculty supervision, including students in medicine, agriculture, and development in an effort to integrate the academic efforts of the students and faculty members with the needs of poor rural communities. They spent the third semester each year of the four-year program working in a community with the local population to understand its needs, gather data, and devise projects to help develop that community. This program produced impressive outcomes, resulting in a number of completed development projects in these communities, mobilizing people in many of them, and creating a demand from rural areas for UDS student placements. Projects included upgrading schools, water improvement, healthcare, and other areas. I read several of the students' final reports on the projects (done in their final year) and they were very thoughtful and excellently done. This was an exciting effort that may well serve as a model for other universities in Africa. The level of student and faculty commitment and excitement about the focus of UDS was the highest I can ever recall encountering anywhere.

Understanding Opposition to the Changes Proposed

The change strategy spelled out in the strategic plan was not without its opponents. Many faculty members opposed the plan from the outset, seeing it as the abandonment of the traditional university role—which indeed it was. There was opposition from the professions as well, especially in medicine, to the integrated approach. Indeed, the medical school was not yet accredited at the time of the plan, in part because it did not have an adequate teaching hospital, although it used facilities at the Tamale hospital. Students had gone on strike in 1997 to force the administration to abandon the integrated approach in favor of a traditional degree program, but without success (Kaburise, 2003: 4). During the negotiations about the change strategy, the medical school threatened to withdraw because their goals for the medical faculty were not listed as the top priority among the changes proposed. Thoughtful discussion and diplomacy, led by Pro-Vice Chancellor Dittoh, eventually brought them back on board.

After many meetings, a great deal of discussion, and broad consultations in the region, the plan for change was approved. The extent of the consultation with people in the rural areas was remarkable, including traditional chiefs and elders, as well as ordinary citizens. Soon, the students too, found the tri-semester plan exciting with its hands-on commitment to work on a development project in a rural area jointly with the local community. Funding for those local plans came from a variety of sources, many local. As the vice chancellor noted several years later, the strategic plan was important in that it "sensitized many stakeholders to its future directions and expectations. Stakeholders within and outside the University system had the opportunity to interact with staff and students on the future of the University."[4] In that way, they also became advocates for the university with the wider community and with government, and thus helped move forward the plan for change.

Implementing the Change Strategy

The strategic plan implementation went well. The tri-semester program was popular with students, faculty members, employers, and participants in the rural communities. All of the first graduates from the program quickly gained employment in related areas. Initial opposition from students, largely because the program was new and different from what they expected, ended quickly as they experienced it. Indeed, students came from other parts of Ghana, even turning down admission to the University of Ghana, Legon, the prestigious flagship institution, to attend UDS because of its program. Similarly, the opposition of some faculty members early on disappeared once they realized how the plan would work and began to participate in it. Female enrollment grew quickly from 12 percent in 1997 to 29 percent in 2003, with an ultimate goal an enrollment of 50 percent women. The budget for the plan was reasonable at $345,000, with most of it realized. In the long run, with help from the European Union, the medical school flourished. The medical school set up a problem-based curriculum following on the Maastricht model,[5] which fit right into the tri-semester program established under the strategic plan, with the first cohort of medical students graduating from the six-year program in 2014.

The university succeeded in blending a practical program with its academic offerings integrating women students in this project as well as giving all students experience with development issues. None of this would have happened without the strong leadership of Vice Chancellor Kaburise and excellent stewardship of the planning process by Pro-Vice Chancellor Saa Dittoh and active support from faculty members and students. The process came close to unraveling several times early on, but their care and diplomacy, plus student and faculty support, held it together and allowed the plan to be completed and implemented. It has served as an important model of student-centered learning and a higher education program that links the rural poor to higher education.

At the same time, it should be noted that the university has continued to be hampered by underfunding—a problem that has plagued Ghanaian higher education in general but late starters such as UDS in particular. In addition, UDS has suffered from frequent changes in leadership following the retirement of Vice Chancellor Kaburise, with each new leader wanting to put his own stamp on the institution and appoint his own deputies, and thus a certain lack of continuity has afflicted UDS over the years.

A Shared Vision for the University for Development Studies

One of the striking things about the UDS case is the extent to which its leaders, both Vice Chancellor Kaburise and Pro-Vice Chancellor Dittoh, inspired a shared vision among faculty members, other administrators, staff, students, and many members of the rural communities in which the university undertook projects with their vision of a university with a pro-poor philosophy, a student-centered curriculum, all closely linked to the rural communities in northern Ghana. As Kouzes and Posner put it, these leaders "have a desire to make something happen, to change the way things are, to create something that no one else has ever created before. . . . They see pictures in their mind's eye of what the results will look like even before they've started their project" (Kouzes and Posner, 2003: 6). They inspire people to share that vision and bring it to reality.

And they have succeeded in doing that in their vision for a transformed higher education institution at UDS and in the strategic plan and the very successful implementation of a new approach to higher education, including their tri-semester field program and the medical school's problem-based curriculum approach. They were not the only leaders of strategic planning to be successful in inspiring a shared vision, but they were especially successful, in many ways similar to those in Afghanistan who mobilized strong support broadly.

Characteristics of Successful Change in Higher Education

As we look back at the successful change efforts at the University of Development Studies, several key characteristics of the leadership stand out: their ability to create a shared vision for the institution, their strong relationship-oriented leadership demonstrating an interest in people, their ability to instill trust, their clear determination and drive, and their ability to mobilize people, as Burns has put it, through goals that motivate and benefit the participants and thus have a transforming effect (Burns, 1978 : 20). What is also striking about this strategic plan is its radical character—setting up a system in sharp contrast to what was the norm in Ghana at that time. It was transformational both in the Burns sense we have noted earlier, but also transformational as Babury and I have emphasized in other cases, bringing about change "which is pervasive and deep in a way that fundamentally alters its structure and some of its major values" (Babury & Hayward, 2014: 2). It focused on a new student-centered academic process; it became much less hierarchical, involving students and faculty in planning the third semester program and the academic curriculum in general; it fostered gender equity, greatly increasing the number of women in a part of the country in which women were often severely disadvantaged; it fostered academic freedom; and it was development-oriented, involving communities in the north both in their own development and in the third-semester program, which they strongly supported. What is particularly noteworthy in terms of fostering change was the success of people at UDS in mobilizing the local communities, including traditional leadership, to work with university student teams and faculty members in a new kind of partnership that helped link rural Ghana to higher education in important ways that enhanced the education process. Although funding was a constant challenge, the university worked closely with the local communities, the regional government, traditional chiefs, and local businesses to link the budget to people in the community, as noted in figure 1.1. UDS leadership understood the importance of these linkages, and this was a key to their success. While at the University for Development Studies the level of funding has never been adequate, the institution has managed to obtain other funding and thus keep its change agenda going with its student-focused third-term program of cooperative development with rural communities continuing and its student-centered academic curriculum still in place.

The situation for higher education generally in Ghana has improved, with the financial situation of the government looking better at the present time although it had a budget shortfall in 2016 due to technical problems in the oilfields. Inflation remains high and financing costs for the government are at about 20 percent. Nonetheless, the economy grew by 4.9 percent in the first quarter of 2016 and more than 6 percent in 2018. Ghana is among the top three African countries ranked in terms of freedom of the press and freedom of speech (World Bank, 2016c: 1), and it has recently successfully carried out new presidential elections, with the opposition candidate, Nana Akufo-Addo, winning. All this bodes well for continued progress in higher education in Ghana generally.

Chapter 11

The University of Malawi

Coalition and Team Building for Effective Change

Keeping All Players in the Project Is a Key to Success and May Require Special Efforts by the Leadership

In a number of institutions and systems, coalition and team building are essential to successful strategic planning, either prior to starting the strategic planning project or at the very outset to ensure there is broad agreement on the goals for change, the process, priorities, and implementation. This was the case in Malawi both at the national system level and especially at the institutional level. At the outset of the process, there was no national higher education strategic plan,[1] and only thoughts about institutional plans at each of the two public universities, the University of Malawi (UNIMA) and Mzuzu University (MZUZU). In addition to the two public universities, there were a number of private universities. They included: the Catholic University of Malawi (CUNIMA), Malawi Adventist University (MAU), the University of Livingstonia (UNILIA), Blantyre International University (BIU), and Mangochi University (DMI).

Higher education in Malawi was in a state of crisis in 2003 when the USAID initiated a request to the Academy for Educational Development (AED) to support strategic planning at the two major public universities. That request was initiated by leaders of the two universities. I was then asked to lead a team there to work with the two public universities on institutional strategic plans. Let's look at the process at one of them, the University of Malawi.

The Context for Change at the University of Malawi

The University of Malawi opened in September 1965 in Blantyre. Ninety students enrolled in the first class. By 1967, the Institute of Public Administration at Mpemba, the Soche Hill College of Education, the Polytechnic in Blantyre, and Bunda College of Agriculture in Lilongwe were incorporated as constituent colleges of the University of Malawi. With the exceptions of Bunda College and the Polytechnic, these colleges moved to Zomba in 1973 to form what is now the Chancellor College campus. In September 1979, the fourth constituent college, Kamuzu College of Nursing, became part of the university. The College of Medicine in Blantyre became the fifth constituent college when it was established in 1991.

In 2003–04, public higher education in Malawi was primarily provided by the two universities (the University of Malawi and Mzuzu University), with the private institutions having few students. Several small private higher education institutions were under consideration. The first two were associated with religious groups. Public universities were autonomous institutions subsidized by government under a separate vote on the government recurrent budget, independent of the budget of the Ministry of Education (Ministry of Education, nd circa 2003: 1.4), but reporting to it. Private institutions received no state subsidy and were largely autonomous.

Understanding the Background to Strategic Planning in Malawi

Access for qualified aspirants to the Malawi public higher education system was severely restricted by limited capacity and can be described as "elitist" in systemic terms. The system hosted a total enrollment of only about six thousand students in 2003, when the strategic planning effort was begun, in a country with a population of about fourteen million. This meant that only about one-fourth of potential applicants could be admitted annually from the secondary school output of about four thousand graduates qualified for university admission. This capacity restriction along with a housing requirement were among the principal causes for the disproportionately high cost of higher education per student, which was reported to be $2,884 per person for the 2003–04 financial year.

The cost of other universities in the region was about one-fourth that amount (Ministry of Education, circa 2003:1. 61).

The major obstacle to increased enrollment was the statutory provision adopted in 1964 that required the University of Malawi to provide free and guaranteed board and lodging to all students. Consequently, dormitory capacity became the limiting factor for the number of students that could be admitted, and this capacity changed little over the years. Although this statutory provision was set aside in 1998, both universities continued to operate according to this practice through most of the period. The situation was exacerbated by the fact that universities are hard-pressed to operate housing and catering as non-core functions of higher education, and the institutions inevitably ended up subsidizing room and board from funds intended for the academic process.[2] That was the case at UNIMA.

In terms of the law, public higher education was free in Malawi, which meant that universities were not able to charge student fees to cover costs. Given the financial crises at both institutions, however, the government acceded to a nominal fee of 25,000 kwachas ($170) per annum for UNIMA and Mzuzu was allowed to charge 55,000 kwachas ($390). The two universities depended on government funding allocations for their operation. However, these were often unpredictable and varied from year to year, sometimes being paid months after they were due. This made long-term planning difficult, as well as complicating expenses for necessities such as maintenance of the physical plant and the purchase of educational equipment. UNIMA and Mzuzu have sought to overcome these constraints to some extent by setting up a program for "parallel students"[3] who pay higher fees and are not provided with housing or food services. This has provided some additional income to both universities.

Public policy regulating higher education was limited, leaving the universities with a level of both formal and default autonomy and a high level of unpredictability. The relationship between the public universities and the Ministry of Education and Vocational Training was opaque and ill-defined. This left the universities feeling ignored and the government deprived of the leverage it would need to steer higher education for the public good. There were no public policies in place to regulate such things as quality assurance, program accreditation and implementation, and institutional accreditation. Malawi, therefore, faced the threat of deteriorating academic standards. There was no body responsible for planning, review, advocacy, or facilitation for higher education nationally. Thus, each institution had to forge its own links with the government—this in a context in which there was no obvious point of entry at the ministry and no section that had ongoing responsibility for it.

Thus, the situation of higher education in Malawi in 2003 was a difficult one. The country was in the midst of a financial crisis, complicated by drought in parts of the country, and the growing scourge of HIV/AIDS, with no medicines generally available in the country to treat it. The numbers of faculty, staff, and students afflicted by the disease was growing. The rate was even higher in secondary schools. The lower levels of HIV/AIDS at universities were in part a function of their successful HIV/AIDS education efforts.

The political situation in the country was in flux, and that made policy decisions for higher education at the national level difficult. The morale at UNIMA was low due to the financial situation, the HIV/AIDS epidemic, drought, and conflicts between several of the constituent colleges—two of which were talking about secession. They thought the solution to their problems was total autonomy from UNIMA. Several of the partner institutions were suspicious that other institutions among them were gaining unfair financial and other advantages from government. This was not an auspicious environment in which to begin work on a strategic plan. Yet the crisis was what led to an effort to start strategic planning and a request to USAID for funding. Fortunately, USAID had access to funding through the AED, sought it, and were asked to provide two experts to help start the planning in 2003.

The Threats of Secession

The strategic planning process for UNIMA that began in 2003 was led by Pro-Vice Chancellor Leonard A. Kamwanja under the leadership of Vice Chancellor David Rubadiri. Both were experienced administrators. Pro-Vice Chancellor Kamwanja was a distinguished academic with a strong research record. Prof. Rubadiri was also a well-known and well-regarded academic, as well as a distinguished poet. Both were widely respected as administrators. The strategic planning committee was led by the pro-vice chancellor joined by the principals of the five participating institutions, Bunda College of Agriculture, the College of Medicine, the Polytechnic, the Nursing College, Chancellor College, by the Registrar, and by several others.

Each of these institutions had carried out its own institutional strategic plan.[4] These were reviewed by the consultants and proved to be very well done. They demonstrated a clear understanding of the process and set out the goals for each institution. On the other hand, the experience of writing their individual plans, plus the high level of discontent about financial problems and central administration control, probably contributed to the talk about secession. When the first meeting of the strategic planning committee took place, including the consultants, two institutions clearly stated their desire to become independent. Several others were giving it some consideration as well.

The crisis over secession was serious. Both institutions believed that they would be better off as independent entities. They felt they would have greater flexibility, more control over their academic life, and an improved financial situation if they were independent. The latter concern was exacerbated by the current financial crisis. Looking at the prospects from the outside, the consultants believed that one of the institutions, with closer ties to political leaders than the other, might well be better off in the short run if it were to be autonomous, but in the long run the consultants saw such a move as leading to a kind of anarchic competition for funds potentially among six entities rather than two, with a cacophony of voices clamoring about financial needs, academic standards, and the programs of higher education generally. The consultants viewed secession as a potential disaster for Malawi higher education at a time when a single coherent message was badly needed to convince political leaders of the importance of higher education generally for national development and for the future of the young people of Malawi.

In many respects, the crisis for UNIMA was like the breakdown of any leadership team that will not function effectively without a unified commitment and collaborative climate (Northouse, 2016: 368–71). As Northouse suggests, an effective team needs to have a unifying goal, be results driven, have a unified commitment to goals, contain members who identify with the goals, and foster a collaborative climate. While the UNIMA strategic planning committee was designed to prepare a strategic plan for the institutions, not all its members subscribed to the goal of a unified UNIMA and therefore were not going to contribute to a collaborative climate or be results driven. Thus, the challenge for Pro-Vice Chancellor Kamwanja and the consultants was either to secure that commitment and the agreement of all the institutions, or to redefine the team in another way, perhaps with an altered membership.

The first meeting of the strategic planning committee was a difficult one, with a general discussion of the problems faced by the institutions, what some saw as the advantages of independence from UNIMA, concerns about centralized financial and administrative control, and the sense of some of the members that the institutions would fare better on their own. Pro-Vice Chancellor Kamwanja started the meeting with a frank and straightforward overview, stating clearly the case for secession, including some of the things the principals were not willing to say about both the challenges and the risks. He made a strong case for staying together, and emphasized that, from his point of view, separation was not realistic. He agreed that they were in crisis but emphasized the need to work together to take charge of the crisis and cooperate on a new direction and solutions, including improving links to the Ministry of Education and making the many major changes needed. That resulted in a very frank discussion, moderated by the consultants, which was detailed about concerns, major issues, and obstacles to progress. The consultants also talked about a variety of options, strategies for actions, and the need to focus on an action agenda for change and to resolve the major issues dividing the institution, if at all possible.

From the outset, it was clear that reaching agreement would take time, and might not ever be possible. The participants agreed that the consultants would visit each of the colleges, the institutions would have consultations with their faculty members, staff, and others concerned, and that after that had taken place, the strategic planning process would continue with whoever wanted to remain a part of UNIMA. The consultants made it clear that if some institutions were going to seek autonomy, there was no point in their continued participation in the process. For two institutions, it was clear that a decision about secession or continued participation as part of UNIMA would require a great deal of debate and time. There were many issues involved, including the need to work out a new funding process, to find a way to deal with what had become the 35 percent shortfall between the government allocation and the funding received, to reach agreement on a division of authority between the center and the institutions, to devise solutions to the lack of financial capacity at many of the institutions, and to establish mechanisms to represent the interests of the institutions to the government. Added to that were a number of changes needed to raise the quality of higher education and update the curriculum. While the tone of the meeting at the beginning was negative and discouraging, with several institutions suggesting that nothing could be done to end the crisis, by the end of the discussion there was a glimmer of hope around the table. Complicating the proposed effort to write a strategic plan for UNIMA was the fact that all of the participants felt overworked with teaching and administrative responsibilities as well as the lack of funding even for travel and per diem for meetings such as this. Thus, the prospect of a continued drain on their time and energy to work on a UNIMA strategic plan and a budget was not an appealing one. Nonetheless, all agreed to discuss the issues within their institutions, meet separately with the consultants, and then meet again in a few weeks.

The consultants then began to meet with the institutional strategic planning committees and other interested individuals at each of the institutions. These involved often difficult discussions. Several of the institutions were ready to declare their independence from UNIMA. Nonetheless, the process had the effect of mobilizing people at each of the institutions to think about what could be done to improve their situation and the costs and benefits of secession—with the consultants stressing their need to take action one way or the other to end the crises. That seemed to instill action in most cases. The consultants also emphasized the difficulties that would occur if each institution worked alone, which would lead to five proposals for funding, five documents of incorporation, and strong competition between all of them for government funding and control over separate policies for each higher education institution—competition that would be settled within the political arena rather than based on decisions by educators. The consultants gave examples from other countries to buttress this case. Part of the success of these discussions was, as one person put it, the no-nonsense assessment by the consultants of the current situation and their summary of where they thought the institutions were individually and where the system was at the present time. While this was happening, the pro-vice chancellor met with the Council of UNIMA and made his strong case for the continued unity of UNIMA and for discussions to rethink the distribution of authority within UNIMA both in finance and administration.

Working on an Accommodation

The individual meetings following the strategic planning meeting provided a jolt on many of the campuses, introducing the realities of possible secession, the costs and risks of operating alone, the depth of the crisis, and the actions that might mitigate the crisis. It was clear that the current structure would be difficult to sustain, even in the short run. There were many liabilities that threatened to hurt, perhaps cripple, some of the institutions, especially since several were already in serious financial situations. The risk of closure of some of them was high since the current government expenditures on higher education were high at about $2,800 per FTE (full-time equivalent), versus an average of about $840 in the rest of Sub-Saharan Africa (without South Africa). That was not sustainable. Government financial support for education was already 27 percent of the total budget, high by most standards.

The consultants suggested that the crisis provided an opportunity to revitalize higher education in Malawi, to increase control by the institutions over it, give the institutions an opportunity to rethink and restructure higher education from the inside, to be in control of the changes they wanted, a chance to be proactive rather than reactive, an opportunity to improve the quality and effectiveness of higher education and make a major new contribution to national development. It was pointed out that they could do that collectively, but not as individual institutions. This would be a major step forward on the route to significant improvements in higher education generally and away from the continued day-to-day crises they were now dealing with while having little to show for it.

Agreement and Moving Forward on a Change Agenda

By the next UNIMA strategic planning committee meeting, after some protracted and heated arguments, ongoing discussions with the consultants and the pro-vice chancellor, there was general agreement to move forward together on the UNIMA Strategic Plan, in large part spurred by the potential cost of secession. The secessionist arguments were dropped, and there was agreement on a united effort to bring about changes all could agree on. This was a major success for the efforts of the pro-vice chancellor and those supporting unity. Participants agreed to: develop a universitywide strategic and financial plan that would focus on the financial problems, shortfalls, and generic problems of funding; rethink the central structure to reflect a different allocation of authority, with decreases in some areas and increases in others; work on questions of governance; consider ways to establish some kind of national structure to help and advocate for higher education; and work together to improve the quality of higher education.

It was agreed that the colleges would have greater autonomy for their academic programs and the management of their own funds. They would provide better and more complete financial information and reporting to the center. At the center, there would be an overall budget submitted to the ministries based on their collective agreement; they would develop an effective advocacy structure for UNIMA to address the government; they would establish mechanisms to improve the quality of teaching and the infrastructure; and the center would be responsible for overall coordination of the activities and policies of UNIMA. These agreements provided an effective way for all the institutions to move forward to prepare the UNIMA Strategic Plan and an action plan for change together as an effective team. A plan of work was agreed upon which would result in a final strategic plan and budget by July 2004.

Lessons about Team Building, Coalitions, and Consensus

One of the things that often is forgotten in preparing for strategic planning is the importance of the planning team. This is especially true in multi-institutional systems and multicollege institutions. The absence or obstruction of one or two members of the team can be crippling. An effective strategic planning effort will be no better than the team involved. The conditions for an effective team suggested by Northouse (2016) are useful to this discussion. I have revised them slightly to encompass six key conditions: (1) clear, elevating goals for the strategic planning process, (2) results-driven structure for the team, (3) competent team members, (4) a unified commitment to the planning process and goals, (5) a collaborative climate, and (6) a commitment to standards of excellence (Northouse, 2016). A strategic planning process that does not meet these conditions will not succeed. Pro-Vice Chancellor Kamwanja and the consultants recognized that and were unwilling to go forward until that kind of agreement was reached, or the team was reconstituted to include only the institutions that accepted them.

There was a second aspect to the process, which was coalition building between the institutions. The strategic planning team needed to be a small, cohesive body with a shared consensus about the goals for change. But at the institutional level, there also had to be agreement on the coalition of institutions that made up the University of Malawi. The process would not have worked with only a coherent team. It had to be supported by strong consensus on the process, the goals for change, and the desired outcomes if progress was to be made. That happened once there was agreement about changes in the central administrative structure, major changes in financial and academic authority between the center and the institutions. Once the costs of secession were clearly understood, as well as the benefits of unity, progress was possible on both coalition building and the creation of a strong team to put the change agenda together in the strategic plan. An effective team was now in place. Overcoming the threat to secede was key to success in team building and in preparing a strategic plan. When that happened, the strategic planning discussion moved forward to build a united UNITRA over the next five years. Success was achieved after thoughtful, albeit sometimes heated, discussion of the likely cost to those who would secede and an understanding of the benefits of unity to all of them. Consensus was achieved and the key conditions of a successful team and a coalition of institutions was agreed to, allowing the strategic planning effort to move forward successfully.

In this case, team building and consensus building took time, facilitated by the thoughtful leadership of Vice Chancellor David Rubadiri and Pro-Vice Chancellor Leonard A. Kamwanja—leadership that was calm, unflappable, logical, and articulate, assisted by two consultants with years of strategic planning experience in many different contexts and countries. Part of what was important to success was the recognition of what it takes to have an effective team and a good working coalition. It was also important that the consultants made clear to those thinking of secession that they could not continue to be part of the planning process if they did secede—that they had to either decide to collaborate on common goals or withdraw. That made the costs of secession immediately clear and cut away some of the romanticism associated with some of the talk of secession. This experience illustrates why sometimes it is necessary to have external advice and structure to help break down a crisis that is on the verge of having devastating consequences for the institutions and the system. Once this crisis was over, the team moved forward to prepare an excellent strategic plan.

Implementing the Change Agenda

The successful higher education changes that took place at UNIMA were in many respects a product of exceptional leadership, which managed to keep the planning team together during a period when secession of two of the constituent colleges was highly likely. Reaching agreement to move forward was a tribute to the excellent leadership of UNIMA by the chancellor and pro-vice chancellor. The first aspects of the change process to be implemented were the administrative changes agree upon, which gave each of the colleges more autonomy in administering their academic programs and over the management of their funds. At the same time, new mechanisms were established to ensure better reporting of expenditures and income to the center so that there was an accurate picture of the finances of the institution as a whole. An overall budget for UNIMA was prepared by the committee, using Cambridge Associates planning software. This was an important success, as it allowed all the participants to agree on budget priorities and the allocation of funds for the institution as a whole. The budget software is especially useful as it allows easy manipulation and changes of each of the categories. It also allows for the addition of a column for inflation and a reserve for contingencies—expense categories that had not been used in the past, which explained in part the financial problems of past budgeting, since without the inclusions of these two categories the budget was not realistic.

There was also agreement that some kind of new mechanism was needed to give the higher education community leverage with government. Early discussions were begun on such a mechanism. It might be done through an association of university vice chancellors, or some mechanism that brought together the leadership of the two public higher education institutions in Malawi to make a stronger case for the financial support they needed to present to parliament, to the Ministry of Education, and to the community at large. In addition, it was agreed that some kind of accreditation process needed to be set up in cooperation with other higher education institutions. While some parts of the change agenda for UNIMA were put in place right away, the overall plan enjoyed only limited success because of lack of funding and lack of expected support from the Ministry of Education and donors.

Unfortunately, the economic situation in Malawi has not improved markedly over the years, and public higher education remains underfunded.

While the GDP (gross domestic product) grew 5.7 percent in 2014, it slowed in 2015 to 2.8 percent, with 17 percent of the population unable to satisfy their basic food requirements in 2015–16. Government corruption resulted in major reductions in donor budget support for government, resulting in substantial deficits that put additional pressure on funding for higher education (World Bank, 2016b: 1).

The World Bank carried out a study of Malawian higher education, published in 2016 (World Bank, 2016b), which was highly critical of the sector. It concluded that:

> The Malawian higher education system's inability to supply sufficient numbers of well-qualified graduates in alignment with the needs of the economy is a major constraint inhibiting the development prospects of the country. In addition to quantitative bottlenecks, there is significant concern with regard to the quality and relevance of existing institutions and programs offered in the Malawian higher education sector. (Mambo et al., 2016: xxv)

The situation at UNIMA has remained little changed from what it was in 2004 and 2006, when we worked with the institutions on the UNIMA change plan and on the national higher education strategic plan, the National Education Sector Plan, prepared for the Ministry of Education and Vocational Training (November 2006). The one change that did occur at UNIMA was that Bunda College of Agriculture, in spite of the earlier agreement, seceded from UNIMA and joined the National Resources College to become the Lilongwe University of Agriculture and National Resources (LUANAR) in 2016. That change proved successful. In 2018 there was renewed talk of breaking up UNIMA, with a proposal being prepared for legislation to do that.[5] At the same time there was strong opposition to that effort, recognizing that it would increase costs and result in counterproductive competition by institutions for funds. Little thought seemed to be being given to the need for increased financial support whether or not UNIMA was broken up. Hopefully, the World Bank review of higher education overall and its report, entitled *Improving Higher Education in Malawi for Competitiveness in the Global Economy* will help bring about badly needed improvements, including increased funding, for the higher education sector as a whole.

Chapter 12

Strategic Planning Challenges at Kabul Polytechnic University (KPU)

I have been so focused on strategic planning that I am dreaming strategic planning.

—Vice Chancellor Mir Fakhruddin, Kabul Polytechnic University

The Context of Kabul Polytechnic University (KPU)

Kabul Polytechnic University (KPU) was founded in 1963 and became one of the leading universities in Afghanistan, carrying out first-rate research on irrigation, hydraulics, and other areas and providing advice and plans for several dams constructed in the country, among other things. By 2006, it had produced 5,043 engineers at the master's and BSc levels. In 2006 it had three faculties, geology and mining, electro mechanics, and construction engineering. It had about 2,700 students at that time and 129 faculty members, of whom seventeen were women. Fewer than fifty students were women.[1] Twenty-five percent of the faculty had PhDs and sixty-eight had master's degrees, with only 7 percent (nine faculty members) having only bachelor's degrees—a very low number at a time when 65 percent of the faculty members in the overall system were teaching with bachelor's degrees. All the female faculty members had master's degrees. The campus had suffered substantial war damage as well as the loss of many faculty members following the Russian invasion and Taliban rule.

Organizing for Major Education Change at Kabul Polytechnic University

The strategic planning program was funded by the World Bank and involved potential access to substantial funding for those of the fourteen invited institutions (including Kabul University, Balkh, Kabul Education University, Herat, and others) that produced high quality strategic plans approved by bank staff. Thirteen of them succeeded in meeting the quality requirements. The strategic planning process was led by KPU Chancellor Mir Fakhruddin and a committee of eight senior administrators and faculty members. They consulted widely with deans, faculty members, staff, and some students during the process. The chancellor was an especially enthusiastic and able leader of this process and had strong support from the committee. The initiative for the planning process came from the Ministry of Higher Education (MoHE) as part of the USAID-funded higher education project, and it was enthusiastically endorsed by university leaders, in part because it came with significant funding for those who submitted viable strategic plans.

During the war years, Kabul Polytechnic had suffered a great deal of damage and lost many of its best faculty members and staff. Their situation in 2006 was laid out courageously and forthrightly at the beginning of the strategic plan for all to see, as follows:

> This university once was equipped with academic and research laboratories in different areas of general and technical engineering that enabled the university and its well qualified faculty to contribute to the overall development goals of training the nation's children and instilling philanthropic objectives that helped develop the country. Twenty-five years of war destroyed most of that capacity and left the University unable to perform as in the past and far behind international engineering and technical expectations in the rest of the world. (KPU, 2006: 1)

The authors of the report went on to describe some of the damage done to the university, its buildings, its loss of staff, and other consequences of war:

> But unfortunately, due to wars in the last years, the classroom buildings and hostel buildings of the students, libraries, training materials, laboratories, electric system, student's dining hall and gymnasium of the university were destroyed or damaged

and some parts of the university are no longer usable. Many members of the teaching staff of the university were compelled to leave the country or to join other non-academic organizations. (KPU, 2006: 1)

They added:

We believe that the reconstruction of war-torn Afghanistan, without the rehabilitation and modernization of Kabul Polytechnic University is nearly impossible because graduates of this institution play such a key role in every part and sector of the economy. (KPU, 2006: 2)

The plan's authors laid out the major changes envisioned by the strategic plan of Kabul Polytechnic University for the next five to ten years in the strategic plan, as follows:

Therefore, our principle [sic] objectives for this strategic plan are: to build up the capacity of faculty members; improve the quality of teaching and learning; increase opportunities to promote science based on the recent developments in science and technology, so that Afghanistan will be the equal of the developed countries of the world. In addition, our overarching goal is to educate qualified engineers who can work with peace, brotherhood, and fairness, free of any religious, language, ethnic, or gender biases. (KPU, 2006: 2)

There were major changes proposed for the next five years that would involve fundamental upgrades to the curriculum, upgrading faculty qualifications for a substantial number of teaching staff, expansion of facilities, and fundamental changes in values when it came to both gender equity and merit hiring and promotions. KPU was especially aware of the critical role engineering would need to play in rebuilding and upgrading the economy.

Beginning to Write the Plan for KPU

The first steps in preparing and writing the strategic plan and the change agenda at Kabul Polytechnic University were difficult to accomplish. The idea of planning was one everyone on the committee agreed with wholeheartedly, as that was indeed a critical part of creating an engineering and construction curriculum. Part of their problem was that some of the powerful senior faculty members involved felt that other than repairs and equipment, everything was fine at KPU. Most faculty members however, especially the younger ones, did not agree. They felt the institution was way behind engineering schools around the region and the world. An additional practical problem for them was that a critical requirement of the World Bank, which was funding the project and some of the plan implementation, was that the plan had to be written in English. No member of the committee had competence in English and only one or two people in the institution had any English at all. Instruction at the university had been mostly in Russian or in Dari. Thus, the strategic planning committee members had more trouble than most institutions in reading some of the directions and understanding some of the workshops held at the ministry, although the latter were in Dari and important documents were translated into Dari. In spite of the challenges, the chancellor and a number of the faculty members on the committee were eager to move forward with the business of putting the change agenda in writing. That commitment and eagerness were reflected in my report on the state of the strategic plan at KPU (Hayward, December 2005).

> Although the Polytechnic was new to the strategic planning process at the time of the workshop, the Chancellor was eager to move forward and start work on the process and development of a plan. During the December workshop, I had several discussions with the Chancellor and encouraged the University to try to get as far as possible before my return visit in mid-January. During that holiday break the strategic planning team began work in earnest on a first draft of the strategic plan which focused primarily on goals for change, objectives and a vision for the future. They communicated with me during this period by e-mail. The draft included the outlines of a mission statement which, with a little more work, would meet their needs. I met with the Chancellor and his team in mid-January at the Polytechnic. The fruits of their labor were evident. They had devoted a substantial amount of time to working on it and in the process, had consulted widely within the university community.

The chancellor confessed to me that the process was becoming all-consuming. He noted that "I have been so focused on strategic planning that I am dreaming strategic planning."[2] In the process of putting the document together, the committee had consulted deans of faculties, the teaching staff, and students. They reported that as a result of the discussions and consultations, a number of significant changes had been made and several new goals and objectives added.

Writing and Rewriting the Plan

Over the next few months the committee worked hard to prepare a draft plan in Dari, and they presented that version to the bank's personnel, who had it translated into English. The first draft was very good for a first draft, setting out goals and objectives. It represented a thoughtful effort to plan for the whole university. Nonetheless, it was badly organized and did not conform to the normal expectations for an institutional strategic plan. While a great deal more work was needed, this draft represented major progress in thinking about the changes needed and writing the strategic plan. Extensive comments were given to help the chancellor and the committee make major revisions. The bank's team came away impressed by the progress and the forward momentum of the Polytechnic. I gave the chancellor extensive comments on the draft. The commitment of the chancellor and his team were clear, as demonstrated by the thoughtful discussions that had taken place since the last consultation. The problems were not related to the changes envisioned but rather to justifying them, laying out a viable implementation plan, and creating a budget; they arose partly as a result of the committee members' limited previous experience with higher education planning. The prospects for a successful strategic planning effort, however, seemed high.

By August, the work of the KPU planning team had borne fruit. During the interval, they had carried out extensive correspondence with the World Bank team and sent several partial drafts for review. They had now found a young faculty member who was able to translate their drafts into English, and that sped up the process. They were very responsive to suggestions, and each draft was a marked improvement over the previous one. Kabul Polytechnic was now ready for a final round of face-to-face meetings to complete their work. The Polytechnic team started the meeting by expressing their appreciation for the learning process that had taken place for all of them. Their hard work had paid off, as demonstrated by this draft. They felt so confident that they started implementation of some parts of the plan in July. The university had purchased several computers, books for the library, prepared plans for teaching laboratories, and were looking forward to receiving funding from the World Bank, contingent on acceptance of their draft plan.

Major Weakness of the Introduction to the Plan and the Lack of a Clear Budget

At the next review of their drafts it became clear that the introduction to the plan was very weak. Indeed, it was confusing and dull. The team was reminded that these first few paragraphs were the first things donors see, and that made it very important to have a strong introduction if they were to attract funding for their change agenda. The current version was not as clear nor as good as it should be and did not reflect the excellent ideas in the plan. Thus, it was suggested that the introductory section should be rewritten in an attractive manner that would be more liable to stimulate interest by donors. At first, the committee members didn't understand what was being suggested, but once they did they saw the problem clearly. The committee was so motivated and enthusiastic at this point that they sat down right away to rework the introduction—although initially without success.

A High-Quality Plan Is Poetry to the Ear

A few days later, I received a call from the chancellor. He said he was coming over to share the new introduction. Indeed, KPU had enticed their poet/engineer, who was quite famous for poetry in a country that loves poetry, to write the introduction. The new introduction was in Dari, and the poet read it aloud in front of us. It was wonderful, flowing verse, in elegant Persian, in a very graceful style, easy to the ears of even those of us who did not understand Persian. The introduction was then translated for the bank team. It was a tremendous improvement even in English, though none of the translations to English over the next few weeks could duplicate the rhythm and meter of the Dari—though several translators tried.

Conclusions

One of the most important lessons received from the Kabul Polytechnic experience is the importance of a well-written plan—especially the plan's introduction. No matter how good the ideas, the goals, the analysis, or how carefully worked out the budget, the plan must be written in a captivating style that will demonstrate its quality to potential funders. The KPU planning committee had excellent ideas, but they had trouble putting them down in ways that would appeal to funders. Once they realized that and solved the problem of clear, readable, appealing presentation, they were successful. The successes of Kabul Polytechnic University in writing an excellent plan for higher education change are a demonstration of what can be done in spite of lack of information about the process at the outset, language problems, disagreement of the old guard on the need for change, and a host of other problems noted earlier. The chancellor of KPU, Prof. Mir Fakhruddin, the strategic planning committee, administrators, faculty members, and the campus as a whole were enthusiastically behind the change plan, eager to make it happen and thus eager to learn how to present it in a way that would gain funding. They were willing to put in the long hours and many drafts on the change plan until they came up with an outstanding and readable plan for the critical changes they deemed essential for the future. It is often forgotten that part of the planning process is a well-written, readable, and convincing strategic plan. Fortunately for KPU, they understood that and worked hard to make their plan meet those requirements.

Without doubt, Kabul Polytechnic University was the most improved of the universities involved in the project. They came to the process confused, discouraged, not sure where they were going or how they were going to get there. They needed extra sessions with the bank's consultants, but they kept at it. The planning committee's leaders were in regular consultation with the MoHE and the consultants throughout the process. The team was committed to successful change and prepared to do what was necessary to get it no matter how hard they had to work to get there. Typical of their commitment to change, the Polytechnic had eight senior staff members working with the bank team. All of them were fully involved in the process. The chancellor was especially good at moving things forward and understanding the issues that needed to be resolved. As a result, the strategic planning process, and the effort put into it, brought substantial change to KPU—change that would not have occurred without that process and effort.

In the end, the plan was reviewed and revised as needed, work was completed before the deadline, the change plan was approved, implementation was begun, and most of the goals were met over the next five years. Their work was outstanding. They were the most improved of all the institutional strategic plans by the end of the planning process and one of the best plans completed.

Most importantly, KPU, more than any other university in the project, saw its role in the national setting as critical. The university's administrators saw higher education as part of the key to transforming Afghanistan after thirty years of war. They were very much aware of the need for what Castells and Himanen discuss as *human development*—"enhancement of the living conditions that make humans human in a given social context" (Castells and Himanen, 2014: 12–13), and the essential role they saw for KPU in making that happen. They saw KPUs transformation as an essential part of the process of transforming Afghanistan's higher education to be able to provide the tools and the training to produce the well-being in Afghanistan that the students and the nation deserved.

The work on a change agenda at Kabul Polytechnic University and the strategic plans designed to make those changes possible demonstrate a commitment to improving the conditions of the nation, enhancing the well-being of the citizens, even in a war environment. People with a vision for change, a commitment to hard work and careful consultation within the university community, produced excellent plans for higher education change written from scratch in a relatively short time, had them approved by the MoHE, and began their implementation even in the modest and not very promising environment of Afghanistan. In the end, what they produced was their own change and implementation plans. And over the next five years they proceeded to put most of their goals in place.

One could not offer a better example of learning, building, and successful planning for major higher education change. In the process, they helped lay the foundation for national development in Afghanistan—contributing to the elements necessary for human development, the affirmation of individual dignity, and changes designed to overcome the injustices of the past. Piece by piece the faculty members, administrators, staff, and students of this institution worked to foster a democratic, open Afghanistan in which all shared in the well-being they believed possible.

Chapter 13

Implications for Leadership and Leading Transformational Change in Developing Countries

Introduction

In trying to understand successful higher education changes and transformations, it is essential to look at the people involved in those changes. What have we learned about leadership of strategic planning in the cases examined? The higher education changes we have examined involve a wide range of leadership experiences, sometimes as the initiators of change, in some cases as the facilitators of strategic plans, the actual planners, the mobilizers of support, and the implementers. In a few cases, successful change was the result of the work of a few leaders. However, in most cases it was a collective effort at many levels and involved broad mobilization of people in support of a strategic plan within the university and/or higher education community. We also saw a few cases where change efforts failed or were less successful than they should have been because of problems at the leadership level, though that was rare. In most of the cases of failure, the causes were issues over which the leaders had no control including several coups d'état.

In our book on strategic planning (Hayward & Ncayiyana, 2003:13), Daniel Ncayiyana and I emphasized the critical role of senior leadership in successful planning for change in higher education. We stated that "the active and enthusiastic support of the vice chancellor, principal, rector, or president, and other senior leaders is essential for successful strategic planning." That statement has been amply borne out in case after case since that time, as demonstrated in examples presented here—both in those that were most successful, and several that were not, with the latter lacking such leadership at some level. Malawi was the best example of this problem with an excellent strategic plan developed by the University of Malawi, but little interest or support at the government level, including the appropriate ministries.

The study of leadership is difficult partly because it is complicated by many types of leaders, different situations, contexts, and conditions. It is often looked on with suspicion, confusion, and distrust. As Cronin notes: "[L]eadership for most people most of the time is a rather hazy, distant and even confusing abstraction. Hence, thinking about or defining leadership is a kind of intellectual leadership challenge in itself" (Cronin, 1995: 28).

In this chapter, I try to make the practice of leadership in higher education a little less confusing by drawing on the cases we have examined and suggesting some ways to look at higher education leadership in the context of higher education change, to identify some of the characteristics, skills, and strategies used. If we are to understand and make sense of higher education change, we need to examine those who lead the change efforts, assess their successes and failures, explore those things that seem to spawn success and those that detract from it. That is especially the case for developing areas where the problems are immense, the stakes high, the challenges great, and the risks of failure substantial. As Thomas Cronin suggests: "Learning about leadership means understanding the critical linkage of ends and means. Learning about leadership also involves the study of the special chemistry that develops between leaders and followers" (Cronin, 1995: 28)," and sometimes between leaders themselves at various levels. We don't like to admit that a "chemistry" exists because it is not "scientific," yet we have seen it between Njabulo Ndebele and the students as the strategic planning process progressed at the University of the North; between Prof. Atta-ur-Rahman and President Pervez Musharraf in Pakistan, which benefited higher education; between Afghan Minister of Higher Education Mohammad Azam Dadfar and Deputy Minister Babury, which led to transformation of higher education there.

As we have looked at leadership in the preceding chapters, I have tried to identify the key characteristics, skills, or traits of successful leaders in planning higher education change at various levels in the higher education institutions and systems we have examined. Let's explore each of them in some detail in the material that follows.

Looking at these cases overall, there also appear to have been important strategies adopted by the successful leaders, either consciously or unconsciously. In general, these strategies were not articulated by these leaders, but became apparent as we looked at what they accomplished. Deputy Minister Babury was not consciously adopting a consensus strategy, but in looking at how he operated, we see that that was clearly a key strategy for him—and it worked well. On the other hand, in Pakistan, Prof. Atta-ur-Rahman and Dr. Sohail Naqvi were overt about their top-down strategy. They believed in being directive and felt that was the only way to move higher education forward with the urgency they believed was needed for success.

Having the characteristics and skills listed does not necessarily make one a good leader. You can have these characteristics and skills and be a failed leader, but they do help explain success. Very few, if any, leaders lacking these characteristics and skills are successful. And, as I have emphasized before, leaders do not succeed or fail by their own actions alone. It is their interactions with other leaders, and the important roles of advisors and followers, which make the actions of leaders possible and are critical to success. As we have seen, followers come at various levels, some being leaders at lower levels of the institution or the system. We have also seen the importance of teams. Much of what we have seen by way of successful strategic planning came from the work of teams.

There are other aspects of leadership that are harder to measure or to explain. How does one measure the success of leaders? George Lenyai, former vice chancellor of Technikon Northern Transvaal in South Africa, suggested it was not just on the basis of outcomes but also of "value added." He argued that as vice chancellor of a historically disadvantaged institution in South Africa, he had to bring students from a much lower learning level, due to poor preparation in primary and secondary school, up to the same level of education at graduation as students from the elite, outstanding primary and secondary institutions.[1] Thus, his institution had to provide a much greater "value added" per student than some of the more prestigious institutions. And it did.

Critical Skills of Higher Education Leaders

By skills, I mean the special qualities, traits, characteristics, or attributes that are the distinguishing features of a person's leadership. Some writers use the term *traits* rather than *skills*. Some refer to characteristics. Yukl defines traits as: "a variety of individual attributes including aspects of personality, temperament, needs, motives, and values" (Yukl, 2014: 140). I will use the term *skills* to encompass all three terms. Let's look at what seem to me to be the most important skills of the leaders we have looked at in the previous chapters. They are:

A Clear Vision for Higher Education

The leader should have a clear vision of the changes desired for higher education, which includes concrete goals for higher education—goals that are measurable, achievable, and well defined. The vision and goals need to be such that they mobilize people to work toward them, to make the changes needed to realize them, and when necessary, to help raise the funds needed to put them in place. Jack Lumby complains that discussions of *vision* suffer from the fact that there is "little evidence of how it works in practice." He suggests that perhaps the idea of a vision is just part of the "current leadership rhetoric" (Lumby, February 18, 2013). How does vision work in practice? In the examples that preceded this chapter, I have tried to show that indeed a *vision* is something more than "rhetoric," that in all of the successful cases of higher education change we have looked at, a vision and related goals have been the foundation for change, usually laid out clearly in the strategic plan. And these visions were built around critical needs for higher education and society that people felt strongly about, including national development, well-being, equality of opportunity, and human dignity.

Among the most successful cases we have examined have involved South Africa and Afghanistan where, as I have shown, major transformations have taken place. In South Africa, higher education moved from a system based on race to one focused on a vision and goals of equality and a multiethnic democracy with all its imperfections. In Afghanistan, the plan focused on changing from a highly centralized traditional structure to one that became increasingly decentralized, participatory, democratic, and merit-based—one in which quality has been improved, accreditation put in place, and significant progress made to include more women in higher education, moving from virtually no women in higher education in 2001 to 22.4 percent in 2016.

One of the particularly successful illustrations of the realization of a vision was the case of the University for Development Studies in Ghana where, under the leadership of Vice Chancellor John Kaburise and Pro-Vice Chancellor Saa Dittoh, the university embraced a vision for higher education based on a pro-poor philosophy and established institutional policies that were student focused, emphasizing teamwork across disciplines, and were dedicated to rural development. That vision for a different type of higher education captivated the whole campus and attracted students from around the country—even some of those who had been admitted to the more prestigious university in Accra. This was a major demonstration of the power of a vision, not only to mobilize a campus but to do the same for rural communities, and to attract many students from across the country. There were those who thought this was just "rhetoric" or a "dream" at the outset, but it was a vision that was realized in concrete terms at the university and in many rural communities throughout Northern Ghana.

Self-Confidence with Modesty

This is perhaps one of the most difficult characteristics or skills to achieve and probably cannot be learned. We have seen many people with great self-confidence, but among them modesty is often lacking. And in most parts of the world, a lack of modesty, when coupled with self-confidence, can be a fatal proposition. It was this combination of self-confidence and arrogance that undermined the efforts of Minister Obaid to take over the strategic planning effort in Afghanistan in 2013. His efforts were ill-conceived from the outset because he was unable to see that his plans were misdirected, those he chose to lead were not competent to carry them out, and their lack of familiarity with Afghan higher education and knowledge about strategic planning would cripple the project. Time was lost, funds were wasted, and the final product was unusable. On the other hand, Deputy Minister Babury, with both self-confidence and modesty, withstood the affronts this effort might have caused, let that process run its course, and then moved to make sure the collective vision laid out in the 2009 strategic plan, and that of the current higher education community, was realized. Similarly, in Madagascar the minister encountered strong opposition to his strategic planning efforts at the outset from both the public and private higher education institutions. The former felt that since they were authorized by the ministry in the first place, they didn't need any further review. Most of the private institutions argued that government shouldn't interfere with their quality, that it was up to the "buyer" to decide. Over several months, the minister made his quiet arguments for accreditation in a modest and self-confident way that won over most of the institutional leaders by saying that we judge the quality of students for admission, so we should also ensure the quality of the institutions to some minimal standard. The students ("buyers") can only make their judgments after they graduate when they look for or take jobs. That is too late. The state has an obligation to ensure minimum higher education quality for them in advance.

The insistence on broad participation in South Africa was in part a reaction against the lack of modesty contained in the apartheid government's education policy, where the leaders "knew" what was good for everyone and did not tolerate questions or dissent. That lack of modesty had angered black leaders for decades. They were committed to a more open, collective decision-making structure.

Relations-Oriented Behavior

In looking at relations-oriented behavior, we are talking about leadership behavior that is closely linked to people, demonstrates an interest in them, and ties people to the leadership. As Yukl points out, "Experiments in field settings found that relations-oriented behavior usually resulted in higher subordinate satisfaction and productivity" (Yukl, 2014: 57). In most of the cases in this study, the successful leaders employed relations-oriented behavior. That was especially pronounced in the leadership of Dr. Sohil Naqvi, executive director of the HEC in Pakistan, that of Dr. Haja Razafinjatovo, minister of education in Madagascar, Prof. M. O. Babury, deputyminister in Afghanistan, and Prof. Njabulo Ndebele, vice chancellor of the University of the North, in South Africa. All of them had relationships with their staff, other leaders, faculty members, and students that were based on active listening, consultation, praise, and interest in what people were doing as individuals. And that paid off in excellent cooperation, achievement of goals, and the ability to overcome differences and move forward. The relationships were productive and positive.

In no case was the success of relations-oriented behavior more evident than at the University of the North in South Africa, an institution with a long history of antagonism between students and administrators, where the military was ensconced on the campus for many years. After some tense moments at the start of the planning process, Vice Chancellor Ndebele developed a relationship with most students, staff, and faculty members that was productive, cooperative, and demonstrated a strong interest and understanding of student, staff, and faculty needs. It paid off with a period of two years without violence on campus and completion of the institution's strategic plan through the careful deliberation of a large committee of about sixty people including students, staff, faculty members, administrators, and others. I witnessed a number of the meetings between the students and the vice chancellor as well as meetings of the strategic planning committee with administrators, faculty members, and students. They were notable for the respect the students showed the vice chancellor in particular, the thoughtful discussions, the willingness to listen, and the ability to discuss differences of opinion without things falling apart. Even some of the administrators and faculty members who started this process as reluctant participants began to adopt a relations-oriented behavior, to good effect. It was an important learning process that was to have long-term significance for the institution and those involved.

In another case, it was the failure of President Ravalomanana of Madagascar to heed the warnings of several of his advisors about the purchase of an airplane and other problems that led him to go ahead with projects that mobilized his opponents and gave ammunition to those who would use illegal means to remove him. He had been a popular leader but these actions mobilized support against him, which he failed to take seriously until it was too late. He had been a major supporter of higher education change. His removal in a coup d'état was a terrible blow to higher education and brought to an end a period of reform and upgrading that was making significant progress in Madagascar.

Personal Integrity and Ethical Behavior

The role and importance of personal integrity, a kind of moral imperative, was critical in all of the successful cases examined. Those leaders who were able to demonstrate their honesty, trustworthiness, openness, and fairness did well as leaders in all the higher education cases examined. In the developing countries at this point in time, personal integrity was especially important in contexts that were often marked by corruption, deceit, secrecy, duplicity, and violence. This was especially the case in South Africa in the context of efforts to end apartheid and bring to its conclusion the long history of violence used to enforce a system based on racial inequality. Personal integrity and ethical behavior became very important to the success of the strategic planning effort at the University of Fort Hare, where Vice Chancellor Sibusiso Bengu, the target of two assassination attempts, had literally put his life on the line standing between police and students at the gates of the university, to defuse a crisis that could have led to death and days of chaos. His integrity made possible the major strides in developing a change plan that moved toward a democratic, open, and fair system of higher education at the university.

The same was true in Afghanistan with the example of Prof. M. O. Babury, who, as deputy minister, had led the effort by the Ministry of Higher Education in 2007 to end corruption in the admissions process and recognized the importance of student concerns for the MoHE. I watched him deal with a case in which students felt they had been mistreated by administrators and came in large numbers to the Ministry to complain. On one occasion there were more than one thousand students chanting and shouting outside the gates of the ministry, with a few throwing stones as well. The deputy minister said he would meet with five students as long as they promised to discuss the matter in his office in a quiet positive manner. Five students were allowed to come into the deputy minister's office and join the deputy minister, the chancellor of that university, several other senior administrators of the MoHE, and me as senior advisor. The deputy minister asked the students to spell out their grievances first and said he would then hear from the chancellor. The issue related to a belief that some students had been discriminated against in an examination by the vice chancellor in a way they ascribed to ethnic discrimination. Deputy Minister Babury listened quietly and wouldn't let any of the other administrators interrupt the students. When they finished, the deputy minister started to ask a few questions of the students but was interrupted by the entrance of the vice chancellor in question. The vice chancellor was furious, red in the face, and sweating profusely. He started shouting at the students, calling them hooligans, ungrateful, and troublemakers. The deputy minister told the vice chancellor to be quiet, to sit still and listen, or to leave. The vice chancellor quieted down reluctantly, but was clearly still very upset and believed the students should not have been allowed in. He continued to mutter about them under his breath until the deputy minister warned him again.

After things quieted down, Deputy Minister Babury asked the chancellor to briefly give his position, which was basically that the students were out of line and the vice chancellor was being maligned by them. The deputy minister noted that he could see that the attitude of the vice chancellor was not productive of any reasonable dialogue and apologized for the tirade by the vice chancellor. The deputy minister then asked the students for suggestions about how the crisis might be resolved. What followed was a very positive discussion, including the admission that some of the students had been wrong in their charge of ethnic bias, but they said it was because the vice chancellor had refused even to hear the students' complaints about the exam. The deputy minister noted that was not appropriate, said he would accept an apology from the students responsible, which was given, and insisted as well on an apology from the vice chancellor for not responding, which was given reluctantly. The matter was thus resolved.

By this demonstration of fairness and integrity, in his willingness to call out a senior administrator who was misbehaving and to insist on a clear and fair discussion, Prof. Babury ended a dispute that might have gone on for days, shut down the university, resulted in damage to university property, and further inflamed student attitudes. It was his personal integrity which had given the students confidence that they would be heard in the first place, and his demonstration of fairness that brought things to a positive conclusion. In the end, a crisis was averted.

Ethical behavior—behavior that is based on a moral value system—is characteristic of personal integrity. There is no single notion of what those values involve. As Northouse has noted, it is difficult to think about a unified ethical theory of leadership. This is partly because there are broad sets of ethical viewpoints (Northouse, 2016: 329) that make it difficult to present a single strategy. It is also because these values may change over time as a result of a leader's own moral development (ibid.: 330). Values are different in every political system. For my purposes then, it is useful to think about ethical behavior as linked to personal integrity and largely defined by what the particular society sees as appropriate or desirable. Ethical leaders are concerned about justice, propriety, rules about decision making, and good governance. Decisions about *right* and *wrong* are clear to these leaders and govern their behavior. The values and notions about what is *just* are embedded in a society and generally shared by its members.

We saw this particularly in South Africa at the University of Fort Hare, where Vice Chancellor Sibusiso Bengu's moral stance against apartheid had a profound impact on students and staff. His bravery in the face of assassination attempts and his willingness to stand between the Ciskei police and the students to prevent violence further heightened what was seen as his moral integrity. That had a powerful effect on some of the staff who had been strong supporters of apartheid. They came to see the power of equality, democratic and participatory values, and in the end apologized to him and others for their previous support of apartheid.

Ability to Adjust to Change; Flexibility

The environment in underdeveloped and developing economies is constantly changing, and effective leaders must have the ability to adjust quickly to changed conditions. It is surprising how many leaders lack that ability to adjust, as has played out in a number of the cases we have examined. A frequently changing environment is a particularly frustrating condition for strategic planning, whereas stability helps give planners the confidence that today's conditions will be constant over at least the next five years. All of the plans we examined were designed to account for at least five years. Ideally, planners can at least make some predictions about the kinds of changes that will take place over the next few years. For example, usually there is good enough data to allow planners to predict student numbers from one year to the next, to predict the number of graduates from secondary school and thus estimate the likely number of students who will want university education, and of that number how many are likely to pass the entrance examination. Planners also need to be able to predict the financial situation, to plan budgets in at least five-year increments with some assurance that the totals are correct. This is especially the case for construction, which usually needs a three- to five-year horizon given the need for land acquisition, environmental assessments in some cases, surveys of the land, preparation of plans, ensuring that the roads, water, and electricity can be ready when needed, laying the foundation, building the structure, furnishing and finishing the building. Major changes in income, lack of availability of material, unexpected changes in student numbers, major weather events, may alter the situation. Leaders must be flexible and adjust to these changing circumstances and plan for them to the extent possible.

The Pakistan case, as noted, went through an extensive series of planning scenarios as part of the risk analysis prepared by the strategic planning team and the World Bank. These scenarios included consideration of different income situations, including state funding, university contributions, donor contributions, among others. The planners laid out generous income scenarios as well as conservative ones and as a result of these variations were able to adjust the plan to conform to their findings that the original plan would cost more than an average income scenario would support. Not only were they prepared to adjust to unknown changes, they tried to predict the kinds of changes that might be faced by going through various scenarios to see what the consequences would be and plan accordingly.

On the other hand, the kinds of challenges faced by some of the institutions and systems we examined proved too much for the leaders in place at that time. We have the examples of both Sierra Leone and Madagascar in that regard. The initial events, as mentioned earlier, were catastrophic coups d'état in both countries. The immediate response was to try to keep the institutions open, which was done in both cases, though in Sierra Leone, Njala University was eventually closed for a time due to the fighting on campus. The national political leadership that followed in both cases was subjected to military rule, which did not lend itself to continuing the existing strategic planning efforts. Even when politics began to be regularized in both countries, the higher education leadership was unable to move forward with effective strategic plans, and some of the plans for change already in place were reversed. Several efforts were made to restart the planning process in Sierra Leone, without success. The plan was not revived in Madagascar, although some of its goals, especially accreditation, did move forward after a period of delays. The universities remained open in Madagascar but with frequent strikes because of lack of funding and other problems with the new government. The accreditation part of the plan was resuscitated in 2013 with new legislation (Ministry of Higher Education and Scientific Research, 2013).

Part of flexibility involves recognition that the timing of a change or announcements about changes, can be critical in certain circumstances; it is sometimes the key to success or failure. We have seen the critical role of timing in several cases examined here. The critical issue for the leader is the ability to recognize when action on certain goals can jeopardize progress. In such cases, it is important to wait for a more auspicious time to move forward with that goal. In other cases, it may be important to move more quickly than planned because the timing suddenly becomes optimal for a certain course of action. The best example of the critical role of timing can be found in the issue of Higher Education Gender Strategy addressed by the Ministry of Higher Education in Afghanistan as part of the effort to move toward gender equity in higher education. As we saw, had the ministry not delayed the plan's release after major parliamentary opposition to gender equity, it would have been reversed and the prospects for gender equity in higher education further delayed. Recognizing the problem, the ministry put the release on hold until July 2016, at which time the gender strategy was promulgated without problems and to strong support.

Determination, Drive, Commitment

The determination by leaders to gain support for particular change goals and for their implementation has been critical to the success of change efforts in almost all of the cases we have examined. In several cases, there was resistance to specific change proposals in strategic plans or some of the related goals. In Madagascar, people thought everything was fine in higher education. There was no need for any changes. What was the point of starting the long process of strategic planning? What they did not understand, although the minister did, was that Madagascar was far behind the rest of Africa and other developing economies in terms of the state of its higher education, and even farther behind most of the rest of the world. The minister, who had traveled a great deal and received his PhD in the United States, was well aware of the gap and pushed the chancellors and others to see that they were lagging and needed to update and upgrade higher education in Madagascar. His personal drive and determination moved the process forward.

Similarly, in the institutional strategic planning efforts in South Africa at the University of the North and at the University of Fort Hare, the initial reaction of some individuals at the institutions was hostility to strategic planning, as they saw it as a threat to the apartheid order—which it was. On the other hand, some anti-apartheid leaders feared that the change process would be taken over by the old apartheid leadership and were unfamiliar with the process proposed. Part of their concern stemmed from fear that the process was "fixed" or set up to prevent change, which indeed had been the case during apartheid, when change was not possible. However, due to the determination of the leaders of the strategic planning processes at both the University of Fort Hare and the University of the North, people from all sides were eventually persuaded to join in the process and successful strategic planning followed. It was the determination, drive, and commitment of the leadership that encouraged progress to be made on the change agenda and led to its realization in the long run.

Reflective Leadership and Strategic Thinking

Reflection is generally not something we think about when we define the skills of leaders. But in undertaking an examination of the change process in many of these examples, the need for reflection becomes clear and with that the importance of strategic thinking, given the environment faced by most of these leaders, and the challenges they confronted in these developing and underdeveloped economies. Pritchard has described strategic thinking as both "the ability to encourage colleagues to reevaluate their assumptions and think more deeply and systematically about the challenges facing the institutions in which they work" and "the ability to tolerate a high level of ambiguity and uncertainty" (Pritchard, 2018: 52–53). In combination, those abilities guided several leaders in exploring areas previously uncharted in their systems and encourage others to do the same. Looking back at several of these cases, we see that the thought and consideration that went into values enshrined by the change goals, into the processes of planning change, and into the strategic plans themselves showed deep reflection and strategic thinking on the part of a number of the leaders. Several of them have left important legacies as part of their strategic planning work—legacies based on clear reflections about the state of higher education in the country, the needs of the people, the requirements for improvement and growth, ways to deal with the major challenges confronted, and strategies for making progress. Let's look at several of these higher education leaders.

Two leaders who have left behind critical legacies of strategic thinking and reflection for higher education are former minister Mohammad Azam Dadfar and Deputy Minister M. O. Babury in Afghanistan, who brought to the Ministry of Higher Education a level of honesty, determination, and moral authority that turned around a troubled ministry and made it possible to lay the foundation for a national strategic plan that turned out to be transformational, as we have seen. They reoriented a ministry that was rife with corruption, full of self-centered staff members, and little interested in quality improvement. The clearest example of their strategic thinking was the focus on quality improvement and accreditation—the latter a process unknown in Afghanistan and for many leaders "un-Afghan." Bringing about accreditation required a rethinking of assumptions by many leaders and faculty members, but at the end of the process the effort was heartily supported by both administrators and faculty members.

One of the first leaders we looked at was Prof. Atta-ur-Rahman, chairman of the Pakistan Higher Education Commission (HEC). He and Dr. Sohail Naqvi, the commission's executive director, were the major forces behind the change process and the strategic plan for Pakistan, the *Medium Term Development Framework: 2005–2010* (MTDF). He and others saw that Pakistan's higher education establishment, unlike that in neighboring India, had largely stagnated since independence in 1947. Prof. Atta-ur-Rahman, in particular, had given years of reflection to the question of what was missing in higher education, had written about it twenty-five years earlier,[2] and had done a great deal of strategic thinking about the direction he felt higher education should take in the future. He and several others had prepared a document laying out the results of that thinking, called "Science and Technology Based Industrial Vison of Pakistan's Economy and Prospects of Growth" (Atta-ur-Rahman et al., circa 2000), which laid out a plan for development. As he wrote in his introduction to the *Medium Term Development Framework: 2005–2010*:

> The world has been transformed in the last several decades into one where knowledge is now the engine for socio-economic development, and the importance of natural resources has greatly diminished. The 5 Year Plan for the Higher Education Sector aims at creating the necessary foundations in which excellence can flourish and Pakistan can embark on the road to develop a knowledge economy. There are three major issues which need to be addressed in the context of higher education sector develop programmes: (a) access (b) quality and (c) relevance to national needs. (MTDF, 2005: 4)

His efforts were intended to change assumptions about higher education, shake people out of their current satisfaction with the status quo, and foster fundamental change. He then worked with the HEC staff and a World Bank team to flesh out the strategic plan to do that, as we saw in chapter 3, with great success.

Njabulo Ndebele is another leader noted for reflection and strategic thinking. He is one of the outstanding thinkers and writers in South Africa today.[3] The focus on ideas, his reflections on problems and how to solve them, was a hallmark of his administrative career at both the University of the North and the University of Cape Town. He was a man of reflection, and that was a key to his success. When I worked with him at the University of the North, I was struck by what he was thinking about at any moment. I would often arrive on the weekend so that we could have some time together to think about the strategic plan. The University of the North had a long history of violence and disruption. Ndebele was the first vice-chancellor to represent the new post-apartheid order, but as he recognized, he nonetheless inherited much of the baggage of the former apartheid-era administrators whose job had been to keep the students in line, with education a secondary concern. He was well aware of that baggage and worked hard to shed it. More than any other leader I worked with in South Africa, his reflections helped him understand that, as he put it, the strategic plan is "about ensuring institutional conditions for the list of things to be done to take the university to the next phase of development in its history. At a certain stage in the life of a university those conditions might be far more important than a program of action" (Ndebele, 2007: 1). He came to realize that the most important condition was a "shared understanding" of a process for working toward those ends. He, and the students, most of the faculty members, and most of the administration, did finally come to a shared understanding that made strategic planning possible and brought peace to the campus for the next two years. He recognized that sometimes *process* is much more important than *outcomes*—once again showing the value of the kind of careful reflection that preceded his work and his actions.

Organizational and Mobilization Skills

It is surprising how many leaders lack organizational skills. The ability to plan in a logical and rational way, get people mobilized to do the work when it is needed, avoid duplication, make sure things are sequenced in an effective way, are all organizational skills needed for success. Probably the most difficult thing to organize in higher education is construction. That in itself has the imponderables of weather, which can be devastating in bad years, but organizational success for construction is also about the logic of building. All this has to be done in the proper order and that takes tremendous organizational skill and experience with construction.

Effective organization usually involves a team effort. However, if it is a skill that major leaders lack, the results can be chaotic. That was the history of higher education in Afghanistan until relatively recently. Far too few leaders have the organizational skills needed to set up, write, and implement plans for major change. There are those who recognize their lack of that talent and hire assistants who can overcome that deficiency for the most part. Those who have good organizational skills have a profound advantage over those who do not.

One of the most critical tools for bringing about higher education change is the ability to mobilize people in support of the changes, to be sure they support the goals and are in tune with the vision for the institution or system. Then comes the need to mobilize people to implement the plan. We are talking about getting people to do something in particular, marshalling support for specific actions, and organizing specific activities. This can be especially difficult in those areas in which major changes are being requested, as with the curriculum, which requires a great deal of work by all faculty members. As we saw in the case of Madagascar, no one believed major changes were needed in the curriculum. Faculty members felt they were as up-to-date as they needed to be and were providing their graduates what they required for life after graduation. The minister initially had a hard time convincing vice chancellors and deans that their academic programs were not up to the quality that was expected internationally. Making that case was especially hard since neither faculty members nor administrators had much contact with universities outside Madagascar, unlike Ghana, for example, which was constantly carrying out exchanges with universities in neighboring Cote d'Ivoire, Sierra Leone, Nigeria, Gambia, and Guinea. In Madagascar, faculty members seldom went to Africa, and if they traveled they were more likely to go to Europe, especially France, which had established the university originally and which was a place where many faculty members still had academic ties from their graduate days. France was the standard for them, the norm against which they measured their academic performance, but they were not perturbed that they were behind France—that was to be expected. Unfortunately, at that particular time, the French were among the laggards in Europe, and Europe was behind the United States.

One master of mobilization was Sipho Pityana, strategic planner at the University of Fort Hare. Part of his success derived from his thoughtful preparation. He knew the talents of everyone, he was a persuasive speaker, and there was a certain charisma about him that made people want to do what he asked. The same was true in Afghanistan, with Deputy Minister Babury. He was adept at mobilizing high-quality faculty members to serve on committees and commissions. People were pleased and flattered to be invited by him to serve. They were proud to be asked and often bragged about it. It was an honor to be asked by Deputy Minster Babury to serve. That is part of what explains the substantial success in achieving the goals of the strategic plan in Afghanistan.

Communications Skills

Not everyone has good communications skills. There are some leaders who survive without them, but the leader with good communications skills has a tremendous advantage over others. Northouse puts it well when he notes:

> With their ability to express a vision strongly and powerfully, communicators can inspire people at all levels. They are good at projecting optimism in times of adversity or crisis and are strongly influential with various constituencies in the organization. (Northouse, 2016: 322)

Good communicators are able to make their points concisely and clearly in a way that seems logical and ordered. Some of the literature suggests that people with good communications skills often "look at the big picture, rather than dealing with details, [which] means that these leaders need others such as strategists and processors, to make their dreams become reality" (Northouse, 2016: 322–323). I have not found that to be the case in higher education. Some of the best communicators in this study were also very interested in, and careful about, details. They did not need "strategists" or "processors" to realize their goals.

As we have seen, there are a variety of characteristics and skills which enhance the chances of success of strategic planning. They are reiterated below in figure 14.1.

Strategies for Higher Education Change

As we look at the leadership of change, it is clear that a number of different strategies have been used by leaders. Some of them were overt and transparent, others not articulated but nonetheless define the actions of the leader in ways we can identify. Let's look at four strategies: transformational, democratic, directive, and collaborative.

Transformational Strategies

In the introduction, I defined transformational change as change that succeeds in fundamentally altering both the structure of a system and some of its major values (Babury & Hayward, 2014: 2). As noted there, I see change as a continuum, with minor changes along the low end of the continuum that are isolated changes (one unit, one department) that may be extensive but do not affect the rest of the university or system. Farther toward the higher end of the continuum are more extensive changes. Finally, at the high end of the continuum is transformational change—"change that is pervasive and deep in a way that fundamentally alters the organization's structure and some of its major values."[4]

We saw examples of a successful transformational strategy's effect on systems in Afghanistan, South Africa, and Pakistan, as well as at institutions in South Africa and Ghana. In those cases, major changes in important values and in structures occurred—in South Africa, by ending apartheid and all it entailed in terms of equality, justice, and upgrading institutions; in Ghana, in a fundamentally different structure of higher education with a focus on rural development, student-centered learning, cross-discipline cooperation, and a pro-poor philosophy. In Afghanistan, the system moved from a traditional hierarchical one to one based on merit, with more decentralized authority and a focus on quality improvement, including faculty development and accreditation. In Pakistan, there was a fundamental reorientation of focus to one emphasizing science, technology, a well-trained faculty, quality research, and a high-quality knowledge-based academic curriculum.

Democratic Strategies

A number of leaders we have examined operated in ways that suggest they were committed to a democratic strategy. Indeed, in South Africa, that was a critical part of what was taking place as part of the anti-apartheid struggle—a demand for democratic processes and equality. Put more broadly, the principles of democracy and freedom were critical to the environment of strategic planning.

The importance of the idea of *freedom* to the development process has been especially well put by Amartya Sen. He writes in *Development as Freedom* that the "freedoms of individuals" are the basic building blocks of development. He goes on to say: "Attention is thus paid particularly to the expansion of the 'capabilities' of persons to lead the kinds of lives they value—and have reason to value. These capabilities can be enhanced by public policy, but also, on the other side, the direction of public policy can be influenced by the effective use of participatory capabilities by the public." This two-way relationship is essential (Sen, 1999: 18). Sen views development as a process of "expansion of substantive freedoms that connect with one another" (ibid.: 8). He suggests that

> [f]reedoms are not only the primary ends of development, they are among its principle means. . . . Political freedoms (in the form of free speech and elections) help to promote economic security. Social opportunities (in the form of education and health facilities) facilitate economic participation. Economic facilities (in the form of opportunities for participation in trade and production) can help to generate personal abundance as well as public resources for social facilities. (Sen, 1999: 11)

Not all efforts to revive higher education will take place in a free environment, but where that is possible, as Amartya Sen (1999) has noted, it fosters a great deal more communication, consensus, and democracy within the development process. That is a tremendous advantage when it is possible.

We saw that most clearly in South Africa, where freedom and democracy were central parts of the anti-apartheid narrative and process. That made a democratic strategy an essential part of preparing any strategic plan. We saw the lengths that were gone to nationally in South Africa to ensure that the process was democratic. At both the University of Fort Hare and the University of the North, establishing agreed-upon democratic procedures for the process was essential to making any progress on the change agenda. Those involved in planning at both the national and institutional levels understood that open, democratic participation was critical to actually moving forward to plan and bring about desired change at both levels. And democratic processes were put in place with substantial success, as we have seen.

One of the fascinating aspects of the Afghan experience in planning was not only the importance of following democratic process, but the fact that higher education, unlike some other parts of the system, operated in a democratic environment. Although there were attacks on freedom of the press, and on opposition in many areas, that did not occur in higher education until 2016, and even then it was a focused Taliban attack.[5] The debates that took place in 2009 during the process of preparing the *National Higher Education Strategic Plan: 2010–2014* were open, democratic, and transparent, with between sixty and one hundred participants working directly on preparing and reviewing the ideas and goals that served as the basis of the strategic plan. Other than one brief outburst by an eastern vice chancellor at the outset, noted earlier, no one attempted to stifle the free discussions of the plan. And indeed, there was opposition to several parts of the change agenda, as noted earlier, including to accreditation, curriculum revision, and gender equity. Only in the latter case did special precautions have to be taken, given the level of opposition of some people to women's education. Nonetheless, the ministry was able to proceed with its efforts to move in the direction of gender equity, as promised in the *NHESP: 2010–2014*, and substantial gains were made.

Directive or Top-Down

In several of the cases we have examined, the change process was overtly "top-down" and directive. The power and authority of the leader is based in part on the position he holds and therefore comes from what is seen as the legitimate right of the leader to give directions and make policy. As Yukl notes, the "[p]osition power includes potential influence derived from legitimate authority, control over resources and rewards, control over punishments, control over information, and control over the physical work environment" (Yukl, 2014: 199). All of the leaders we have examined had a degree of personal power. But whether or not that is usable to bring about substantial change depends a great deal on how the leader exercises that power. That usually means that it is used with skills such as the ability to mobilize people and outstanding communicative skills.

The directive or "top-down" strategy was most clearly used in the case of Pakistan, as noted earlier. It was a conscious decision by the leadership that the changes had to be directed from the Higher Education Commission if they were to take place in a reasonable amount of time. There was, nonetheless, a considerable degree of consultation throughout the course of implementation of the change plan, and the strategic plan itself was the result of an extensive review. Success could not have been achieved from the top down only.

Collaborative Strategy

A collaborative strategy is a highly participative process, which involves a great deal of discussion at all levels of higher education, input from those affected by the plan, and broad-based review of the process along the way. This is often linked with a democratic approach to change as well.

The best example of a collaborative strategy can be seen in the work on the national strategic plan for higher education in South Africa, which we discussed earlier. Every effort was made to ensure that there was broad input into the process and changes planned at every level. That included posting drafts on the internet and encouraging people to send in written comments—which they did. The payoff was a process which was seen as legitimate, contrasting markedly with that of the apartheid government, where the plans had been prepared and enforced from the top. The structure of higher education and the values it enshrined for the nonwhite population were prepared by those in control—the white minority government, without consultation. In the postelection period, under the ANC, the new plans for change that produced a transformed system were based on collaboration, openness, transparency, with a commitment to equal opportunities for all people.

A useful way to think about a strategic planning leadership is set out in figure 13.1, which provides a description and suggests the

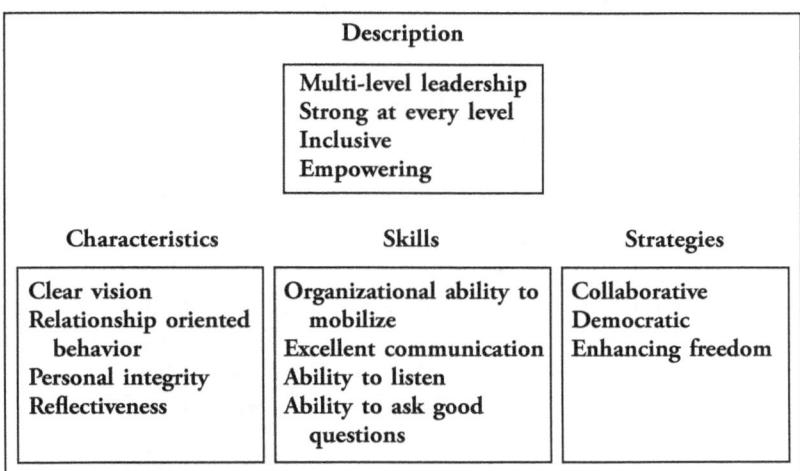

Figure 13.1. Leadership in Strategic Planning. *Source:* Washington, DC: Fred M. Hayward.

characteristics, skills, and strategies of the most successful leaders of change through strategic planning examined in this study. In the most successful strategic planning efforts, leadership is multilevel, strong at every level, inclusive, and empowering. The dominant characteristics of that leadership include a clear vision, relationship-oriented behavior, personal integrity, determination, and reflectiveness. Critical skills include good organizational abilities, capacity to mobilize support, excellent communications skills, ability to listen, and ability to ask good questions. With a few exceptions, a successful leader's strategies are collaborative, democratic, and designed to enhance freedom.

Conclusions

In this chapter, I have tried to unpack higher education leadership into some of its component parts, skills, characteristics, and strategies used by the leaders in the eight countries and twelve cases examined in this study. Are there particular kinds of leaders who are more likely to succeed? I do not think it is possible to identify them by type, but it seems to me that there are a number of skills, characteristics, and strategies that foster success. They are laid out in figure 14.1 above. All of the successful changes we have discussed were facilitated by leaders at various levels with a mix of skills and characteristics. Understanding the skills, characteristics, and strategies that helped them succeed in bringing about changes, ranging from modest alterations of processes to major transformation of a higher education system based on a detailed strategic plan, helps us recognize what seems to work well in various environments in the underdeveloped and developing world and what does not. Adopting those skills and characteristics, or using those strategies, will not guarantee success, but hopefully it will help clarify what Cronin has suggested people see of higher education leadership most of the time, as "a rather hazy, distant and even confusing abstraction" (Cronin, 1995: 28). In none of the examples looked at here was there a "heroic leader" who singlehandedly established a plan, gained support for it, and oversaw successful implementation. As Estela Bensimon and Anna Neumann put it so well: "[A]s the world grows more complex . . . it is likely that we will stop thinking of leadership as the property or quality of just one person. We will begin to think of it in its collective form: leadership as occurring among and through a group of people who think and act together" (Bensimon & Neumann, 1994: 2). Good leadership is required at many levels, including in the universities, if a plan is to succeed. That leadership must be spread throughout the system, not only in the ministry, but in the university administration and also among the faculty, staff, and students.

Chapter 14

The Nature of Change and Transformation in Higher Education in Developing Countries

The changes chronicled here represent a remarkable range of goals for a better life through improvements in higher education. For some change involved adjusting the existing system in specific ways such as greater efficiency or a more student-centered focus. For others, the vision was for a fundamentally altered higher education system in terms of the values it enshrined, expanded participation, and major changes in the curriculum—changes of the kind we saw in South Africa and Afghanistan, which transformed entire systems—changes that fundamentally altered the structure of the systems and many of their major values (Babury & Hayward, 2014: 2). Some of those involved in the process saw these efforts as vital to the transformation not only of higher education but to the development of the nation as a whole. As discussed, in two of the cases, the change efforts failed (Sierra Leone and Madagascar) due to military intervention. Several other cases were only modestly successful (Malawi and Uganda), primarily because of financial shortfalls, which reflected both national political weaknesses and economic crises. All of these examples took place in underdeveloped and developing economies facing an extensive range of financial, social, and political challenges. While each of these cases is unique, there are some general lessons they suggest about both the successes and challenges for higher education change.

Most of the cases had transformational components in their strategic plans. They were not just aimed at reproducing what already existed—even in the least ambitious of them, in Sierra Leone. They sought significant changes, in values in ways that would improve quality and install extensive change that would be long lasting. In the most ambitious of them, as in South Africa, they sought to create a system of equals unbiased regarding race, gender, or ethnicity—to end a hierarchical, racist, discriminatory system in both higher education and society. In Pakistan, the strategic plan was designed to reorient the whole higher education system by moving it from a self-replicating, stagnant one to a system that aspired to create a knowledge economy that would occupy a place among the top higher education systems in the world.

Human Development and Higher Education Change

One of the most striking aspects of several of the successful change processes is that they occurred in especially difficult environments—an ongoing war, tough economic circumstances, violence and intimidation, major campus conflicts, political interference, and other pressures. What is remarkable about these particular situations is that the magnitude of the challenges seems to have helped facilitate change efforts, mobilize support, spark participation, encourage action, and breed success. Many of the changes sought demonstrated deep concerns about the human condition that proved to be powerful drivers of higher education transformation. Here, I am talking about human development much as Castells and Himanen do, as "a process of enhancement of the living conditions that make humans human in a given social context." As they note, it involves the quality of life, which includes security, food, education, health, as well as "job creation, work quality, and environmental sustainability" (Castells & Himanen, 2014: 12–13). As people found higher education failing to meet development needs they sought changes they hoped would help overcome those deficiencies. That effort was especially clear in the cases of South Africa, Pakistan, and Afghanistan, but we also saw it in the other change efforts.

In South Africa and Afghanistan, the contexts in which the change process occurred included major conflicts about values and beliefs that had become life and death matters related to the society as a whole as well as to higher education. And that made some aspects of the change agenda personally dangerous to those participating in it. They became the targets of threats and ongoing violence in both countries. For outsiders, it is easy to overlook the power and extent of threats and intimidation.

Yet, they were present every day with tremendous consequences for those involved and their families, causing some to flee, while others were arrested and spent time in jail, and some were killed.

We saw some of the consequences of the struggle environment in both Afghanistan and South Africa in student dropouts, mental health problems, suicide, and fear, as well as the loss of faculty members and staff. Yet at the same time the demands for dignity, equality, and well-being trumped the threats and fear in the long run for most major participants, though those legacies remained.

The conditions in both countries created powerful forces for change. People realized that without major changes in higher education, the possibility that they might live in a society that provided better opportunities and well-being for all its citizens was impossible to achieve. These goals were reflected in the visions put forward for higher education in both countries, which reflected the desire to create the conditions for a high-quality higher education establishment that would help the nation meet basic human needs: well-being, equality, freedom, justice, and human dignity. The search for human dignity should be emphasized. People not only wanted economic well-being, they wanted to be treated with dignity and respect—something that was absent not only in apartheid South Africa but in the experience of the poor in most of the countries we have examined. People sought recognition of their individual worth (Castells & Himanen, 2014: ch. 10). Access to education was seen as part of the solution. Many people were willing to put their lives on the line for that because the consequences of lack of access were abundantly clear.

The vision for change in most of these cases reflected these concerns about human development, dignity, well-being, and equal opportunity in a variety of ways. The focus on admission, relevance, and national development reflected an effort to open opportunities to those who had been left out. The focus on access did not always come from below. Indeed, in Madagascar, it grew out of a finding by the minister, as noted earlier, based on his research that revealed that only a few students came from the poorer segments of the population. That led him to propose loan schemes and other ways to help poor families afford higher education in an effort to open higher education access to the poor. Similar worries were expressed in Pakistan, along with concerns about whether or not students from poor families could afford the university fee raises proposed to help fund the planned changes. In Ghana, concerns about opportunities at the University for Development Studies led to a major program based on a "pro-poor strategy" in rural communities based on both teaching and outreach plans and the third-term program.

Sometimes the poor, undereducated, and uneducated are forgotten in higher education thinking about change, in part because most administrators, faculty members, and students are from the upper and upper-middle classes. That makes it easier to ignore or forget about the poor. However, the change efforts at UDS in Ghana, the plans in South Africa, in Afghanistan, in Pakistan, and pre-coup Madagascar, contained a major focus on finding ways to be inclusive, including student loan plans, scholarships, and other funding mechanisms. Those involved in these strategic plans for change envisioned transformation, not modifications of the existing system—transformation that was both extensive and deep, involving altering key values in the system. It remains to be seen whether or not the focus will shift as time goes on, as it seems to have done in the BRICs, to the middle and upper classes that are their main supporters, rather than to the poor and the masses (Carnoy et al., 2013: ch. 9). To some extent, that is already happening in several of the countries we have examined.

Freedom and Higher Education

Among the lessons learned is that a certain level of freedom was critical to the ability to bring about the desired changes in higher education in all the successful examples examined here. It was especially essential to Afghan higher education transformation under wartime conditions. It is what allowed the thorough discussion of values involved in some of the changes, attacking underlying beliefs and challenging unexamined assumptions and their consequences. Importantly, there was greater freedom in the academic community than in the society as a whole. And it was that which allowed planning to take place to put together a National Higher Education Strategic Plan in 2009 that fostered transformation, that made a commitment to gender equity, and that recognized the importance of merit as a basis for recruitment and promotion, as it already was for admission. Stimulating those changes was the widespread fear that without major upgrades to the quality of higher education, national development would not occur in Afghanistan. Academic freedom in this case was a basic building block in planning the kind of education needed for national development.

One of the lessons learned from the Afghan experience was the critical role that academic freedom played in allowing the change exercise to take place that produced the very successful *National Higher Education Strategic Plan: 2010–2014*. The process was successful in large part because of a broadly participatory change strategy, both at the outset and later on. Higher education leaders worked hard to ensure that academic freedom was central to the work of all higher education institutions. This was a major task in a war environment. Indeed, the level of freedom of speech, action, and writing was considerably higher in the universities than it was in Afghanistan as a whole and in the press in particular. There were ninety-five attacks against the press in 2015, and the Freedom House Press Freedom Score for Afghanistan was a poor 62 out of 100 (0 is best and 100 is worst) (Freedom House, 2016: 1–2). Part of the success in establishing and maintaining academic freedom in Afghan higher education was the broad commitment to it by academics and by the government.

In most of the situations we have examined, it was not necessary to initiate a physical struggle for the freedom needed to discuss and foster higher education changes, as was the case in South Africa. However, in several cases there were few mechanisms available to express demands for change or venues where that was possible. Part of the anger among academics in both Malawi and Uganda was the consequence of their inability to operate in higher education with the access, freedom, and impact needed to make progress both institutionally and nationally. There were the cases in which freedom was totally curtailed in Sierra Leone and Madagascar due to military coups, losses that still have a negative effect on the quality of higher education in those countries.

Democracy and Higher Education

The democratic values that played a critical role in the successes of almost all of the cases we have discussed were related to academic freedom, and I want to highlight them here as a lesson learned, since their role is often missed in democratic societies because it is part of their normal culture and inherent in their higher education institutions, and is thus assumed. The development of democratic values and procedures has been critical to the success of the strategic planning process in several of the cases we looked at, following years of oppression, violence, and intimidation. In democratic societies, we notice when someone tries to ram something through a committee or a senate, but normally we don't think about the critical importance of democratic processes. Yet, democratic processes were important to the success of higher education change in every one of the cases we examined. Successful higher education change almost always grows out of extensive discussions about goals, values, and priorities as part of the strategic planning process. Those discussions can be difficult in any environment, but as we have seen they were especially difficult in the apartheid universities of South Africa, as demonstrated by the cases of the University of Fort Hare and the University of the North. Success only came after there was agreement on process, and that process enshrined democratic values, openness, and equal participation for everyone involved. Its importance was equally clear to the success of Afghanistan strategic planning.

Competition and Catching Up

Many of the change agendas we have discussed were driven in part by the desire to catch up with neighbors, the region, or higher education internationally. Often, as in Pakistan, Madagascar, and Afghanistan, it was based on a sudden shocked realization about how far behind their universities were compared to those in neighboring countries. That was the case of the reaction of many academics in Pakistan to the publication in 2000 of World Bank's *The Peril and the Promise*. Their shock at learning about their poor reputation internationally helped mobilize a major change effort. In the sciences in particular, there was stunned disbelief that their institutions were not ranking among the top institutions in Asia, or even close to those in India. That realization worked to foster major changes that would bring some of Pakistan's universities up to world-class quality. In Madagascar, the stimulus was the appointment of a new minister of education who had studied in the United States and traveled widely. He let the universities know that they were way behind the rest of the world and especially Africa, which they tended to look down on. And that mobilized support for change. In Afghanistan, after thirty years of war, it was common knowledge that their former lead in the rankings of academic excellence in the region had disappeared long ago and they were far behind their colleagues, because of war, purges, killings, restrictions on faculty members, lack of interest by the Taliban government, and limited funding. That understanding helped motivate the extensive changes that were implemented, following up on the goals of the national strategic plan, which resulted in real transformation.

Competition proved to be a powerful motivator for higher education change in a number of places when people realized how far behind they were in comparison to other institutions and in particular academic fields. The loss of status embarrassed some leaders and academics and reminded others of the cost of being uncompetitive. In Pakistan, part of the motivation was the desire not to always be dependent on the West for major innovations in science and technology. Becoming competitive was an effective stimulus in Pakistan, whose higher education system, in spite of starting out on a par with India's in 1947 as part of the same system, was way behind India in quality in 2001—virtually unchanged from what it had been in 1947. That created an impetus for a successful push for rapid growth, improvement, and transformation of the system. Competition between institutions was also an important driver of change in Afghanistan, as shown in the case of Kabul Polytechnic University as they undertook work on their institutional strategic plan.

Political Involvement in Higher Education

Active interest in higher education on the part of national political leaders has been a critical variable for successful strategic planning and change in higher education in a number of cases examined. While it has not been as extensive as in the case of the BRIC states, where it has been seen by Carnoy et al. as the major driving force for higher education change (Carnoy et al., 2013), it has been substantial, especially in South Africa and Pakistan. For example, the role of President Musharraf in supporting higher education change in Pakistan at the outset was very important to the initial successes of that effort. His commitment to high-quality higher education, assistance with the legal framework, and support for a substantial amount of funding were vital to success. Presidential involvement in Afghanistan did not play the same major role, but President Karzai intervened at several critical junctures to help the strategic planning and change process move forward, and his financial support for faculty development was critical. Similarly, President Ashraf

Ghani has provided strong support for the Higher Education Gender Strategy and on behalf of the new National Higher Education Strategic Plan: 2016–2020.

Presidential support for higher education change in Madagascar was also very important at the outset, though the removal of the president at the time of the coup brought much of that support to an end. Similarly, President Momoh helped initiate the development plans for the University of Sierra Leone, though once again a coup and years of chaos and corruption after that scuttled the plans for rehabilitation and change. In South Africa, the strong support of the ANC leadership for higher education change was critical to the transformation that took place in the national system of higher education, as reflected in revised institutional strategic plans in the cases of the University of Fort Hare and the University of the North.

In contrast, the lack of strong support for higher education from the political leadership in Uganda and Malawi contributed to limiting the success of the strategic planning efforts in both countries and led to only partial implementation of their strategic plans for change. The total absence of support by the political leadership in Sierra Leone for more than fifteen years following the coup thwarted efforts to rebuild and improve the University of Sierra Leone. Similarly, in Madagascar, neglect of higher education by the political leadership after the coup there has had a similar effect, although the newly elected leadership in 2016 seems to be moving in the direction of helping facilitate badly needed higher education change and development after years of neglect.

While I had been aware of the importance of finance in success of the strategic planning process, I had underestimated its significance prior to writing this manuscript. One of the key differences in strategic planning between the developed and underdeveloped nations is the greater fragility of the changes in the latter. In the West, we talk about lack of adequate funding, and there is never enough. But the crises of funding in even the most successful of the cases examined here are only a hair's breadth away from lapsing into disaster in ways that are constantly hanging over the heads of the universities and the higher education systems that contain them. My budget as an associate dean of social sciences at the University of Wisconsin-Madison was greater than the budget for the whole system of thirty-six public universities in Afghanistan. In another example of the consequences of financial shortfalls, the higher education system in Madagascar did not hire any faculty members for more than a decade because of a shortage of funds. There are many other such examples. As noted elsewhere, there is a critical need for a concerted effort to figure out how to improve the funding situation for higher education in underdeveloped and developing nations around the world. Much more attention needs to be paid to this crisis.

Recognition of the Role of Higher Education in Development

The critical role of high-quality higher education in national economic and political development has been recognized and touted since 2002. Both the World Bank and UNESCO have been particularly active in trying to make that clear to governments and institutions of higher education in developing economies (World Bank, 2002; UNESCO, 2006). Yet, in several of the cases reviewed, the political elite, and to some extent the higher education community itself, did not recognize the critical role of high-quality higher education in fostering national development. That was most egregious in Sierra Leone, where following a major effort by the Momoh government that never achieved fruition, for the last seventeen years no government has recognized, or acted upon, the strong evidence of the powerful relationship between development and high-quality higher education. It also seems clear that in neither Malawi nor Uganda has the government acted in ways that would suggest recognition of this strong relationship. It may also be that the higher education community failed to make a strong enough case for those findings in Uganda, though they certainly did in Malawi. While information about the link between high-quality higher education and national development has been talked about and written about[1] in those countries, there is no evidence that their importance has been heeded by their governments. Thus, both higher education and development have suffered.

In general, however, the strong relationship between high-quality higher education and national development is recognized by the leaders of higher education even if not by political leaders. Given the economic conditions in most developing economies and the demand for growth, it is surprising that more government effort is not put into improving the quality of higher education generally. Indeed, the declining levels of funding for higher education in most of the cases we have examined are evidence that suggest that if political leaders are aware of the relationship, they do not see it as important enough to compel them to focus more resources on supporting and building high-quality higher education.

Higher Education in War and Conflict Situations

An important lesson of this study is that major higher education change can take place even in the most difficult conditions, including war. Most of us think of such changes as taking place after war, the Civil War, World War II, the war in Iraq.[2] What is clear about several of these cases, especially Afghanistan, is that transformation can take place even in the midst of war. How did that happen? Part of the success in Afghanistan had to do with the fact that for the most part higher education, unlike primary and secondary education, did not become a target of war between 2001 and 2016, except for two targeted attacks (one in Kandahar the other in Nangarhar), each aimed at a particular person, not the institution. The ministry successfully kept the presence of war off the campuses until that time or kept it at such a low profile that it did not disrupt classes. Political activity on campus was not allowed, and that policy was generally followed. There were some student demonstrations near campuses that suffered from violence and attacks, but those were about non–higher education issues. It was not until two faculty members were kidnapped, on August 8, 2016, near the American University campus that the situation changed. Shortly thereafter, on August 25, the Taliban attacked the campus, killing more than a dozen people including students, faculty members, security, and police who rushed to their aid, as well as the three attackers. That attack was no doubt inspired in part by the fact that this was a U.S.-supported institution, and in part that it was a higher education institution teaching both men and women and in English.

Part of the success of strategic planning in Afghanistan was attributable to the fact that higher education stayed out of politics; though its leaders did not support the Taliban and opposed the war, they stayed out of public discussion about the issue. Some of the chancellors were active in their opposition to the Taliban, as was the chancellor at Nangarhar, who had to deal with its efforts to organize on campus. He therefore became the object of several, unsuccessful assassination attacks, but in general the focus of higher education was on access and quality improvement. After the Taliban, the Islamic State and other small local groups did attack schools, especially girls' schools, in large numbers.[3] The war did put pressure on higher education and have an effect on progress. People were aware of the many demands on the budget exacerbated by the war, relating to health issues, transportation, primary and secondary education, and a host of other needs. People wanted to make substantial progress with the postwar possibilities in mind and also to ensure that today's students had a higher education that would prepare them for the future.

The struggle against apartheid in South Africa had gone on for decades primarily as a guerrilla war. It had devastating consequences for the black population in terms of repression, imprisonment, death, restrictions, and lack of opportunities. Unlike the case in some conflicts, the anti-apartheid organizations' goals for higher education were clear and had been worked out carefully in discussions within the ANC over the years: equality, respect, opportunities for high-quality education at all levels, widespread participation in policymaking, and an end to restrictions based on race and gender. The national elections in April 1994, when they concluded, brought relief to almost everyone. Having been involved in working on the final counts of the election, I will never forget the celebration by people of all races that took place outside the electoral commission office where I was working, people hugging each other, singing, and joyous, and then Nelson Mandela came to join the celebration in an ecstatic victory celebration at the Carlton Hotel.

The coups in Sierra Leone and Madagascar were a different kind of military intervention in that there was not a lot of violence, which, initially at least, resulted in very few deaths. Indeed, some people celebrated the coups, but both resulted in long periods of strife, insecurity, instability, and a halt to the progress on reform and upgrading higher education. Indeed, education and much else was ignored and higher education deteriorated to an extent from which it still has not recovered at the time of writing. Military intervention, and the governments that follow it, seldom help improve higher education or provide the other conditions necessary for successful education reform. The military far too often uses its power to increase its income, corrupt various aspects of government, and stifle free speech and academic freedom. War, such as that in Afghanistan, affects almost every family with the loss of life and injury to civilians and family members in the military or police. Since 2001 at least 28,000 Afghan civilians have been killed and more than 50,000 wounded.[4] While the number of Afghan police and soldiers killed is no longer released, it is estimated that at least 5,000 were killed last year (2018). Almost every Afghan has lost family members or close friends.

The war has left Afghanistan with the highest level of Post-Traumatic Stress Disorder (PTSD) in the world—something that affects more than half of the higher education students at some point during their studies (Babury & Hayward, 2013).

War and civil strife affect almost every aspect of life in Afghanistan, create a high sense of insecurity, and almost always curtail the freedoms, including freedom of speech and the press, so essential to high-quality higher education. They also suck up vast amounts of funding for arms and equipment, and very often lead to levels of corruption in the armed forces and police of a magnitude not seen before. And who is to police the policemen and the military? Generally, no one can. Thus, in spite of the successes in Afghanistan and South Africa in particular, we need to recognize that those successes came at high cost. As one higher education leader said to me in Afghanistan, "All of us are suffering for some level of PTSD."

Careful Strategic Planning with Consensus on Goals and Objectives for Change

An important lesson from the most successful cases discussed here is the critical importance of careful strategic planning, which helped focus attention on what had to be done to bring about change, on who was responsible for each of the goals, on what had to be done to implement change, on the order of implementation, and on steps to be followed in forwarding the process. As we have seen, a key to successful change is consensus on the goals and objectives for change. Without that, there will be little or no progress. While that seems straightforward, we have also seen that this is not always that easy. The challenge to gaining such consensus was most starkly expressed in South Africa, especially in the cases of the University of the North and the University of Fort Hare, where the issue was lack of consensus about the process. The battle against apartheid had been fought nationally, and brought Nelson Mandela and the ANC to power, but the battle was far from won in the minds of many people in positions of authority in the country and on the campuses—especially those at some of the historically black institutions, which had largely been run by Afrikaners, many of whom were still in place as administrators and faculty members and had seen their jobs primarily as consisting of keeping order and exercising control. Most of these people in leadership and faculty positions were fearful of losing power, wanted to maintain their entrenched positions at the institutions, and were determined to undermine efforts to change the system and the culture on campus. They were particularly alarmed by the notion of broad participation and "change from below" in what had, under apartheid, been a very hierarchical system with the minority whites in charge and seeing themselves remaining at the top.

What was impressive about the leaders and activists at both the University of the North and University of Fort Hare, was their patience, persistence, and thoughtfulness in working to bring everyone possible to the table to work out a new plan for higher education at each institution. This effort was complicated on the anti-apartheid side by the existence of the "highly politicized students," as Sipho Pityana noted (Pityana, 1997: 7), who were expecting immediate rewards from their efforts in the struggle now that a victory had been achieved. They were wary of further discussions with the old order and wanted results. Yet, it was essential to bring them to the table as well. Part of what Vice Chancellor Sibusiso Bengu and Sipho Pityana were able to do was to use a kind of moral imperative—to wrap the goals of equality, participation, consensus, and democracy around the moral authority of the struggle, undoing the injustices of racism and unequal education, in ways that embarrassed and won over many of apartheid's defenders. This led to apologies for the past from some of the faculty members and staff as well as commitments to the new order, as we saw in the chapters on South Africa. Eventually, the leaders succeeded in getting almost everyone to the table. That involved making sure that the process as well as the goals and objectives were clear and agreed to by everyone. That was where the "shared understanding" that Vice Chancellor Ndebele emphasized became so important. And with time, patience, and discussion agreements were reached.

Other efforts in other countries to gain consensus were not as difficult to pursue, although the Malawi effort came close to collapse. There, the battle was over control of the academic aspects of the university, decentralization, and financing. Once those differences were resolved, the strategic planning process moved forward relatively easily.

These cases demonstrate how important it is that all the major plan goals are agreed to by most, if not all, faculty members, staff, administrators, and in many cases students. The latter were key to agreement in South Africa. As we have seen, until agreement happens, little progress can be made. Pakistan, at the outset, and Madagascar, early on, as well as the

University for Development Studies in Ghana, demonstrate clearly how those disagreements hold up the process, and if unresolved can destroy any hope of progress. These cases also demonstrate the advantage of the early involvement of a broad spectrum of people in the institutions at all levels in the discussion of the strategic plan and its goals. Sometimes, the disagreements are more a function of the newness of the ideas than a disagreement on principles. Time and understanding are often key to success in the long run.

What is striking, as we look back at each of these change agendas, is the similarity of their goals. All of the plans sought quality improvement (usually with accreditation), upgraded curricula, improved relevance in terms of jobs and development needs, faculty development (more faculty members with master's and PhDs), increased student access (especially for the disadvantaged), improved gender equity, infrastructure upgrading and expansion, improved information technology and access to it, and more effective and efficient governance.

Lessons about Financing Change

All of the cases examined here demonstrate in different ways both the importance of linking the budget to the change plan, and the critical need to carefully develop a realistic budget in terms of expected expenditures, along with realistic assumptions about income. Failure to do so inevitably leads to failure or at least minimal success. Two of the cases examined here, those of Sierra Leone and Uganda, lacked the financial support needed to move forward. In the case of Sierra Leone, most of that was the result of a coup d'état and the ravages that followed. In Uganda, as we saw, it was the failure of leaders to agree on a budget plan, as well as differences of opinion about priorities, and a lack of strong linkages with the Ministry of Finance. It was also a function of confusion about the responsibilities of the National Council for Higher Education and the Ministry of Education and the inability of those in power to sort that out in a way that allowed the strategic plan to be fully funded and implemented.

We also saw that budget and political problems in Malawi sabotaged the excellent strategic and budget plan of the University of Malawi once its leaders had solved their internal difficulties. In that case, although the strategic plan had a well-prepared budget, expected state funding did not materialize. Thus, much of the plan for change was stillborn. This is another example of how important national political leadership can be for success of the higher education change agenda.

These cases demonstrate the centrality of careful budget planning to successful strategic planning for higher education change—budget planning that includes detailed calculations of costs, timing of expenditures, sources of income, priorities, expected income, a risk analysis, and ongoing assessments that allow for changes when costs or income levels diverge from what was planned. The care and time put into working out a budget, doing a risk analysis, checking and rechecking the sources of funding, and allowing for shortfalls, will pay dividends in the long run and help ensure success in higher education strategic planning for change and transformation. Nonetheless, it would be a mistake to assume that financial problems are only a matter of planning. As noted earlier, all of the cases examined here faced actual or potential financial problems. They were all in a fragile position in that regard in ways that are not easy to solve. The pressures on national budgets were severe in many other areas too, including health, transportation, housing, primary and secondary education, and in many cases such as Afghanistan, Pakistan, and South Africa, defense and security. The choice to increase funding for higher education usually came at a cost to other levels of education and to other budget priorities. Unlike much of the West, increasing cost substantially to students was not a realistic option for most underdeveloped nations given the low per capita income, though some ostensibly free higher education was not viable in systems that aspired to high quality. South Africa has made a move for free higher education for poor first-year students, but the World Bank thinks that is not viable in the long run,[5] although some educators think it can be made successful by changing priorities.[6]

Institutionalizing the Change Process

If higher education change is going to have any long-term effects the process itself needs to be institutionalized and, secondly, the changes envisioned in the plan need to become part of the ongoing operation and history of the system or the institution. Thinking about institutionalizing the change process is an activity that should be undertaken from the start of the planning process. The usual way to do that, as we have seen, is through the establishment of a permanent strategic planning office or similar entity that has the function of oversight of strategic planning and can help ensure that the changes desired are put in place and followed over the years.

Effective strategic planning should be viewed as a continuous process. A plan is prepared, implementation begins, the implementation is monitored by the planning office, records are kept about its successes and challenges, problems are resolved or changes made when needed, and progress is followed up by people in the office throughout the time period of the plan. Toward the end of the planning period, plans are begun for the next strategic plan based on the successes of the change efforts in the current plan, unmet goals, and new challenges and needs that are on the agenda for change. As we have seen, when that does not happen, as in Afghanistan, a great deal of time and money is wasted. More importantly the change process should always be seen as ongoing, with new challenges and questions to be resolved.

Conclusion

What Does This Study Suggest for Higher Education in Underdeveloped and Developing Countries in the Future?

As I look back on the examples we have discussed in the preceding chapters, four critical issues for the future of higher education in underdeveloped and emerging economies are clear. They are: (1) There is a financial crisis in higher education—that higher education in almost all the cases examined here suffers from levels of funding that are too low to provide the quality needed for national development in the long term. That creates a broad range of negative consequences, including hindering efforts to improve higher education and build national economies. (2) Educators must do a better job of making the case for strong support for high-quality higher education. They are responsible for the inadequate funding in many, though not all, of the cases examined. If higher education leaders do not make the case for adequate support, who will? (3) There is need for more opportunities for, and participation in, formal professional training programs for university presidents, chancellors, deans, and other leaders, to professionalize them and raise their ability to respond to the increasingly complex challenges facing higher education. Higher education is becoming increasingly technical, with progressively complex financial issues, the need to understand extensive information technology, the growing role of legal challenges, and the greater expectations of specific outcomes in terms of employment. (4) The growing divide between the rich and the poor, with its implications for access to higher education, employment, national development, and stability must be addressed.

The Critical Need to Increase Funding for Higher Education in Underdeveloped and Developing Countries

In almost all the cases examined here the level of funding for higher education was below the minimum necessary for the high-quality higher education required to promote economic and social development in the host country. The average level of funding in the cases examined here was only $840 per capita. While the amount required for a quality education will vary by country, it is, by any accounting, at least two or three times that amount. And, of course, its impact depends on how effectively it is spent. But the basic crisis of underfunding is undeniable.

Many writers, including this one, have been addressing the need to increase funding for higher education in underdeveloped and developing countries for years. In some real sense, "there is never enough funding," so the call for it is often ignored as clichéd. Yet, as we have seen, the consequences of underfunding in some countries has been devastating in ways that often go unrecognized and unresolved. In other countries, the consequences, while less severe, nonetheless limit the ability of universities to produce graduates with the training needed for economic, social, and political development.

What are the areas in which insufficient funding for higher education hurts quality and national development?

- The scarcity of faculty members with PhDs or even master's degrees is the principal problem. Among the countries examined, this was most pronounced in Afghanistan, where at the end of the Taliban period only 35 percent of faculty possessed advanced degrees—a problem no doubt attributable to the long-running war, but also to the cost of acquiring a PhD, which needed to be pursued abroad, since there were no advanced degree programs offered in the country at that time. We see similar problems elsewhere. The fact that faculty members without advanced degrees are teaching obscures the fact that they are not fully qualified, they do little or no research, and often they have no more training than the students they teach. The cost to upgrade their qualifications is substantial, and includes funding for replacement staff. Pakistan did the most impressive job in recognizing and dealing with this problem, sending more than nine hundred faculty members abroad for PhDs during their strategic planning period, with another 4,500 working on advanced degrees at home.

- Limited financing is responsible for restricting opportunities for access in several of the countries we have examined, including Malawi, Uganda, and Afghanistan. This tends to particularly affect the admission of women, who need adequate, safe housing. Sometimes the effort to solve the access problem leads to increased admission in numbers without appropriate expansion of facilities, faculty and staff.

- Quality instruction requires access to well-equipped laboratories, libraries, and other research facilities as well as information technology and textbooks, and as we saw, there were serious deficiencies in almost every case we examined, with physics being taught without functioning laboratories in Afghanistan, limited access to the internet in many countries, and students in Sierra Leone, Afghanistan, and Ghana forced to sit on the floor or stand outside classrooms while class was in session, or take examinations outdoors because of lack of chairs and space within. These problems have profound negative consequences on the quality of student learning.

- In general, faculty salaries are low, often requiring teachers to take second jobs in order to survive. The need for a second job is devastating in many ways, not least that it cuts into the time available to advise students, carry out research, or prepare new material. It is often overlooked that faculty salaries have an international rather than a national comparative base.

- There are many issues that affect the ability of graduates to gain employment, but, as we saw in a number of cases, the poor quality of the curriculum is usually a major factor.

- Many of the universities in the cases we examined, notably those in Madagascar, Uganda, and Afghanistan, have suffered the loss of their best faculty members and many of their best graduates due to the poor conditions. Most of those lost will never return, constituting a huge waste of national resources and potential.

- The low completion rates for students in South Africa, Uganda, Sierra Leone, Madagascar, and elsewhere are another consequence of underfunding, which inhibits the availability of remedial assistance in higher education. It too constitutes a large waste of both resources and human potential.

- Little or no research funding was available in many of these cases (South Africa and Pakistan are exceptions), which helps explain the limited amount or complete lack of research into national problems and the poor training for research at the undergraduate and graduate levels, and constitutes at least part of the reason why these countries are so far behind the rest of the world in knowledge creation.

- All of this adds up to an overall failure to develop knowledge societies in most of the underdeveloped and developing world, and a failure to foster the full creativity and potential for innovation among its young people, thus squandering a vast global resource.

The sad fact is that the consequences of these and other financial shortfalls become cumulative over time: underfunded primary and secondary schools produce underprepared students, who, if they get into universities, often fail to advance to graduation or need costly remediation, which is unavailable thanks to the poor overall quality of university education, especially in science and technology, where the lack of research opportunities and its impact on the quality of teaching hinders development, and so it goes.

What is clear is that almost all of the countries examined here are faced with the need to make a significantly greater investment in higher education. As I noted earlier, the case for the critical importance to national growth of high-quality higher education was made in 2002 by the World Bank in its important study *Constructing Knowledge Societies: New Challenges for Tertiary Education*. In that document, it was stressed that: "social and economic progress is achieved principally through the advancement and application of knowledge." The study emphasized: "Tertiary education is necessary for the effective creation, dissemination and application of knowledge and for building technical and professional capacity" (World Bank, 2002: viii–xix). The bank's staff also noted at that time that "[m]ost universities in developing nations function at the periphery of the international scientific community, unable to participate in the production and adaptation of knowledge necessary to confront their countries' most important economic and social problems" (World Bank, 2002: 59). That continues to be the case almost two decades after publication of this World Bank study. Thus, it is urgent that these countries put more funding into higher education if they are to be able to carry out the development so desperately needed and provide their young people with the opportunities to develop to their full potential. Funding should be more targeted than it is now to ensure that universities offer high-quality graduate education producing the research and well-trained PhDs needed to help foster economic development generally. In the long run, we all benefit from more nations offering access to high-quality higher education and its resulting contributions to their economies, their political stability, and the well-being of their citizens.

The tragedy today is that too few national political leaders seem to understand the importance of such investment, as we can see from the cases we have examined. Indeed, in many of these countries government funding for higher education has decreased in recent years, including Ghana, South Africa, Uganda, Afghanistan, and Madagascar. In South Africa, government funding for higher education decreased from levels covering 49 percent of the cost of a university education in 2000 to 40 percent in 2013. At the same time, student fees grew from 24 percent of the overall cost to 33 percent (Cloete, 2016: 28). As noted earlier, currently the government has a plan to abolish fees for first-year students, but as the World Bank has noted, that may not be sustainable. In some of the examples we reviewed, government funding was regressive, something that governments seem not to have understood. In most cases, regressive funding imposes a higher tax burden on the poor while the funds gained go primarily to subsidize students from rich and middle-class families, who comprise the vast majority of higher education students in all underdeveloped and developing countries. In addition, where there are increased fees, they usually saddle poor students and their families with burdensome loan debts for years to come.

Student fee debt problems in South Africa have recently sparked demonstrations, violence, damage to universities, closures, and a crisis for government, with the problem unresolved in the long run (Cloete, 2016: 28). Patrinos and others have suggested that a better answer to the student debt problem is to find other modes of funding higher education input from students, suggesting the adoption of a system derived from income-based repayment of income-contingent student loans repayable after graduation, as has been done successfully in Australia (Patrinos, 2015).

The responses to the funding crises will no doubt have to be different in each county. In some cases, it is clear that governments are underfunding higher education, as Cloete and others suggest, with low expenditures as a percentage of GDP. Those countries need to be encouraged to increase their expenditures as an investment in national development, knowing also that the multiplier effect is high in terms of the return on such investments in higher education. For some countries, increased student participation in covering some of the costs of higher education will be appropriate. The new Higher Education Strategic Plan for Afghanistan has proposed that students from middle- and upper-class families pay the cost of their board and room at the university, which is now free. The assumption of that cost consumes 28 percent of the budget in Afghanistan—an amount that could at least be cut in half by charging students from middle- to higher-income families for board and room. Those expenses could be charged on a sliding scale, anywhere from 10 to 100 percent starting with those in the lower-middle income range and rising according to the students' ability to pay. Increased contributions by students are also being considered in Malawi and several other countries. When students contribute they tend to take their studies more seriously. Similarly, loan schemes should be considered with a careful look at income-contingent repayment, as Patrinos has suggested (Patrinos, 2015), perhaps starting one year after employment. And there are many other ways by which more income could be directed to raise the quality of higher education, including entrepreneurial efforts by institutions, which proved successful in Pakistan, where university income covered 21 percent of the costs of higher education.[1]

The process of providing funding for high-quality higher education will also require greater targeting of funding. We have seen some examples of that, especially in Pakistan, Afghanistan, and South Africa with their focus on supporting "elite institutions" through various funding mechanisms, including research and publications in South Africa, institutional differentiation in Afghanistan, and science centers and state of the art equipment in Pakistan. This does not have to mean lower quality for the country's second-level institutions, but rather it engages a division of labor in terms of costly programs, including graduate education. Nonetheless, we have not seen the level of differentiation that has taken place in the BRICs with their push for world-class quality institutions, though that has been discussed in Pakistan, South Africa and Afghanistan, as well as Madagascar in an earlier era. The effort to set up a world-class graduate institution in Africa with five campuses (in Algeria, Kenya, Cameroon, Nigeria, and South Africa) through the Pan-African University is a recent effort to move in that direction, though it is in the early stages and faces substantial challenges (Hayward et al., 2018).

The mechanisms for funding higher education are many. What is clear is that most countries in the underdeveloped world are not making a concerted effort to fund higher education at a level that will provide the quality of graduates they desperately need for national economic and social development. Not only is that costly in terms of lack of economic growth, it is likely to pave the way for increased unemployment, failure of the rule of law, and the kind of unrest we have seen in a number of countries that has resulted in destruction, loss of life, and dislocation, but little long-term change. Now is the time to increase the quality of tertiary education in the underdeveloped and developing world to improve the life chances of the nations' young people and the opportunities for national development.

What I want to emphasize is the huge waste of human potential—potential that might make major contributions to improving the economic and social conditions of these nations and fostering growth, political stability, and public well-being, which are adversely affected by both lack of sufficient numbers of places in higher education institutions and high-quality institutions (as we noted in Egypt). The numbers adversely affected are growing quickly and will continue to grow because of population growth, higher levels of primary and secondary education, recognition of greater employment opportunities for university graduates, as well as higher salaries. It is therefore critical that a major effort be made in many more underdeveloped and developing nations to reverse the underfunding trend and create the conditions for the high-quality higher education so important to national development. We have seen some remarkable successes in a number of the cases examined here. It is essential to foster more of them.

Educators Must Do a Better Job Making the Case for More Financial Support for Higher Education in Underdeveloped and Developing Economies

A key to acquiring increased financial support for higher education is that higher education leaders in developing and underdeveloped economies must make a stronger case for increased financial support for higher education than they have in the past. Almost no one is currently making that case, with a few exceptions such as the Higher Education Commission in Pakistan, the Centre for Higher Education Trust[2] (CHET) in South Africa, and a few others. Making the case for higher education is not something the leaders of higher education do well in many countries. Even in the United States, higher education leaders have been slow to make the case effectively. They have assumed it was self-evident. But that is not true anywhere, especially given the other, conflicting demands for funding. If educators don't make the case for adequate funding, who will? Yet, by and large, even in the West, we hear the same arguments and excuses for failure to increase funding—that higher education "is elitist," that it is not productive, that it only benefits the individual student, that faculty members do not work very hard, that higher education is not run in a businesslike fashion, that it needs to be reformed. Those arguments must be refuted. Few if any of the people who make those claims propose solutions that lead to adequate support, either financial or otherwise, for higher education in general.

The situation in underdeveloped and developing countries is much more challenging. As we have seen, the average level of support in the cases examined here is appallingly low at $840. On the other hand, several Asian countries including Japan, South Korea, Singapore, and China have invested heavily in higher education, thereby substantially reducing or eliminating poverty and unemployment. This improved quality has served "to prepare the workforce to take advantage of the high wage manufacturing jobs created by globalized investment. This was complemented by public investment in infrastructure to continue to attract foreign investment" (Nabi, 2016: 2). The debts incurred as a result of that investment were largely offset by increased development revenue. The result was new jobs and greatly improved economies. This should serve as a model for developing and underdeveloped economies.

The failures of most of the developing and underdeveloped world to do the same, as reflected in the inadequate amounts of money being invested in higher education there, guarantees that most of these nations will continue to have substandard higher education and, thus, their economies will remain weak, while thousands of bright young students who otherwise might contribute to national development will not be able to do so. Even those getting a higher education may not receive one with sufficiently high quality to make them marketable, or one that provides the quality of graduates needed overall to help boost national development, or even, for some of them, to find entry-level employment. As a result, we will continue to see the kinds of unrest, violence, and anger we recently saw in the Middle East spread to other parts of the world, as well as a continuation of the mass migration out of Africa and Asia by large numbers of young people searching for work and security.

In the long run, inaction is likely to guarantee growing violence, terrorism, and decay worldwide. It need not be that way, but it is critical that education leaders make a major effort to make a strong case to the public, to politicians, and to donors in order to acquire the funding needed for high-quality higher education in underdeveloped and developing economies, both to foster economic and social development and to guarantee stability. Efforts such as these have met with success in several of the cases we examined, as well as, more recently, in parts of Asia. Surely, a major financial commitment to quality higher education can be implemented in more underdeveloped and developing economies.

The Need for Professional Higher Education Leadership Training

Substantially more professional training opportunities for higher education leaders are badly needed in the developing and underdeveloped world. While we have seen examples of outstanding leadership, these cases also demonstrate the need to develop more professional leaders at all levels. As James R. Davis put it: "An important challenge for colleges and universities today is the cultivation of leadership itself in all corners of the organization, so that collectively the resources of the institution can be marshalled to address the issues spawned by the new era" (Davis, 2003: xvii). We have seen that need expressed clearly in many of the cases examined here. The financial constraints highlighted above make it even more important that leaders be able to maximize what resources they have available to them. It was remarkable, for example, what Afghan higher education was able to do with very limited resources. In some places, higher education leaders have received some formal training, and the help of consultants and experts. In others, lessons were learned on the job, and sometimes, unfortunately, through mistakes along the way.

As higher education around the world becomes more complex, reflecting in particular the impact of globalization and the levels of worldwide economic interdependence that have resulted as a consequence, higher education leadership requires greatly enhanced training in order to understand and be able to deal with a growing range of issues, beginning with those that address the production of knowledge societies, access to networking and information technology, dealing with economic challenges and personnel issues, including a host of legal issues regarding gender equity, fundraising, risk assessment, new requirements governing the environmental impacts of higher education construction, research, protection of human subjects, and other issues.

The developing world would benefit from access to something like the American Council on Education's Fellows Program, a year-long training program for promising young faculty members who have demonstrated an interest in administration. It provides training, including workshops, around the country on higher education issues, plus a mentorship during the year with a prominent senior administrator (usually a college president or vice president) and a great deal of hands-on experience. More than 80 percent of those who have participated are now university presidents or senior administrators. Along those lines, it is good to see the Association of African Universities beginning to provide some leadership training. More is needed. Harvard University hosts an excellent summer program for new university presidents, to fill them in on the latest issues, legal challenges, and other key areas they need to understand. Similar programs should be set up for administrators in underdeveloped and developing areas of the world to give them an advantage as they move into position or continue to serve as senior university administrators. It is imperative that that training include focus on strategic planning for higher education change and transformation.

Among the most obvious deficiencies among higher education leaders in the cases studied here concerned finance. Few of the administrators had received any training in that area, with the notable exception of those in Pakistan, and their work was made much more difficult by their lack of knowledge in critical financial management, human resources, construction, and fund raising. Even in South Africa, with its excellent budget system, there was no training program for senior administrators, a shortcoming that was to haunt universities and technikons over the years. The Organization of African Unity was setting up such a program, but it is not clear how successful that has been. The Council for Higher Education Transformation (CHET) was one of the few NGOs that focused on capacity development, research, training, and publications about higher education in a wide range of areas.[3]

The cases examined in this study demonstrate the need for strong, well-trained leaders with vision, drive, and organizational skills in higher education. While some of these attributes can be obtained on the job, much of the information related to finance, human resources, law, and construction cannot. Also, greater efforts must be made to protect leaders from threats and attacks, not only for their own safety but to demonstrate to aspiring leaders that they will be protected and rewarded for their service. Leadership training is a critical starting point for improved leadership in developing and underdeveloped economies. At the same time, as we have seen, every successful case examined here was also a team effort. That calls for broad leadership training on campuses as well.

Attacking the Growing Divide between Rich and Poor and Its Consequences for the Future of Higher Education Is Critical

It is especially worrying that so many underdeveloped and developing countries suffer from growing economic inequality, which causes anger and dissatisfaction and the spread of unemployment, in particular among uneducated and undereducated young people—a segment of the population that is rapidly increasing in number as these countries continue to fail to satisfy the need among their population for higher education. As Piketty points out, "In the long run, the best way to reduce inequalities with respect to labor as well as to increase the average productivity of the labor force and the overall growth of the economy is surely to invest in education" (Piketty, 2014: 306–307). Contrary to earlier assertions, investment in higher education has a much larger multiplier effect in the developing world than investment in primary and secondary education (Patrinos, 2015). This fact alone should encourage governments to increase their investment in quality higher education. In emphasizing the high rate of return from university education, Harry Patrinos added that "[h]igh private returns signal that tertiary education is a good private investment" (ibid.), which, if true, should encourage private investment in quality higher education alongside public resource allocation.

In most of the cases examined here, the principal beneficiaries of access to higher education are students from middle- and upper-income groups, in some cases, just the nation's elite, which means that a large number of students finish their education in high school or even sooner, and, predictably, find it hard to access employment. Of those students from a low-income background who do manage to gain admission to higher education, many of them and their families incur debts that take years to repay. And if they remain unemployed, the debt can become a survival trap for years to come.

The dropout rates in the countries examined where the data are available are high. In Madagascar, 50 percent of university students fail in the first year, in South Africa only 6 percent graduate within five years and 72 percent do not graduate at all (Cloete, 2016). This exacerbates an already skewed income distribution. These problems need to be attacked. Most distressing is that the little evidence that exists on the family incomes of university students demonstrates that only a small percentage of students in higher education in developing countries come from low-income families. Thus, growing numbers of unemployed youths from low-income groups, many with substantial education debts, are angry, discouraged, and ripe for mobilization by radical groups such as Al Qaeda, Al Shabaab, and ISIS. This problem is growing rapidly, as widely reported (Wadud, January 27, 2017).

Even in countries such as Afghanistan and Malawi, where higher education is theoretically free—that is, without tuition or charges for room and board—there are real costs to students for travel, books, supplies, clothing, and other related needs, which keep many potential students out of higher education. I estimated recently that the out-of-pocket costs for a male student in Afghanistan are about $1,150 per year and for a woman student about $1,400, the higher amount reflecting the higher cost of clothes. That is a lot of money in a country where the average per capita income was $634 a year in 2016, and it prevents many students from seeking further education beyond the high school level (World Bank, 2016e). While the attraction of terrorism is a worry, the real concern should be the potential cost of the lack of opportunities for large numbers of young people, who might otherwise contribute to national development.

Exacerbating the growing gap between rich and poor in most of the countries we have examined is the position of women, who are among the poorest of the poor since in many cultures they often face additional discrimination based on their gender and for the same reason are less likely than men to gain a higher education. There has been excellent progress in gender access in some places such as Madagascar, South Africa, and, recently, Afghanistan, the problem remains acute generally. Any society that excludes large segments of its population from education is eliminating talented people from many of the potential benefits of society and their potential contributions to development. Not only is inclusiveness important in admissions, it is critical in policymaking, where we observe the paucity of women in senior administrative positions that exists in higher education. Women must be provided with training and mentoring so that their participation in administrative positions can be effective. We have seen in South Africa, in spite of major efforts to overcome the racism and sexism of apartheid, that the percentage of people of color in higher education, while increasing, has not reached equality on a per capita basis with the white population, even years after the end of apartheid. In South Africa, the participation of women in undergraduate education is now equal to men, but even there, where gender equality has been a goal from the outset, few women are in senior management positions.

Importantly, growing inequality around the world "is a matter of policies and politics" (Stiglitz, 2015: 416), as Stiglitz correctly states. These are problems that can be solved. Long-term inequalities in access spur unemployment. The lack of a policy voice exacerbates an individual's sense of hopelessness. To prevent that, underdeveloped and developing areas need to do a better job of ensuring equal access to higher education and its governance regardless of gender, race, religion, region, or income. While South Africa, Afghanistan, and several other countries have worked to improve access, but there is still a long way to go to achieve equality and to provide more representative access in policymaking.

Solutions to income inequality are especially hard to achieve, with only a few promising experiments to draw on as examples, such as the income-based repayment schemes mentioned earlier. The question of how to pay for increased access to education for those who lack the minimum funding is difficult. As Piketty notes, "Unfortunately, the data available for addressing issues of educational cost and access in the United States and France are extremely limited." He notes that this is in spite of the fact that both countries give great importance to education to foster social mobility and subscribe to meritocracy (Piketty, 2014: 307). The situation is much worse in the underdeveloped and developing world. What then can we expect from them? The problem must be attacked.

Final Thoughts about Higher Education Change and Transformation

Successful change has resulted from a commitment to human development, and that needs to continue in the future. Such a commitment requires: a focus on well-being, equal opportunities, dignity, justice, and education; a desire for freedom—the space that makes discussion possible, enhances lives, and fosters the ability to develop as one wishes; a belief in democracy—participation, openness, and accountability; a recognition that high-quality higher education is essential to producing national social, economic, and political development; and a desire for equal access to higher education as a condition for long-term development in society.

All of the examples explored in this book took place in countries struggling with poverty, privation, limited health care, and economic hardships for large numbers of their citizens. Many of their citizens also experienced discrimination based on religion, race, ethnicity, gender, or individual beliefs. They sought a different order—one based on justice and fairness. High-quality higher education was seen as part of the solution to building a different kind of society.

In all of the successes chronicled here, the development, discussion, decision making, and implementation of the plans for change happened in a relatively free and open environment. Sen is correct when he suggests that freedoms of individuals are the essential building blocks of development (Sen, 1999). Even in Afghanistan, where freedom of the press is an ongoing battle, the academic environment was free and open throughout this period—a tribute to both the leadership of the higher education sector and the successes of the government in keeping higher education policy largely free of political conflict. In South Africa, we saw that the process did not move forward on the campuses we examined until a free, open, and participatory environment was assured.

I had assumed that I would find striking differences in the process of strategic planning between national and institutional experiences. That was not the case, with the exception of finance. The demands on planners, the issues related to the choice of change goals, questions of implementation, oversight, and conditions for success are very similar. In contrast to my original assumption, both the scale and extent of changes in the cases we have examined here do not bear out my expectations of major differences except in terms of the much greater access to funding at the national in contrast to the institutional level.

※

We have seen examples of remarkable higher education change in a number of different countries—some of which have operated in the most inhospitable environments one can image yet with striking success. We have seen successes based on the determination, creativity, and dedication of people at many levels. And there have been some failures. We have discussed the importance of high-quality strategic plans closely linked to well-crafted and properly funded budgets. Yet, even the successes will flounder in time, if higher education is not adequately funded over time and high quality achieved and maintained. The time frame for that is short in some of these examples and the lack of urgency in many of them is worrying and potentially devastating. I hope some of what is said here will help spur a greater sense of urgency.

Finally, I hope this examination of a number of interesting examples of efforts to bring about higher education quality improvement, change, and transformation in underdeveloped and developing economies through well-developed strategic plans will encourage others by providing ideas and examples that will stimulate their own creativity and help as they carry out the challenges of higher education change in the future anywhere in the world as well as provide useful information about successes elsewhere in the world. These cases provide models, examples, lessons, and suggestions of what can be achieved by those committed to quality improvement and positive change in higher education.

Notes

Preface

1. The American Council on Education (ACE) is a membership organization with more than 1,700 member institutions that looks after the interests of higher education and is a major coordinating body for higher education policy in Washington, D.C. Among its programs were efforts to encourage universities to focus on internationalization, gender equity, and quality improvement.

Introduction

1. Some writers, such as Birnbaum, Robert, (1992), *How Academic Leadership Works: Understanding Success and Failure in the College Presidency*, second edition, San Francisco: Jossey-Bass, avoid that problem by doing a five-year longitudinal study, others make good use of historical data such as that by Michael Cohen and James March, (1986), *Leadership and Ambiguity*, second edition, Boston: Harvard University Press.

2. Drawing on my work and that of M. O. Babury: Hayward, Fred, and M. O. Babury, (2014), "Afghanistan Higher Education: The Struggle for Quality, Merit, and Transformation," *Planning for Higher Education Journal*, v. 42. no. 2, January–March 2014, p. 2.

3. Ibid. In a four-part typology used in the *On Change* project the four quadrants are: adjustments, isolated change, far-reaching change, and transformational change.

4. See also Kellerman, (2016), who suggests that the "leadership industry is dedicated to searching for a savior, a single individual who is apotheosis of the "great man" or great woman" (p. 181).

5. Fragile states are those whose governments are not able to guarantee security, health care, education, or other basic services. According to the World Bank there were thirty-three fragile states in 2013 including

Afghanistan and Sierra Leone. World Bank, (2013), "Twenty Fragile States Make Progress on Millennium Development Goals." News release, May 1, downloaded from: www.worldbankorg/en/news/press.release/2013/05/01/twenty-fragile-states-make-progress-on-millennium-development-goals.

6. For a very useful study of networks and their influence on change see: Castells, Manuel, (2015), *Networks of Outrage and Hope: Social Movements in the Internet Age*, second edition, Cambridge: Polity Press.

Chapter 1. The Critical Role of High-Quality Higher Education for National Development

1. BRICS (or earlier, before South Africa joined, BRICs) is an acronym of emerging economies that includes Brazil, Russia, India, China, and later South Africa. They are seen to be at similar levels of development. They have met each year to discuss economic and other issues since 2009.

2. *Education for All* was a program led by UNESCO with a goal of providing basic education for all children around the world by 2015.

3. IMF, (2018), *Regional Economic Outlook: Sub-Saharan Africa, Domestic Revenue Mobilization and Private Investment*, Washington, DC: IMF, p. 1, notes that growth in Burkina Faso, Côte d'Ivoire, Ethiopia, Ghana, Guinea, Rwanda, Senegal, and Tanzania grew by 6 percent or more in 2017.

4. Pakistan is one of the few to have an effective system of rewards for high-quality faculty members. It is tied to the tenure system introduced with the strategic plan, as discussed in chapter 3.

5. For a discussion of SWOT analysis see Hayward and Ncayiyana, (2003), *Strategic Planning: A Guide for Higher Education Institutions*, Cape Town: Centre for Higher Education Transformation, pp. 38–40.

6. For a more detailed discussion of strategic planning see ibid., p. 3.

7. I attended a number of meetings in which senior higher education or ANC leaders, who tried to intervene, were reminded that they could not speak again until everyone had a turn who wanted one. Several of the meetings included students from the universities.

8. As Peter Northhouse emphasizes with leaders having the "knowledge and abilities [that] are needed for effective leadership." Northhouse, (2016), *Leadership: Theory and Practice*, Seventh Edition, Thousand Oaks, California: Sage, p. 43.

9. The key question is, Do the higher education policy and the changes planned "meet the needs of conflict-affected populations for inclusive and quality education in equitable ways that do not contribute to grievances, intergroup tensions or conflict?" INEE, (2003), "INEE Guidance Note on Conflict Sensitive Education," New York: INEE, p. 18.

10. Recently there were 200,000 vacancies in Egypt while many times that number of people in those fields were unemployed. They did not meet the qualifications of employers in their own fields, mostly a function of the poor quality of the education they received. Ghafar, (2016), "Educated but Unemployed: The Challenge Facing Egypt's Youth," Washington, DC: Brookings, pp. 4–5.

11. See the discussion of transformational leadership in Kezar, Carducci, and Contreras-McGavin, (2006), *Rethinking the "L" Word in Higher Education: The Revolution of Research on Leadership*, San Francisco: ASHE, Wiley, pp. 34–35.

12. Burns writes that "transforming leadership raises the level of human conduct and ethical aspirations of both leader and led, and thus it has a transforming effect on both." Burns, (1978), *Leadership,* New York: Harper and Row, p. 20.

Chapter 2. Prelude to Planning in Higher Education

1. For a more extensive discussion of this period in Sub-Saharan Africa see Hayward and Ncayiyana, (2014), "Confronting the Challenges of Graduate Education in Sub-Saharan Africa and Prospects for the Future," *International Journal of African Higher Education*, vol. 1, no. 1, pp. 173–216.

2. Interview by the author with President Siaka Stevens during June 1984.

3. The Asian data should be looked at with some skepticism since it suffered from the same types of problems of data that Jerven noted for Africa.

Chapter 3. Leading Change in Pakistani Higher Education

1. Some of this section draws from my earlier piece, "Political and Economic Instability and Higher Education Transformation in Pakistan," *International Higher Education*, vol. 54, Winter 2009, pp. 19–20.

2. In the 2015 rankings of Asian universities, India had nine in the top one hundred and Pakistan had none. See IELTS, (2015) "The Top 250 Universities in Asia 2015," Cambridge, England: British Council, pp. 9–13.

3. Personal communications by the author with Atta-ur-Rahman, January 7, 2017.

4. Interview with Prof. Atta-ur-Rahman by the author, August 4, 2016.

5. TTS stands for Tenure Track System.

6. The author was part of one of those teams in 2005–06.

7. Interview with Atta-ur-Rahman, August 6, 2016.

8. Interview with Atta-ur-Rahman, August 2016.

9. Ibid.

Chapter 4. Afghan Higher Education

1. These included the Commission on Quality Assurance and Accreditation, the Curriculum Commission, and the Commission on Rules and Responsibilities.
2. Interview by the author of a faculty leader, October 2013.
3. In 2012, it was reported by Afghanistan's Ministry of Education that "550 schools in 11 provinces where the Taliban have strong support had been closed down by insurgents." See Reuters, "Afghan School Attack: Students, Teachers Poisoned in Takhar Province," *Huffington Post World*, May 24, 2012.
4. In an excellent book on learning, Jane Vella lists twelve principles for learning, including safety. See especially part I: Vella, (2002), *Learning to Listen, Learning to Teach: The Power of Dialogue in Education Adults: Revised Edition*, San Francisco: Jossey-Bass.
5. For the final report and recommendations, see Hayward and Amiryar, (2003), "Final Report: Feasibility Study on Private Sector Involvement in Tertiary Education in Afghanistan," Washington, DC: Academy for Educational Development and the International Development Agency of the World Bank.
6. A review committee was set up in 2013–14 to review private higher education at the request of President Karzai. That review was carried out on 256 faculties around the country and the committee recommended that eleven be closed and nineteen put on notice that they must improve in a semester or be closed or merged. Unfortunately, interference by the then minister prevented that from taking place and the problem remained in 2016.
7. For a more complete discussion of the transformation in Afghanistan, see Hayward, (2015), *Transforming Higher Education in Afghanistan: Success Amidst Ongoing Struggles*, Ann Arbor: Society for College and University Planning.
8. See for example: MoHE, "Current State of the Implementation of the National Higher Education Strategic Plan: 2010–2014, September 26, 2011. Unpublished report prepared by the Higher Education Project.
9. Early in the discussions about the strategic plan in Afghanistan, there was some objection by several vice chancellors from the South. They made their objections known, but gained no support, and the process moved forward.

Chapter 5. Bringing National Education Transformation to South Africa

1. "Black," in this context, is used to refer to part of the majority population of South Africa that was discriminated against. Historically, the group was divided into African, Coloured, and Indian/Asian. The term *black* is also

used to describe people of "black" African descent, in contrast to Coloured and Indian, which is sometimes confusing.

2. A few students were admitted with permission of the minister of education or through other dispensations, but by 1953 only 1,064 Africans had graduated from a university since 1652 (Moleah, 1993, pp. 415–416).

3. The term *coloured* referred to people of mixed race. A recent, fascinating article (Quintana-Muret et al., [2010–11]), has explored the origin of the Coloured population. The authors conclude that their origins are primarily found in five population groups: Khoisan, Bantu, European, Indian, and Southeast Asian. The predominant group was the Khoisan peoples (more than 60 percent), with an almost negligible maternal contribution by Europeans. The major group contributions in the early days were from "massive maternal contributions of Khoisan peoples and the almost negligible contact with respect to their paternal counterparts." The overall picture of the South African Coloured population today reflects mainly early contact with Europeans but minimal contact with European women. The major early contact was between Khoisan and African males and autochthonous Khoisan females (Quintara–Muret, 2010–11).

4. Part of this discussion draws upon an unpublished piece written by the author, Teboho Moja, and Nico Cloete in 1955 entitled "Change in Higher Education," which was a think piece on strategic planning funded through a Ford Foundation Pilot Project on higher education change in South Africa.

5. Part of the national effort to encourage a dialogue was the suggestion that each campus set up a *Transformation Form* which would have strong representation from students and staff. However, there was confusion about how much authority it would have, how it would work with other governance bodies, and in the end the few that were set up were not successful and were discontinued on most campuses.

6. Kezar and Lester present an interesting, if far too brief, discussion of "collective leadership" in contrast to "top-down" leadership, seeing it as a "dramatic departure" in the literature on leadership. I see its importance particularly in the South Africa case—indeed, it proved critical to success. Adrianna Kezar and Jaime Lester, (2011), *Enhancing Campus Capacity for Leadership: An Examination of Grassroots Leaders in Higher Education*, Stanford, CA: Stanford University Press, pp. 6–7.

7. Dr. B. E. (Blade) Nzimande was ANC Minister of Higher Education from 2009–2017.

8. Funding for the historically black institutions, designed to make up for the inadequacies of funding in the past.

9. Paraphrased from a speech by Minister SME Bengu, "Review of Transformation in Higher Education: 1994–1999," January 26, 1999, Pretoria: Department of Education, pp 1–3.

10. I attended a number of meetings in which senior higher education or ANC leaders, who tried to intervene, were reminded that they could not speak again until everyone had a turn who wanted one. Several of the meetings included students from the universities.

11. Because of the apartheid system, most primary and secondary schools in predominately black areas had inferior curricula and less well trained teachers. All levels of education were affected by the differential funding of apartheid, with the schools for white children receiving far more funding than the others, per capita.

12. The analysis noted here is discussed in more detail in Pilot Project Consortium, (2001), *Implications of the New Higher Education Framework*, Cape Town: CHET, chapter 2.

Chapter 6. Three Cases of Institutional Transformation in South Africa

1. The author was project director of the South Africa Project, funded through the American Council on Education by the Ford Foundation and USAID.

2. At the request of the participating vice chancellors, each institution chose an American university president from a list of candidates prepared by ACE to serve as its senior associate, visiting the institution twice a year for at least two weeks each time, for two years. This was a major contribution on the part of the presidents, for whom being away from campus for one month a year was a major sacrifice.

3. He had been warned by ANC intelligence units on two separate occasions that there was a team out to kill him. He managed to swerve his car the first time they tried, so the shooter missed. The perpetrators were arrested before they could act on the second occasion. He had broken with the leadership of Inkatha some years earlier in a disagreement over methods. The second attempt was thwarted when a student tipped off security that armed assassins were on campus and they were caught before they could attack the vice chancellor.

4. The ethic of justice paradigm focuses on social justice, human freedom, and the equal rights of all people. For an excellent short discussion of the ethics of justice paradigm see: Joan Shapiro and Jaqueline Stefkovich, (2011), *Ethical Leadership and Decision Making in Education: Applying Theoretical Perspectives to Complex Dilemmas*, New York: Routledge, p. 11.

5. Confidential interview with one of the finance specialists sent to clear up the problems, March 2018.

6. Journals established primarily to make money, with low standards for acceptance of articles, and often fake boards and review processes. The government has worked to end that practice.

7. For a detailed analysis of the merger process and policies leading to its failure see Dinkwanyone Kaglema Mohuba and Krishna Govender, (2016) "The Merger of Historically Disadvantaged Tertiary Institutions in South Africa: A Case Study of the University of Limpopo," *Cogent Business Management*, no. 3.

8. Personal communication with Professor Njabulo Ndebele, 2007.

9. Working with the South Arica Project facilitated by the American Council on Education and funded by the Ford Foundation and USAID from 1993 to 1997.

10. Njabulo Ndebele, (2007), "Strategic Planning at the University of the North—South Africa: 1993," personal communication to the author February 28, 2007.

11. Each institution in the project was able to choose an American university president from a list of willing presidents who would work with the vice chancellor and his staff on the strategic plan, going to South Africa at least twice for two weeks each year. Delores Cross was president of Chicago State University.

12. A particularly South African type of demonstration knee high jog in which the participants dance while moving forward shouting slogans and demands, usually pumping their fists at the same time.

13. That program included $309,783 in funding for "student success and development," including tutorials, improved English proficiency, training staff on alternative methods of instruction, skills programs, supplementary instruction, with fifty-seven total programs. See David Bleazard, (1997), "Summary of Earmarked Funding Projects Related to the Strategic Objectives," Cape Town, South Africa: Peninsula Technikon.

14. The funding added for research projects was $202,644. See ibid.

15. Personal communication with former rector Brian Figaji, November 15, 2016.

16. Site visit by the author and others with senior staff of the Ministry of Higher Education and the institute staff at Cape Peninsula University of Technology, March 6–14, 2018.

Chapter 7. Challenges for Higher Education Change in Sierra Leone

1. The team consisted of Dr. James T. Riodan, an economist and associate director of MUCIA, Professor Russell T. Odell, professor of agronomy emeritus, and the author, a professor of political science at the University of Wisconsin, Madison.

2. Fourah Bay College had been funded by the Colonial Office, the Church Missionary Society, and other sources but was taken on as the

responsibility of the Government of Sierra Leone as a national institution in 1954. See, C. P. Foray, (1979), "An Outline of Fourah Bay College History: 1827–1977," Public Lecture, October 26, 1977, Sesquicentennial of Fourah Bay College. p. 24.

3. A report in *West Africa* suggested that Sierra Leone's was among the lowest in Africa. Its literacy level in 1990 was only 15 percent, compared to Tanzania with 85 percent, Nigeria 42 percent, and Guinea 48 percent. *West Africa*, February 5–11, 1990, pp. 170–171.

4. Which later became a political party until 2007.

5. I was serving as advisor to the president in support of his efforts to return the country to a multiparty democracy. It had become a one-party state legislatively under former president Siaka Stevens.

6. Interview with President Momoh, April 1992.

7. I am indebted to Jimmy Kandeh for this and other updates on the higher education situation in Sierra Leone, September 2, 2018.

8. In 1993, the National Patriotic Front of Liberation initiated an investigation into the finances of the Fourah Bay College and found mismanagement of finances, irregularities with examinations, and reported that there had been no financial audit for the last ten years. In spite of the report, little was done to correct or improve the situation. See: Daniel J. Paracka Jr., (2003), *The Athens of West Africa: A History of International Education at Fourah Bay College, Freetown, Sierra Leone*, New York: Routledge, pp. 230–231.

9. For an excellent description of this corruption see Jimmy Kandeh, (2008), "Rogue Incumbents, Donor Assistance and Sierra Leone's Second Post-Conflict Elections of 2007," *The Journal of Modern African Studies*, vol. 46, no. 4, pp. 603–635.

10. Ecomog stands for the Economic Community of West African States Monitoring Group.

11. Ministry of Education, Science and Technology, (2007), "Sierra Leone Education Sector Plan: A Roadmap to a Better Future," especially chapter 8, "Meeting Our Human Resources Needs through Higher Education."

12. Arab News (2018), "IMF Agrees to New Loan Program for Sierra Leone," *Arab News*; downloaded February 19, 2019, from http://www.arabnews.com/node/1414131/business-economy.

13. Personal communication from Jimmy Kandeh, September 2, 2018.

Chapter 8. Fostering Higher Education Change in Uganda

1. Ugandan tertiary education institutions included: 25 universities (4 public, 10 licensed private, 11 unlicensed private); 12 national teacher's colleges;

6 technical colleges; 5 colleges of commerce; 3 agricultural colleges; 1 forestry college; 2 cooperative colleges; 2 hotel and tourism colleges; 13 medical training institutions; 3 vocational training colleges; 2 aeronautical institutes; 1 land survey institute; 2 fishery institutes; and 9 theological institutes.

2. This represents a summary of concerns expressed by the executive director, A. B. K. Kasozi in his introduction to the conference, July 25–30, 2004. See Kasozi, (2004), p. 6.

3. Personal correspondence between Prof. Kasozi and the author, September 3, 2004.

4. Ian Bunting, Nico Cloete, and François van Schalkwyk, (2014), *An Empirical Overview of Eight Flagship Universities in Africa: 2001–2011*, Cape Town: CHET, emphasize that it came second in knowledge production after Cape Town in its study of flagship universities.

Chapter 9. Madagascar

1. The author was that consultant, and I spent a good deal of time in Madagascar over the next few years.

2. This section draws some material from an earlier work: Fred Hayward and Hanitra Rasoanampoizina, (2007), "Planning for Higher Education Change in Madagascar," *International Higher Education*, number 46, Winter 2007, pp. 18–20.

3. There was some evidence of French government involvement in the coup. See for example: "Dear France, Thank You for the 2009 Coup," *Madagascar Express*, March 5, 2012.

4. This was also manifest in their unhappiness, publicly expressed, that an American was now advisor to the Minister of Higher Education, rather than the usual Frenchman. The author was that advisor.

5. The author witnessed the march from a nearby restaurant and the shooting that followed.

6. Independent contact with employees in the Ministry of National Education and Scientific Research, August 2016.

Chapter 10. Ghana

1. Commenting on the tri-semester work in the communities, one commenter stated: "We are happy that your students live with us in our local homes when they come. That way we are able to know each other." There were other positive comments about the projects that resulted. UDS, (2003), *Strategic Plan: 2003-2008, Third Draft*, Tamale: University for Development Studies, p. 21.

2. The author provided that consultation through the Carnegie Corporation during the period October 2002 through April 2003, making several trips to the area and visiting each of its campuses.

3. This was built around a three-term system each year with the first two being regular classes and the third the field work with teams as described above. Thus, the discussion of the "tri-semester field plan."

4. Kaburise, John, personal communication, February 17, 2007.

5. A student-centered multidisciplinary model of medicine.

Chapter 11. The University of Malawi

1. The author and Dr. Daniel Ncayiyana would be asked to assist with a national higher education strategic plan a few years later in 2006, with USAID funding their participation through the Academy for Higher Education Development (AED).

2. This section draws from material in the report by the author and Daniel Ncayiyana, See Fred Hayward and Daniel Ncayiyana, (2006), "Report on the National Education Sector Plan Project Malawi: 30 October–18 November 2006," Washington, DC: World Bank.

3. These students have records that make them eligible for admission but are below the cutoff point for fully subsidized admission.

4. These plans were very well done and demonstrated a good understanding of what was required for a useful strategic plan. That for the college of medicine, for example, "Strategic Plan: Towards 2020," focused on increasing the number of doctors produced to sixty a year, emphasizing clinical specialists, promotion of research, student-focused learning, expansion of land and infrastructure, and increasing its staff to accommodate needs. See: College of Medicine, (2004), "Strategic Plan: Towards 2020," Blantyre: College of Medicine, p. 3.

5. For an interesting article on that possibility, see Joy Ndovi, (September 2018), "Students Pin Hopes on Successful University Unbundling," University World News, downloaded September 10, 2018, from http://www.univeristy.worldnews.com/article.php?story=20180904.

Chapter 12. Strategic Planning Challenges at Kabul Polytechnic Institute

1. There are no data for women student numbers in 2006, but in 2010 the total number of women was fifty-four, amid 588 males, or 9.2 percent of the students in that year according to MoHE data, and it was probably about that number in 2006.

2. Comments to the author, January 2006.

Chapter 13. Implications for Leadership and Leading Transformational Change in Developing Countries

1. Personal communication with Vice Chancellor George Lenyai of Technikon Northern Transvaal, 2005.
2. Personal communication with Prof. Atta-ur-Rahman, August 6, 2016.
3. Among his books are *Fools and Other Stories*, which won the Noma Award, and *Rediscovery of the Ordinary: Essays on South African Literature and Culture*, as well as many articles and commentaries.
4. I am indebted to Eckel et al. for this description, in P. Eckel, M. Green, B. Hill, and W. Mallon, (1999), *On Change III: Taking Charge of Change: A Primer for Colleges and Universities*, Washington, DC: American Council on Education. Retrieved January 9, 2014, from: www.osu.edu/eminence/assets/files/On_ChangeIII.pdf.
5. This was the attack on American University Afghanistan on August 24, 2016, in which several students and faculty members were killed as well as a number of police and security force members who responded. It was preceded a few weeks earlier by the kidnapping of two faculty members, one American, one Australian, who remained in captivity at the time this is written in 2019.

Chapter 14. The Nature of Change and Transformation in Higher Education in Developing Countries

1. In Uganda, the link between high-quality higher education and national development was discussed extensively in the higher education workshop of chancellors and heads of higher education institutions hosted by the Uganda National Council for Higher Education in 2004, and in Malawi during work on the national higher education strategic plan in 2006.
2. For example, see Savo Heleta, (2015), "How to Rebuild Higher Education in Countries Torn Apart by War," based on "Higher Education in Post-Conflict Societies: Settings, Challenges and Priorities," in *Handbook of Internationalisation of European Higher Education*, Vol. 1, Stuttgart: Raabe Verlag.
3. A major effort has been made to keep education out of war around the world. See for example GCPEA, (2012), "Lessons in War: Military Use of Schools and Other Education Institutions during Conflict," New York: Global Coalition to Protect Education from Attack.
4. No one has accurate figures on civilian or military deaths in Afghanistan, but these numbers are probably low. See CBS, (2018), "Civilian Casualties Down, Airstrike Deaths Up in Afghanistan," (2018); downloaded February 14, 2019, from https://www.cbsews.com/news/afghanistan-us-coalition-airstrikes-civilian-deaths=casualti....
5. See the discussion of the free higher education plan that would support nine out of ten students, and which the World Bank thinks is not viable,

suggesting several other options. World Bank, (2019), "South African Economic Update: Increasing South African Tertiary Education"; downloaded February 20, 2019, from http://www.worldbank.org/en/country/southafrica/publication/south.

6. For an interesting article that suggests that free higher education is possible in South Africa see the piece by long-time educator Saleem Badat, (2010), "South Africa: Free Higher Education—Why Not?" *University World News*, March 28, 2010, p. 1.

Conclusion

1. Entrepreneurial efforts can also be a trap with high costs as we have seen in many such failed efforts in the United States and elsewhere. They need to be carefully considered and assessed before embarking on them.

2. Formerly called the *Centre for Higher Education Transformation*.

3. See, for example, the CHET publications on higher education finance, governance, and strategic planning, www.chet.org.za.publications.

Works Cited

Altbach, P. (2011). *Leadership for world-class universities: Challenges for developing countries*, New York, NY: Routledge.

Arab News (2018). IMF agrees new loan program for Sierra Leone. *Arab News*; downloaded February 19, 2019, from http://www.arabnews.com/node/1414131/business-economy.

Aring, M. (2012). Report on skills gap. Paris, France: UNESCO.

Atta-ur-Rahman, Kemal, A., Siddiqui, R. et al. (circa 2000). *Science and technology based industrial vision of Pakistan's economy and prospects of growth*. Islamabad, Pakistan: Pakistan Institute of Development Economics.

Babury, M. O., & Hayward, F. (2013, September 26). A lifetime of trauma: Mental health challenges for higher education in a conflict environment in Afghanistan. *Education Policy Analysis, vol 21*(70).

Babury, M. O., & Hayward, F. (2014, January–March). Afghanistan higher education: The struggle for quality, merit, and transformation. *Planning for Higher Education Journal, vol. 42*(2).

Babury, M. O., & Hayward, F. (2017). Challenges for higher education in Afghanistan in nurturing economic development. In *Going global: Building nations, connecting cultures*, Vol. 6. London, UK: British Council and Institute of Education Press.

Badat, S. (2010, March 28). South Africa: Free higher education—why not? *University World News: Africa Edition*, p. 1.

Bailey, T. (2014). *The role and functions of higher education councils and commissions in Africa: A case study of the Uganda National Council for Higher Education*. Cape Town, South Africa: Centre for Higher Education Transformation.

Bengu, S. M. E. (1999, January 26). *Review of transformation in higher education: 1994–1999*. Pretoria, South Africa: Department of Education.

Bensimon, E., & Neumann, A. (1994). *Redesigning collegiate leadership: Teams and teamwork in higher education*. Baltimore, MD: Johns Hopkins University Press.

Birnbaum, R. (1992). *How academic leadership works: Understanding success and failure in the college presidency,* 2nd ed. San Francisco, CA: Jossey-Bass.

Bleazard, D. (1997). Summary of earmarked funding projects related to the strategic objectives. Cape Town, South Africa: Peninsula Technikon, internal document.

Bloom, D., Canning, D. & Rosenberg, L. (2011). Demographic change and economic growth in South Asia. Program on Global Demography of Aging, Working Paper no 67, Harvard, downloaded, July 8, 2016, from: www.hsph.harvard.edu/pgda/working.htm.

Bunting, I. (1994). *A Legacy of inequality: Higher education in South Africa.* Cape Town, South Africa: UCT Press.

Bunting, I., & Cloete, N. (2007). *Governing access.* Cape Town, South Africa: Centre for Higher Education Transformation.

Bunting, I., Cloete, N., & van Schalkwyk, F. (2014). *An empirical overview of eight flagship universities in Africa: 2001–2011.* Cape Town, South Africa: CHET.

Burns, J. M. (1978). *Leadership.* New York, NY: Harper & Row.

Carnoy, M. et al. (2013). *University expansion in a changing global economy: Triumph of the BRICs?* Stanford, CA: Stanford University Press.

Castells, M. (2012). *Networks of outrage and hope: Social movements in the internet age.* Cambridge, MA: Polity Press.

Castells, M., & Himanen, P., eds. (2014). *Reconceptualizing development in the global information age.* Oxford, UK: Oxford University Press.

CBS. (2018). Civilian casualties down, airstrike deaths up in Afghanistan; downloaded February 14, 2019, from https://www.cbsews.com/news/afghanistan-us-coalition-airstrikes-civilian-deaths=casualti...

Centre for Higher Education Transformation. (2001). *Implications of the new higher education framework.* Pretoria, South Africa: CHET.

Centre for Higher Education Transformation. (2002). *Transformation in higher education: Global pressures and local reaction in South Africa.* Cape Town, South Africa: CHET.

Clark, B. (1998). *Creating entrepreneurial universities: Organizational pathways of transformation,* Issues in Higher Education. New York, NY: Elsevier.

Cloete, N. (2009). Comments on the CHE's The State of Higher Education Report: 2009. Cape Town, South Africa: CHET.

Cloete, N. (2016). Free higher education: Another self-destructive South African policy. Centre for Higher Education Transformation; downloaded July 4, 2016, from: http://chet.org.za/files/Higher%20education%20and%20Self%20destructive%20policies%2030%20Jan%2016.pdf.

Cloete, N., Bunting, I. & Bailey, T. (2017). Fort Hare at its centenary: University functions in post-apartheid South Africa. *Development Southern Africa.* London, UK.

Cohen, M., & March, J. (1986). *Leadership and ambiguity: The American college president*, 2nd ed. Cambridge, MA: Harvard University Press.
College of Medicine. (2004). *Strategic plan: Towards 2020*. Blantyre, Malawi: College of Medicine.
Collier, P. (2007). *The bottom billion: Why the poorest countries are failing and what can be done about it.* Oxford, UK: Oxford University Press.
Cronin, T. (1995). Thinking and learning about leadership. In J. T. Wren, *Leader's companion: Insights on leadership through the ages.* New York, NY: Free Press.
Curaj, A. et al., eds. (2015). *Mergers and alliances in higher education: International practice and emerging opportunities.* New York, NY: Springer.
Dandy, D. (2015, December 1). Tears of Fourah Bay College—the University of Sierra Leone. *Sierra Leone Telegraph*; downloaded, May 24, 2016, from www.thesierraleonetelegaph.com/?p=10951.
Davis, J. (2003). *Learning to lead; A handbook for postsecondary administrators.* Washington, DC: American Council on Education.
Deltombe, T. (2012, March). La France, acteur-clé de la crise malgache. *Le Monde diplomatique.*
Department of Education. (1997). *Higher education action, 1997.* Cape Town, South Africa: Department of Education.
Department of Education. (2005). *White paper on education and training.* Cape Town, South Africa: Department of Education.
Department of Education. (2006). *Green paper on higher education transformation.* Pretoria, South Africa: Department of Education.
Dewar, B., Massey, S., & Baker, B. (2013). *Madagascar: Time to make a fresh start*, London, UK: Chatham House.
Diplomat. (August 2018). Pakistan's economic crisis; downloaded August 15, 2018, from https://the diplomat.com/2018/08/pakistan's economic crisis.
Dunya News. (2016, September 8). HEC to send 10,000 scholars to U.S for PhD studies. *University World News*; downloaded September 12, 2016, from http://dunyanews.tv/en/Pakistan/352551-HEC-to-send-100000scholars.
Eckel, P., Green, M., Hill, B., & Mallon, W. (1999). *On change III: Taking charge of change: A primer for colleges and universities.* Washington, DC: American Council on Education; retrieved January 9, 2014, from: www.osu.edu/eminence/assets/files/.
Economist Intelligence Unit. (2014). High university enrollments, low graduate employment: Analyzing the paradox in Afghanistan, Bangladesh, India, Pakistan, and Sri Lanka. London, UK: *The Economist*.
Eisenhower, D. D. (1957). From a speech at the National Defense Executive Reserve Conference in Washington, DC, on November 14, 1957, downloaded on September 1, 2016 from http://herdingcats.typedpad.com/my_welog/2016/02/quote-of-the-day.

Foray, C. P. (1979). An outline of Fourah Bay College history: 1827–1977. Public Lecture 26, October 1977, Sesquicentennial of Fourah Bay College.
Figaji, B. (2007). Strategic planning at Peninsula Technikon. Personal correspondence with the author.
Freedom House. (2016). Afghanistan freedom of the Press 2016; downloaded January 17, 2017, from https://freedomhouse.org/report/freedom-press/2016/afghanistan.
Gardner, T. (2014, January 20). Fourah Bay College: The decline of Sierra Leone's "Oxford in the Bush." *The Salone Monitor*, Freetown, Sierra Leone.
Gasikara, T. (2015). Madagascar—Dossier Special Coup D'état du 17 Mars 2009. World Press; cited from http://tsimoki Gasikaraworldpress/2015/03/17 madagascar-dossier-special-coup-detadu17mars2009/.
GCPEA. (2012). *Lessons in war: Military use of schools and other education institutions during conflict*. New York: Global Coalition to Protect Education from Attack.
Ghafar, A. A. (2016). *Educated but unemployed: The challenge facing Egypt's youth*. Washington, DC: Brookings.
Ghani, A., & Lockhart, C. (2008). *Fixing failed states: A framework for rebuilding a fractured world*. Oxford, UK: Oxford University Press.
Ghumman, K. (2006, May 29). QAU faculty awaits TTS implementation. *Dawn*.
Goldman, C., & Salem, H. (2015). *Getting the most out of university strategic planning: essential guide for success and obstacles to avoid*. Santa Monica, CA: Rand.
Government of Afghanistan. (2009). *National higher education strategic plan: 2010–2014*. Kabul, Afghanistan: Ministry of Higher Education.
Government of Afghanistan. (2016). *National higher education strategic plan: 2016–2020*. Kabul, Afghanistan: Ministry of Higher Education.
Government of India. (2016). University and higher education. New Delhi: Government of India; downloaded on August 1, 2016, from http://mhrd.gov.in/university-and-higher-education.
Government of Sierra Leone. (2012). The agenda for prosperity: Sierra Leone's third generation poverty reduction strategy paper (2013–2018); downloaded May 25, 2016, from: http://www.undp.org/content/dam/sierraleone/docs/projectdocuments/povreduction/undp_sle_The%20Agenda%20for%20Prosperity%20.pdf.
Government of South Africa. (1959). *Extension of Universities Act, Act No 45*. Cape Town, South Africa: Government of South Africa.
Graham-Harrison, E. (2014, February 24). New Afghan law to silence victims of violence against women. *The Guardian*.
Green, M., & Hayward, F. (1997). Forces for Change. In M. Green (Ed.), *Transforming higher education: Views from leaders around the world* (pp. 3–26). Washington, DC: American Council on Education.

Hall, M. (2015). Institutional culture of mergers and alliances in South Africa. In Adrian Curaj et al. (Eds.), *Mergers and alliances in higher education: International practice and emerging opportunities*. New York, NY: Springer.

Hayward, F. (1995). Sierra Leone: First steps in the return to multiparty democracy. In Marion Doro & Colin Legum (Eds.), *Africa Contemporary Record*, vol. 22, 1989–90, New York, NY: Holmes and Meier.

Hayward, F. (1998). Sierra Leone: Reestablishing multiparty democracy. In Colin Legum (Ed.), *Africa Contemporary Record*, vol. 23, 1990–92. New York, NY: Africana.

Hayward, F. (2002). Report to the Carnegie Corporation: Strategic and Financial Planning at the University for Development Studies, the University of Education at Winneba and preliminary discussions with the Committee of Vice Chancellors and the National Council for Tertiary Education. Unpublished document.

Hayward, F. (2004, October). The Uganda strategic plan for higher education 2003–2005: Strengths, challenges, and prospects for implementation. *The Uganda Higher Education Review, vol. 1*(1), 28–31.

Hayward, F. (2005). Progress report on KPU strategic plan. Unpublished report.

Hayward, F. (2008, April-June). Strategic planning for higher education in developing countries: Challenges and lessons. *Planning for Higher Education, vol. 36*(3).

Hayward, F. (2009, Winter). Political and economic instability and higher education transformation in Pakistan. *International Higher Education, vol. 54*, 19–20.

Hayward, F. (2015). *Transforming higher education in Afghanistan: Success amidst ongoing struggles*. Ann Arbor, MI: Society for College and University Planning.

Hayward, F., & Amiryar, S. (2003). *Feasibility study on private sector involvement in tertiary education in Afghanistan*. Washington, DC: Academy for Educational Development.

Hayward, F., & Babury, M. O. (2014, January-March). Afghanistan higher education: The struggle for quality, merit, and transformation. *Planning for Higher Education Journal, vol. 42*(2).

Hayward, F., & Babury, M. O. (2015, Summer). Rebuilding higher education in Afghanistan. *International Higher Education*, no.81.

Hayward, F., Dumond, B., & Slack, P. (2018). Draft Pan African University strategic plan: 2019–2023, Addis Ababa, Ethiopia: Pan African-EU Partnership, unpublished manuscript.

Hayward, F., & Kandeh, J. (2001). Sierra Leone: War and continued decay. In Colin Legum (Ed.), *Africa Contemporary Record*, vol. 25 (pp. B167–B187). New York, NY: Holmes and Meier.

Hayward, F., Moja, T., & Cloete, N. (1995). Change in higher education. Unpublished document.

Hayward, F., & Ncayiyana, D. (2003). *Strategic planning: A guide for higher education institutions*. Cape Town, South Africa: Centre for Higher Education Transformation.

Hayward, F. & Ncayiyana, D. (2006). Report on the national education sector plan project Malawi: 30 October–18 November 2006. Unpublished report.

Hayward, F., & Ncayiyana, D. (2014). Confronting the challenges of graduate education in Sub-Saharan Africa and prospects for the future. *International Journal of African Higher Education, vol. 1*(1).

Hayward, F., & Rasoanampoizina, H. (2007, Winter). Planning for higher education change in Madagascar. *International Higher Education*, no. 46, pp. 18–20.

HEC Press Release. (2005). Atta forms committee to look into the issue of fake degrees. Islamabad: Higher Education Commission; downloaded August 17, 2005, from: http://www.hec.gov.pk/,/htmls/presss%5Frelease/May2005/03.htm.

Heleta, S. (2015). How to rebuild higher education in countries torn apart by war. Based on Savo Heleta, Higher education in post-conflict societies: Settings, challenges, and priorities. In *Handbook Internationalisation of European Higher Education*, Vol. 1. Stuttgart: Raabe Verlag.

Higher Education Commission. (2000). *Higher Education Commission report*. Islamabad, Pakistan: HEC.

Higher Education Commission. (2003). *HEC Annual Report*: 2002–2003. Islamabad, Pakistan: HEC.

Higher Education Commission. (2005). *Higher education medium term development framework: 2005–2010*. Islamabad, Pakistan: HEC.

Higher Education Commission. (2008). *Higher Education Commission report: 2002–2008*, Islamabad, Pakistan: HEC.

Hill, L., & Lineback, K. (2011). *Being the boss: The 3 imperatives of becoming a great leader.* Boston, MA: Harvard Business Review Press.

Hyuha, M. (2017). Uganda: Reversing the decline in higher education. *University World News*; downloaded July 3, 2017, from: http://wwwuniversityworldnews.com/article.php?story=2017062712.

IELTS. (2015). *The top 250 universities in Asia 2015.* Cambridge, UK: International English Language Testing System, British Council.

International Development Association. (2009, May 5). *Program document for a proposed credit in the amount of SDR 66.9 million (US million 100 equivalent) to the Islamic Republic of Pakistan for a higher education support program.* Washington, DC: World Bank.

International Monetary Fund. (2018). *Regional economic outlook: Sub-Saharan Africa, domestic revenue mobilization and private investment.* Washington, DC: IMF.

International Network for Education in Emergencies. (2013). *INEE guidance note on conflict sensitive education.* New York, NY: INEE.

Jerven, M. (2015). *Africa: Why economists get it wrong.* London, UK: Zed Books.

Kabul Polytechnic University. (2006). *Strategic plan*. Kabul, Afghanistan: KPU.
Kaburise, J. (2003). The UDS experience with developing an alternative approach to tertiary education. Paper presented at the *Regional Training Conference on Improving Tertiary Education in Sub-Sharan Africa: Things that work!* Accra, September 23–25, 2003.
Kandeh, J. (2008). Rogue incumbents, donor assistance, and Sierra Leone's second post-conflict elections of 2007. *The Journal of Modern African Studies, vol. 46*(4), pp. 603–635.
Kasozi, A. B. K. (2004), Capacity training workshop National Council for Higher Education. Unpublished presentation at the workshop for higher education.
Kasozi, A. B. K. (2016). *The National Council for Higher Education and the growth of the university sub-sector in Uganda, 2002–2012*. Dakar, Senegal: CODSRIA.
Kellerman, B. (2012). *The end of leadership*. New York, NY: Harper Collins.
Kerr, C. (1994). *Higher education cannot escape history: Issues for the twenty-first century*. Albany, NY: State University of New York Press.
Kezar, A., Carducci, R., & Contreras-McGavin. (2006). *Rethinking the "L" word in higher education: The revolution of research on leadership*. San Francisco, CA: ASHE, Wiley.
Kezar, A., & Lester, J. (2011). *Enhancing campus capacity for leadership: An examination of grassroots leaders in higher education*. Stanford, CA: Stanford University Press.
Khan, A. (2010a, September 29). Pakistan: Universities boycott prompts funds offer. *University World News*, no. 141.
Khan, A. (2010b, October 3). Pakistan: Politics, not floods, divert university funds. *University World News*, no. 142.
Kouzes, J., & Posner, B. (2003). *An administrator's guide to exemplary leadership*, San Francisco, CA: Jossey-Bass.
Langa, P., Wangenge-Ouma, G., Jungblut, J., & Cloete, N. (2016, February 26). South Africa and the illusion of free higher education. *University World News*, Issue 402.
Lebbie, J. (2012). University of Sierra Leone concludes retreat. *Politico SL News*, p. 1; downloaded from: http://politicosl.com/2012/06/university-of-sierra-leone-concluses-re.
Lumby, J. (2013, February 18). Leadership in higher education: This much we (don't yet) know, *The Guardian*; downloaded August 20, 2015, from: www.theguardian.com/higher-educatiln-network/blog/2013/fe.
Madagascar Express. (2012, March 5). Dear France, thank you for the 2009 coup. *Madagascar Express*; downloaded May, 24, 2016, from: htttp://Madagascar-express.blogspot.com/2012/03/dear-france-thank-y.
Makhubu, N. (2014). New medical university set to open. *IOL Newsletter*, Gauteng, South Africa; downloaded January 25, 2018, from: https//www.IOL.co.za/newsletter.

Mambo, M., Meky, M., Tanaka, N. & Salmi, J. (2016). *Improving higher education in Malawi for competitiveness in the global economy.* Washington, DC: The World Bank.

Marcum, J. & Kamba, W. (1997). *Review of project on strategic planning for historically disadvantaged universities and technikons in South Africa.* Washington, DC: American Council on Education.

Ministry of Education, Malawi. (nd circa 2003). *Public expenditure review.* Lilongwe, Malawi: Ministry of Education.

Ministry of Education, Pakistan. (2002). *Task force on improvement of higher education in Pakistan.* Islamabad, Pakistan: MoE.

Ministry of Education and Vocational Training. (2006). *The national education sector plan, Malawi.* Lilongwe, Malawi: Ministry of Education.

Ministry of Education, Science, and Technology. (2007). *Sierra Leone education sector plan: A roadmap to a better future.* Freetown, Sierra Leone: Government of Sierra Leone.

Ministry of Education and Sports. (2003). *Uganda strategic plan for higher education: 2003–2015.* Kampala, Uganda: NCHE.

Ministry of Higher Education. (2009). *National higher education strategic plan: 2010–2014.* Kabul, Afghanistan: Ministry of Education.

Ministry of Higher Education, Afghanistan. (2011). *Current state of the implementation of the national higher education strategic plan: 2010–2014.* Kabul, Afghanistan: Higher Education Project.

Ministry of Higher Education. (2015). *Policy on elimination of discrimination and sexual harassment in universities and institutions of higher education.* Kabul, Afghanistan: Ministry of Higher Education.

Ministry of Higher Education, Afghanistan. (2016a). *Higher education gender strategy.* Kabul, Afghanistan: Ministry of Higher Education.

Ministry of Higher Education, Afghanistan. (2016b). *National higher education strategic plan: 2016–2020.* Kabul, Afghanistan: Ministry of Higher Education.

Ministry of National Education and Scientific Research. (2007). *Document de strategie: Réforme de l'enseignement post fundamental.* Draft of September 9, 2008. Antananarivo, Madagascar: Ministry of National Education and Scientific Research

Mohuba, D. K., & Govender, K. (2016). The merger of historically disadvantaged tertiary institutions in South Africa: A case study of the University of Limpopo. *Cogent Business Management,* no. 3.

Moja, T. & Hayward, F. (1999). Higher education policy development in contemporary South Africa. *Higher Education Policy,* vol. *13*(4), pp. 335–359.

Moja, T., & Hayward, F. (2001). The development of South African higher education policy: 1994–1997. In Yusuf Sayed & Jonathan Jansen (Eds.), *Implementing education policies: The South African experience.* Cape Town, South Africa: University of Cape Town Press.

Moja, T. & Hayward, F. (2005). The changing face of redress in South African higher education: 1990–2005. *Journal of Higher Education in Africa, vol. 3*(3), pp. 31–56.

Moleah, A. (1993). *South Africa: Colonialism, apartheid, and African dispossession.* Wilmington, DE: Disa Press.

Moodie, A. (2010, October 3). South Africa: Advancing women in higher education. *University World News,* Issue 63; downloaded August 8, 2016, from: http//www.universityworldnews.com/article.php?story=2010100210.

Nabi, I. (2016, June 30). Globalization: What the West can learn from Asia. Brookings; downloaded from http://www.brookings.edu/blogs/future-development/posts/s016/05/3.

National Commission for Higher Education. (1996). *National Commission on Higher Education: A framework for transformation.* Parow, South Africa: CTP Printers.

National Council for Higher Education. (2005). *The state of higher education and training in Uganda 2005: A report of data collected from institutions of higher learning.* Kampala, Uganda: NCHE.

National Council for Higher Education. (2008). *Other tertiary institutions (quality assurance) regulations, 2008. Arrangement of regulations.* Kampala, Uganda: NCHE.

National Council for Higher Education. (2011). *The state of higher education and training in Uganda 2011: A report on higher education delivery and institutions.* Kampala, Uganda: NCHE.

National Council for Higher Education. (2015). *The state of higher education and training in Uganda 2005: A report of data collected from institutions of higher learning.* Kampala, Uganda: NCHE.

Ndebele, N. (2007, February 28). Strategic planning at the University of the North, South Africa: 1993. Personal communication to the author.

Ndebele, N. S. (nd). Biography; downloaded May 3, 2016, from http://www.njabulondebele.co.za/biography/.

Ndovi, J. (2018, September 7). Students pin hopes on successful university unbundling. *University World News*; downloaded September 10, 2018, from http://www.univeristy.worldnews.com/article.php?story=20180904.

Neelakantan, S. (2007). Spending on higher education has gone up, but critics say academic standards have gone down. *Chronicle of Higher Education, vol. 53*(20).

Norimitsu, O. (2016, August 5). ANC suffers major election setback in South Africa. *New York Times*; downloaded August 9, 2016, from http://www.nytimes.com/2016/08/06/world/africa/south-africa-election

Northhouse, P. (2016). *Leadership: Theory and practice*, 7th ed. Thousand Oaks, CA: Sage.

Paracka Jr., D. (2003). *The Athens of West Africa: A history of international education at Fourah Bay College, Freetown, Sierra Leone.* New York, NY: Routledge.

Patrinos, H. (2015). Higher education: Returns are high but we need to fund it better. World Bank Education blogs; downloaded June 30, 2016 from: http://blogs,worldbank.org/education/print/higher-education-returns-are-high-we-need-fun.

Phosa, Y. (2015). Higher education in South Africa review: Council on Higher Education briefing. *Higher Education in South Africa Review*; downloaded August 9, 2016, from: http//pmg.org.za/committee-meetings/32351.

Piketty, T. (2014). *Capital in the twenty-first century*. Cambridge, MA: Harvard University Press.

Pilot Project Consortium. (2001). *Implications of the new Higher Education Framework*. Cape Town, South Africa: CHET.

Pityana, S. (1997). Sipho Pityana on strategic planning. Interview by Maria Carrington, assistant director of the South Africa Project. In *South Africa Project: 1993–1997 project summary*. Washington, DC: American Council on Education.

Pritchard, J. (2018). Developing institutional strategy. In Tony Strike, *Higher education strategy and planning: A professional guide*. New York, NY: Routledge.

Quintara-Muret, L., Harmant, C., Quach, H., Blanovsky, O., Zaporozhchenko, V., Bormans, C., van Helden, P. D., Algeria-Hart, M., & Behar, D. (2010, April 9). Strong maternal Khoisan contribution to the South African coloured population: A case of gender-biased admixture. *The American Journal of Human Genetics* 86, 611-620.

Reuters. (2012, May 24). Afghan school attack: Students, teachers poisoned in Takhar Province. *Huffington Post World*.

Riodan, J., Odell, R., & Hayward, F. (1990). *Project to revitalize the University of Sierra Leone*. Madison, WI: Midwestern Universities Consortium (MUCIA).

Sen, A. (1999). *Development as freedom*. New York, NY: Random House.

Shapiro, J., & Stefkovich, J. (2011). *Ethical leadership and decision making in education: Applying theoretical perspectives to complex dilemmas*. New York, NY: Routledge.

Stiglitz, J. (2015). *The great divide: Unequal societies and what we can do about them*. New York, NY: Norton.

Strike, T. (2018), *Higher education: Strategy and planning: A professional guide*. New York, NY: Routledge.

Tahir, P. (2017). Education spending in Pakistan. *The Express Tribune*; downloaded February 8, 2019, from: https://tribune.com.pk/story/14909411/education-spending-pakistan/.

UNESCO. (2006). *Toward knowledge societies*. Paris, France: UNESCO Publishing.

University for Development Studies. (2003). *Strategic plan: 2003–2008, third draft*, Tamale, Ghana: University for Development Studies.

University of Fort Hare. (1994). *Strategic plan: Goals and plan of Work III, September 1994–August 1995*. University of Fort Hare and American Council on Education, unpublished.

University of the North. (1994, September 14). *Strategic planning goals and plan of work III*. University of the North and the American Council on Education, unpublished.

Vella, J. (2002). *Learning to listen, learning to teach: The power of dialogue in educating adults*: Revised ed. San Francisco, CA: Jossey-Bass.

Wadud, M. (2017, January 27). Graduate unemployment "is stoking religious extremism." *University World News*, Issue 444; downloaded February 1, 2017, from: http://www.universityworldnews.com/article.php?story=2017012618.

Walsh, D. C. (2006). *Trustworthy leadership: Can we be the leaders we need our students to become?* Kalamazoo, MI: Fetzer Institute.

West Africa. (1990, February 5–11). Sierra Leone. *West Africa*, p. 170–171.

World Bank. (1997). *Revitalizing universities in Africa: Strategy and guidelines*. Washington, DC: World Bank.

World Bank. (2000). *Higher education in developing countries: Peril and the promise*. Washington, DC: World Bank.

World Bank. (2002). *Constructing knowledge societies: New challenges for tertiary education*. Washington, DC: World Bank.

World Bank. (2005). *National reconstruction and poverty reduction—The role of women in Afghanistan's future*. Washington, DC: World Bank.

World Bank. (2006). *Higher education policy note: Pakistan, an assessment of the medium-term development framework*. Washington, DC: World Bank.

World Bank. (2009). *Accelerating catch-up: Tertiary education for growth in Sub-Saharan Africa*. Washington, DC: World Bank.

World Bank. (2013, May 1). Twenty fragile states make progress on millennium development goals. News release; downloaded from www.worldbankorg/en/news/press.release/2013/05/01/twenty-fragile-states-make-progress-on-millennium-development-goals.

World Bank. (2015). South Asia, now the fastest-growing region in the world, could take greater advantage of cheap oil to reform energy pricing. Press release; downloaded on September 8, 2016 from: http://wwwworldbankor/en/hews/press-release/2015/04/13/south-as.

World Bank. (2016a). Afghanistan unemployment rate: 1991–2016. Washington, DC: World Bank; downloaded from: http//www.tradingeconomics.com/afghanistan/unemployment-rate.

World Bank. (2016b, April). Overview of Malawi; downloaded from http://wwwworldbank.org/en/country/malawi/overview.

World Bank. (2016c). Ghana overview; downloaded January 13, 2017, from http://www.worldbank.org/en/country/ghana/overview.

World Bank. (2016d). Madagascar overview; downloaded January 13, 2017, from http://www.worldbank.org/en/country/madagascar/overview.

World Bank. (2016e). Education statistics—all indicators, retrieved on July 26, 2016, from: http://worldbank.org/data-catalog/ed-stats.

World Bank. (2016f, December). Uganda overview; downloaded January 13, 2017, from http://www.worldbank.org/en/country/uganda/overview.

World Bank. (2018a). The World Bank in Africa: Overview; downloaded January 29, 2018, from www.worldbankk.org/en/region/afr/overview.

World Bank. (2018b). The World Bank in Asia. Washington, DC: World Bank.

World Bank. (2019). South African economic update: Increasing South African tertiary education; downloaded February 20, 2019, from http://worldbank.ort/en/country/southafricapublication/south.

Worldreader. (2015). Literacy in Ghana; downloaded April 27, 2016, from www.worldreader.org/wp-contact/uploads/2015/07/ghana - literacy.pdf.

Yukl, G. (2014). *Leadership in organization*, 8th ed. Noida, India: Person Education.

Index

Academy for Educational Development. *See* AED
Academy for Higher Education Development, 254
ACE (American Council on Education), ix–xi, 86, 94, 96, 111, 245, 250–51, 255, 259–60, 264, 266–67
ACE project, x, 65, 96, 104, 108, 111, 117
AED (Academy for Educational Development), 54, 64, 169, 172, 248, 254, 261
Afghan Higher Education, 53, 57, 59, 61, 63, 65, 67, 69, 71, 73, 75
Afghanistan, x, 8–11, 14–18, 20–23, 26–27, 29, 53–56, 63–67, 70–75, 192–94, 203–6, 213–14, 216–20, 222–24, 230–31, 233–35, 240–42, 248, 257–61, 263–64
  private sector involvement in tertiary education in, 248, 261
  transforming, 188
Afghanistan freedom, 260
Afghanistan Ministry of Higher Education, 147, 199
Afghanistan's Ministry of Education, 248

Afghanistan unemployment rate, 267
Afghan School Attack, 248, 266
Africa Contemporary Record, 261
African Development Bank in Abidjan, 129
African economies, 17, 30
African Higher Education, 247, 262
African National Congress, 80
African students, 90, 103
African Unity, 239
African Universities, 235, 238
Afrikaners, 224
Algeria, 9, 235
All Peoples Congress (APC), 130, 132
Altbach, P., 14–16, 257
American Council on Education. *See* ACE
American Council on Education's Fellows Program, 238
American Council on Education's South Africa Project, 112
American University Afghanistan, 255
American university presidents, 94, 112, 250–51
Amiryar, S., 65, 261
ANC, 90, 92, 95, 97, 209, 223–24, 265
ANC government, 100

269

ANC intelligence units, 250
ANC leadership for higher education change, 220
ANC Minister of Higher Education, 249
Apartheid South Africa, 215
APC (All Peoples Congress), 130, 132
Arab Bank for Economic Development in Africa, 133
Arab News, 252, 257
Arab Spring, 9
ASHE, 247, 263
Asian countries, 39, 236
Asian universities, 247
Aslami, Hassan, xi, 55, 60
Asmal, Kadar, 100, 111, 120
Athens of West Africa, 252, 265
Atta-ur-Rahman, 33–36, 45–49, 190–91, 202, 247, 255, 257

Babury, Mohammad O., 15, 54, 56–59, 68–70, 72, 190–91, 193, 196, 204
Babury & Hayward, 167, 206, 213, 224
Badat, Aslam, 256–57
BADEA, 133
Baghlan University, 60
Bailey, T., 138–39, 257–58
Bangladesh, 9, 259
Bantu, 249
Bantustan, 96, 101
Bengu, Sibusiso, x, 84, 95–97, 99–102, 196–97, 257
Bensimon, Estela, 85, 210, 257
Berger, Joseph, xi
Bio, Julius Maada, 132
Birnbaum, R., 5, 245, 258
BIU (Blantyre International University), 169–70, 254, 259
Black Consciousness Movement, 95

Blantyre International University (BIU), 169–70, 254, 259
Bleazard, D., 111, 251, 258
Bloom, D., 29, 32, 258
Botswana, 103
BRIC governments, 14, 219
BRICs, 13–14, 216, 235, 246, 258
British Aid, 156
British Council, 247, 262
Brutus, Dennis, 95
Bunda College, 170, 172, 180
Bunting, Ian, 78, 89–91, 147, 253, 258
Burkina Faso, 246
Burns, J. M., 3–5, 27, 167, 247, 258

Cambridge, 246–47, 258–59, 262, 266
Cambridge Associates, 100, 179
Cameroon, 9, 235
Cape Peninsula University of Technology, 120–21, 251
Cape Technikon, 120
Cape Town, 25, 87, 89, 147, 246, 250–51, 253, 257–60, 262, 264, 266
Cape University of Technology, 111, 119, 121
Carnegie Corporation, xi, 17, 164, 261
Carnoy, M., 13–14, 216, 219, 258
Castells, M., 22, 188, 214, 246, 258
Castells & Himanen, 102, 214–15
Catholic University of Malawi (CUNIMA), 169
Centre for Higher Education Transformation (CHET), 25, 87, 89, 246, 256–58, 262
Centre for Higher Education Transformation Pilot Project, 86
CEPD, 80
Challenge Facing Egypt's Youth, 247

Chancellor College, 170, 172
Characteristics of Successful Change in Higher Education, 167
CHE, 258
CHET (Center for Higher Education Transformation), x, 7, 114, 236, 239, 250, 253, 256, 258, 266
Chicago State University, 251
China, 22, 236, 246
Church Missionary Society, 251
Ciskei, 95–96, 101, 197
Ciskei funding, 94
Clark, Burton, 7, 258
Cloete, Nico, 88–91, 94, 101, 103, 106, 233–34, 240, 249, 253, 258, 261, 263
CODSRIA, 263
Cohen, Michael, 245, 259
College of Medicine and Allied Health Sciences, 125
Collier, Paul, 17, 259
Constructing Knowledge Societies, 17, 267
Council for Higher Education Transformation, 239
Critical Role of Strategic Planning for Change, 23
Critical Skills of Higher Education Leaders, 191
Cronin, Thomas, 190, 210, 259
Cross, Delores, 108, 251
CUNIMA (Catholic University of Malawi), 169
CUNY, 96
Curaj, Adrian, 259, 261

Dadfar, Mohammad Azam, 15, 56–57, 190, 201
Dandy, D., 133, 259
Davis, James R., 237
Davis, Josephine, 96
DeLauder, William, 112

Delaware State University, 112
Democratic Strategies, 206
Department of Education, 81–82, 90, 249, 257, 259
Development Studies, xi, 161, 166–67, 216, 261, 266
Dewar, B., 156, 259
Dittoh, Saa, xi, 165–66, 193
Dunya News, 49, 259
Durham University in England, 61

Ebola epidemic, 11, 131, 133
Ebola epidemic in Sierra Leone, 8
Eckel, Peter, 7, 255, 259
Ecomog, 132, 252
Economic Community of West African States Monitoring Group, 252
Economist Intelligence Unit, 15, 259
Education Commission, 148, 262
Egypt, 15, 22, 27, 235, 247
Essa, Mohammed, 65
Ethical Leadership, 197, 250, 266
Ethiopia, 9, 17, 151, 246, 261
European Higher Education, 255, 262
European Union, 113, 165
Extension of Universities Act, 260

Fakhruddin, Mir, 181, 187
Faryab University, 61
Fayez, Sharif, 54, 65
FBC (Fourah Bay College), x, 11, 31, 123–29, 133–34, 251–52, 259–60, 265
Feasibility study on private sector involvement in tertiary education, 248, 261
Female Students, 60, 62
Figaji, Brian, 111–15, 117–20, 251, 260
Financing Change, 226

Foray, Cyril P., 126, 252, 260
Ford Foundation, x, 17, 94, 124–25, 250–51
Ford Foundation Pilot Project, 249
Fort Hare, 93–98, 100–103, 112, 196–97, 200, 204, 207, 218, 220, 224–25, 266
Fort Hare Strategic Plan, 100
Fourah Bay College, 127, 252
Fourah Bay College. *See* FBC
Fourah Bay College and Njala University College, 124–25, 127–29
France, 155, 157, 204, 241, 257, 259, 266
Freedom and Higher Education, 216
Freedom House, 217, 260
Free Higher Education, 256
French government involvement, 253
French interests, 151, 155
Funding Higher Education, 63

Gambia, 9, 124–25, 204
Gardner, T., 133, 260
Gasikara, T., 155, 260
GCPEA, 255, 260
GDP, 29, 39–40, 151, 180, 234
Gender Challenges, 60
George Washington University, 65
Germany, 43, 60, 74–75, 155
Ghafar, A. A., 27, 247, 260
Ghana, 9, 11, 16–17, 27, 29, 31, 161, 163, 165, 167–68, 204, 206, 215–16, 231, 233
Ghani, Ashraf, 17, 63, 73–74, 219–20, 260
Ghazni University, 61
Ghumman, K., 38, 260
Goldman, C., 25, 260
Govender, Krishna, 251
Government of India, 260

Government of Sierra Leone, 133, 252, 260, 264
Graham-Harrison, E., 62, 260
Green, Madeleine, xi, 18, 22
Green Paper on higher education transformation, 259
Guinea, 130–31, 204, 246, 252
Guinean troops, 130

Handbook Internationalisation of European Higher Education, 262
Hayward, Fred, x, 16, 18, 24–25, 29, 60, 129–30, 140–43, 245–48, 253–54, 257, 260–62, 264–66
Hayward & Amiryar, 54
Hayward & Babury, 50
Hayward & Kandeh, 132
Hayward & Ncayiyana, 31, 68, 189
HDIs (historically disadvantaged institutions), 85, 93–94, 107, 111, 118
HEC (Higher Education Commission), x, 33–38, 41–43, 45–50, 154, 194, 202, 208, 259, 262
HEC Annual Report, 35, 262
HEC budget, 48–49
HEC staff, 36, 38–39, 202
Hedayet, Mujtaba, xi, 68–69
Heleta, Savo, 255, 262
HEP (Higher Education Project), 54, 61, 68, 70, 248, 264
Higher Education Change, 47, 53, 66, 74, 125, 127, 129, 131, 133, 135, 205
Higher Education Commission. *See* HEC
Higher Education Commission in Pakistan, 28, 148, 236

Higher Education Gender Strategy, 199, 220
Higher Education in War and Conflict Situations, 222
Higher Education Journal, 245, 257, 261
Higher education leaders and faculty members, 30
Higher Education Project. *See* HEP
Higher Education Transformation, 7, 25, 87, 89, 239, 246–47, 256–58, 262
Higher Education Transformation Pilot Project, 86
Higher Educatrion Commission (HEC), 38, 40, 43, 48, 50, 262
historically disadvantaged institutions. *See* HDIs
HIV/AIDS, 140, 142–43, 172
HIV/AIDS education efforts, successful, 172

ICT, 45, 140–41
IELTS, 247, 262
IMF, 31–32, 129, 156, 246, 252, 257, 262
India, 15–16, 33–34, 39, 43, 47, 218–19, 246–47, 259–60, 268
Indian universities, 34
INEE guidance note on conflict sensitive education, 246, 262
Inkatha Freedom Party, 96–97, 250
Institut Catholique, 154
Institutionalization and Sustainability of Higher Education Change, 66
Institutional Transformation, 95, 97, 99, 101, 103, 105, 107, 109, 111, 115, 117, 119, 121
International Development Agency, 248

International Development Association, 38, 262
International Higher Education, 247, 253, 261–62
Internationalisation, 255
International Monetary Fund, 262
International Network for Education in Emergencies, 262
Iraq, 22, 222
ISAF military forces, 63
ISIS, 22, 240
Islamic Republic of Pakistan, 262
Islamic State, 222

Jansen, Jonathan, 264
Japan, 236
Jerven, Morten, 17

Kabbah, Ahmad Tejan, 132
Kabul Donor Group, 61
Kabul Education University, 182
Kabul Medical University, 62
Kabul Polytechnic University. *See* KPU
Kabul University, 61, 182
Kaburise, John, 161–64, 166, 254, 263
Kahane, Adam, 106
Kama, Seretse, 103
Kamran, Naim, 35
Kamuzu College, 170
Kamwanja, Leonard A., 172, 178
Kandeh, Jimmy, xi, 132, 252, 261, 263
Kankor, 58
Karim, Razia, xi
Karzai, Hamid, 57, 62, 69, 73–74, 219, 248
Kasozi, A. B. K., xi, 138–39, 143–45, 147–48, 253, 263
Kaunda, Kenneth, 103

Kellerman, B., 4, 245, 263
Kellogg Foundation, 94, 96
Kenya, 9, 235
Kerr, Clark, 23, 263
Kezar, Adrianna, 26, 84–85, 247, 249, 263
Khoisan and African males and autochthonous Khoisan females, 249
Khost University, 61
Koroma, Ernest, 132, 134
Koroma, Johnny Paul, 132
Koroma government, 133–34
Koso Thomas, Kosonika, 126
Kouzes, J., 4, 166, 263
KPU (Kabul Polytechnic University), 11, 181–88, 219, 254, 261, 263
KPUs transformation, 188

Leading Change in Pakistani Higher Education, 33, 35, 37, 39, 41, 43, 45, 47, 49, 51, 247
Lebbie, J., 133, 263
Legum, Colin, 261
Lenyai, George, 96, 98, 102, 191, 255
Lester, Jaime, 249
Liberia, 129–30
Lilongwe University of Agriculture and National Resources (LUANAR), 180
Limpopo, 104, 109, 251, 264
Lockhart, Clare, 17
LUANAR (Lilongwe University of Agriculture and National Resources), 180
Lule, Yusuf, 103
Lumby, Jack, 192
Lutheran World Foundation, 96

Madagascar, x, 8–9, 11, 13, 151–59, 193–95, 199–200, 204, 213, 217–18, 220, 231–33, 240–41, 253, 259–60
  higher education, 151, 159, 200
Madagascar Action Plan, 152
Madagascar overview, 267
Makerere University, 137, 147, 150
Makhubu, N., 109, 263
Malagasy, 155
Malawi, 18, 20, 26, 29, 169–71, 173, 177, 179–80, 217, 220–21, 231, 234, 264, 267
  higher education in, 1, 169–70, 172, 176
Malawi Adventist University (MAU), 169
Malawi National Education Sector Plan Project, 254, 262
Malawi Strategic Planning, 170
Mambo, M., 180, 264
Mandela, Nelson, 84, 94–95, 97, 100, 103, 223–24
Mangochi University, 169
March, James, 245
Margai, Albert, 123
MAU (Malawi Adventist University), 169
Mauritius, 9, 154
Mbeki, Govan, 95
Medical University of Southern Africa, 104
Medium Term Development Framework. See MTDF
Medunsa, 109–10
Mergers and alliances in higher education, 259, 261
Middle East, 22, 27, 237
Midwestern Universities Consortium, x, 131, 266
Ministry of Education and Sports, 138–39, 145, 264
Ministry of Education and Vocational Training, 171, 180, 264

Ministry of Education in South Africa, x
Ministry of Finance, 66, 74, 144–45, 155, 226
Ministry of Higher Education. *See* MoHE
Ministry of Higher Education and Sports, 138, 140
Ministry of National Education and Scientific Research, 154, 157, 253, 264
Ministry of Women's Affairs, 59, 61–62
M. L. Sultan, 86
Modern African Studies, 252, 263
MoHE (Ministry of Higher Education), 53–56, 59–68, 71, 74–75, 182, 187–88, 196, 201, 248, 251, 260, 264
Mohuba, D. K., 264
Moja, T & Hayward, F., 79–80, 85
Moja, Teboho, 106, 249, 261, 264–65
Moleah, A., 249, 265
Momoh, Joseph, x, 123–24, 126, 129–32, 134, 220, 252
Momoh government, 134, 221
Moral Imperatives, 58, 102
MTDF (Medium Term Development Framework), 35, 39–40, 42, 44–46, 49, 202
MUCIA (Midwest Universities Consortium for International Activities), x, 124, 131, 251, 266
MUCIA team, 126–27, 133–34
Mugabe, Robert, 95, 103
Musharraf, Pervez, 34, 36, 44–47, 190, 219
Mzuzu University, 169–71

Namibia, x, 94, 112

Nangarhar University, 60–61, 222
Naqvi, Sohail, 34–35, 45–46, 48, 191, 202
National Commission, 56, 81–82, 84, 88, 118, 265
National Council, xi, 11, 137, 142, 149, 226, 263, 265
National Council for Higher Education. *See* NCHE
National Council for Tertiary Education, 261
National Education Policy Investigation (NEPI), 80
National Higher Education Strategic Plan, 26, 57–59, 66, 68, 75, 208, 216, 248
National Patriotic Front, 129, 252
National Research Foundation, 114
Ncayiyana, Daniel, xi, 16–17, 24–25, 119, 189, 246–47, 254, 262
NCHE (National Council for Higher Education), xi, 11, 81–82, 84, 118, 137–39, 142–50, 226, 255, 257, 263–65
NCHE standards, 138–39
Ndebele, Njabulo, 103–4, 106–7, 109, 190, 194, 202–3, 251, 265
Ndovi, Joy, 254
Neelakantan, S., 265
NEPI (National Education Policy Investigation), 80
Netherlands, 9
Neumann, Anna, 85, 210
New challenges for tertiary education, 17, 232, 267
New York University, xi
NGOs, 14, 54, 62, 239
NHESP, 57, 59, 67–68, 70–71, 208
Nigeria, 32, 124–25, 130–31, 204, 235, 252
Njala College, 124–26, 132, 199
Njala University College. *See* NUC

Njala University College and Fourah Bay College, 134
Noma Award, 255
Norimitsu, O., 90, 265
Northern Ghana, 162, 166, 193
Northouse, P., 15, 46, 173, 177, 197, 205, 246, 265
Norway, 60
NPFL, 130
NUC (Njala University College), x, 124, 127–29
Nyerere, Julius, 103
Nzimande, Blade, 80
Nzimande, M. Y., 249

OAU (Organization of African Unity), 121, 126, 239
Obaid, Obaidullah, 69, 193
Odell, Russell T., 251, 266
Open access system, 43
Organization of African Unity (OAU), 121, 126, 239
Oxford, 258–60

Pakistan, ix–x, 16–17, 20, 22, 28–29, 32–34, 36, 38–39, 41, 43–50, 144, 202, 206, 214–16, 218–19, 234–36, 246–47, 259, 261–64, 266–67
  higher education change, 33, 46, 51, 219
  Task Force on Improvement of Higher Education, 264
Pakistan education spending, 266
Pakistan Higher Education, 33, 35, 37, 39, 41, 43, 45, 47, 49, 51, 247
Pakistan Higher Education Commission, 202
Pakistan Institute of Development Economics, 257
Pakistan Muslim League, 49
Pakistan National Strategic Plan, 34, 38, 42, 202, 257
Pakistan's universities, 43, 49, 218
Pan African-EU Partnership, 261
Pan African University, 119, 121
Pan African University Draft, 261
Paracka Jr, Daniel J., 252, 265
PASA (Post-Apartheid South Africa), 80
Patrinos, H., 234, 239, 266
Peninsula Technikon, 11, 28, 86–87, 93, 111–13, 115–21, 251, 258, 260
Peninsula Technikon and Cape Technikon, 86, 111, 113, 120
PERI (Programme for the Enhancement of Research Information), 154
PhDs, 20, 33, 35, 38, 43, 48, 53, 128, 147, 226, 230–31
Philippines, 39
Phosa, Y., 88, 266
Piketty, T., 239, 241–42, 266
Pilot Project Consortium, 87, 250, 266
Pityana, S., 93, 95–99, 101, 204, 225, 266
Polytechnic, Kabul, 170, 172, 184–85, 187
Posner, James, 4
Post-Apartheid South Africa (PASA), 80
Post-Traumatic Stress Disorder (PTSD), 224
Pritchard, J., 5, 201, 266
Private Higher Education, 55, 57, 64
Professional Higher Education Leadership Training, 237
Programme for the Enhancement of Research Information (PERI), 154

PTSD (Post-Traumatic Stress Disorder), 224

al-Qaeda, 22, 240
Quaid-i-Azam University (QAU), 38
Quality Higher Education, 13, 15, 17, 19, 21, 23, 25, 27
Quintara-Muret, L., 266

Rahman, Atta-ur, 33–37, 44, 46–49, 191, 202, 247, 255
Rajaonarimampianina, Hery, 157
Rajoelina, Andry, 155–56
Rajoelina, Ratsiraka, 155
Ramaphosa, Cyril, 90
Rasoanampoizina, Hanitra, 253
Ravalomanana, Marc, 152, 155, 157, 195
Razafinjatovo, Haja Nirina, x, 152, 194
Recruitment and Retention of Top Faculty Members, 19
Reddy, Jairam, 84
Revitalizing universities in Africa, 267
Revolutionary United Front (RUF), 129
Rhodes campus in East London, 101
Rhodes University, 100
Riodan, James T., 125–28, 134, 251, 266
Rubadiri, David, 172, 178
RUF (Revolutionary United Front), 129
Russia, 58, 181, 184, 246
Rwanda, 246

SAAQ (System d'Accréditation and d'Assurance Qualité), 158
Saharan Africa, 11, 16–17, 30–32, 123, 147, 149, 176, 246–47, 262, 267

Salmi, Jamil, 264
Saudi loan, 134
Sayed, Yusuf, 264
Scientific Research, 154, 157, 199, 253, 264
Scotland, 95
SDR, 262
Sen, Amartya, 206–7, 242, 266
Senegal, 17, 246, 263
Sesay, Abu, 126
sexual harassment, 56, 63, 67, 264
Shapiro, Joan, 250, 266
Sharia Law Faculty, 61
Sierra Leone, ix–xi, 5, 8–9, 11, 15, 18–19, 31, 123–35, 199, 220–21, 231–32, 251–52, 257, 259–61, 263–67
invaded, 130
Upgrade and Change Higher Education, 126
Sierra Leone and Madagascar, 13, 199, 213, 217, 223
Sierra Leone Education Sector Plan, 133, 252, 264
Sierra Leone Higher Education Change, 123, 251
Sierra Leone People's Party, 132
Sierra Leone's Third Generation Poverty Reduction Strategy Paper, 133
Singapore, 236
SLPP, 130
Social Movements, 246, 258
South Africa, ix–x, 8–11, 14, 16–17, 20–21, 77–79, 81–85, 92–95, 99–104, 120–21, 191–92, 194–95, 206–7, 213–14, 216–18, 223–25, 232–36, 240–42, 248–51, 256–66
South African cases, 26, 110
South African Higher Education, 87, 89, 91, 95, 215, 249, 255–56

South Africa participation rate in higher education, 91
South Africa Project, 96, 106, 111–12, 119, 250, 266
South Africa Review, 266
South Africa student fee debt problems, 234
South Arica Project, 251
South Asia, 15, 29–32, 258, 267
Southeast Asian, 249
Southern African Development Community, 157
South Korea, 236
Sports, 138–40, 145, 264
Sri Lanka, 259
Stanford, 249, 258, 263
STEM fields, 101
Stevens, Siaka, 31, 123, 129, 247, 252
Stiglitz, J., 241, 266
Strasser, Valentine, 130–31
Strategic Planning Challenges, 181, 183, 185, 187, 254
Strategic Planning Model, 25
Strategies for Higher Education Change, 205
Strike, Tony, 2, 266
Sultan Technikon, 86–87
Sweden, 43
Switzerland, 96
SWOT Analysis, 25, 246
Syria, 22

Tahir, P., 51, 266
Takhar Province, 248, 266
Takhar University, 61
Taliban, 22, 53–54, 62, 73, 219, 222, 248
Taliban attack, 58, 208
Taliban period, 66, 181, 230
Tambo, Oliver, 95, 97
Tanzania, 103, 246, 252

Technikon Northern Transvaal, 191, 255
Technology Based Industrial Vision, 34, 202
Times Higher Education Supplement, 9
Transformation Form South Africa, 78, 249
Transformation in Higher Education in Developing Countries, 213, 255
Transforming Higher Education, 2, 4, 6, 8, 10, 12, 14, 16, 18, 20, 22, 24, 26, 28, 30
TTFPP (Third Trimester Field Practical Programme), 162
Turay, Abdul Karim, 126
Turfloop Farm, 103
Turkey, 22
Tutu, Desmond, 97, 117

UDS (University for Development Studies), xi, 11, 27, 161–68, 192, 216, 226, 253, 261, 263, 266
UDS student placements, 164, 168
UDUSA (Union of Democratic University Staff Associations), 80
Uganda, xi, 9, 11, 137, 139, 141–51, 217, 220–21, 226, 231–33, 252, 255, 257, 261–65
  Change in Higher Education, 137
  Fostering Higher Education Change, 137, 139, 141, 143, 145, 147, 149, 252
  state of higher education and training in, 265
Uganda enrollment in higher education, 137
Uganda Strategic Plan, 139, 148–50, 261, 268

UNESCO, 13, 17, 54, 72, 221, 246, 257, 266
UNILIA (University of Livingstonia), 169
UNIMA (University of Malawi), 11, 143, 169–75, 177–80, 190, 226, 254
UNIMA Strategic Plan, 173, 176–78, 180
Union of Democratic University Staff Associations (UDUSA), 80
United Kingdom, 156, 257–60, 262–63
United Nations Development Program, 133
United States, x, 4, 9, 43, 49, 70, 96, 124–25, 131, 200, 204
University for Development Studies. *See* UDS
University for Development Studies in Ghana, 27, 192, 226
University of Cape Town, 147, 202
University of Fort Hare, x, 93–97, 100–103, 112, 197, 200, 204, 207, 218, 220, 224–25
University of Ghana, 165
University of Livingstonia (UNILIA), 169
University of Malawi. *See* UNIMA
University of Malawi and Mzuzu University, 170
University of Natal, 86–87
University of Sierra Leone, x, 124–25, 127, 129, 131–34, 220, 259, 263, 266
University Support and Workforce Development Program (USWDP), 61
University World News, 9, 254, 256–57, 259, 262–63, 265, 267

USAID, x, 54, 61, 63, 66, 72, 74, 124–25, 169, 172, 250–51, 254
USWDP (University Support and Workforce Development Program), 61

van Schalkwy, F., 253, 258
Vella, Jane, 60, 248, 267
Vocational Training, 171, 180, 264

West Africa, 124–25, 252, 265, 267
West African States Monitoring Group, 252
Western Cape, 111, 120
White Paper South Africa, 82
Women's Affairs, 59, 61–62
World Bank, x–xi, 30, 32, 38–44, 53–54, 63–66, 69–70, 129, 149, 154–56, 180, 184–86, 221, 232–33, 245–46, 254–56, 267–68
World Bank's Higher Education in Developing Countries, 13, 44
World Bank's Revitalizing Universities in Africa, 17
Worldreader, 161, 268
World War II, 222

Xhosa, 95

York College, 96
Yukl, G., 4, 191–92, 194, 208, 268

Zahid, Hasir Aslam, 48
Zambia, 103
Zimbabwe, 103
Zululand, 96
Zuma, Jacob, 90, 92

www.ingramcontent.com/pod-product-compliance
Lightning Source LLC
Chambersburg PA
CBHW020641230426
43665CB00008B/262